# No Tears to the Gallows

# NO TEARS
## to the GALLOWS
### the

## THE STRANGE CASE
## OF FRANK MCCULLOUGH

# MARK JOHNSON

M&S

**Canadian Cataloguing in Publication Data**

Johnson, Mark David, 1949-
  No tears to the gallows: the strange case of Frank McCullough

Includes index.
ISBN 0-7710-4417-8

1. McCullough, Frank, d. 1919.   2. Murderers – Ontario – Toronto –
Biography.   3. Police murders – Ontario – Toronto.   4. Toronto (Ont.) –
Social conditions.   I. Title.

HV6535.C33T67  2000      364.15'23'092      C99-933013-6

We acknowledge the financial support of the Government of Canada through
the Book Publishing Industry Development Program for our publishing
activities. We further acknowledge the support of the Canada Council for the
Arts and the Ontario Arts Council for our publishing program.

Map by Visutronx
Typeset in Minion by M&S, Toronto

Printed and bound in Canada

McClelland & Stewart Inc.
*The Canadian Publishers*
481 University Ave.
Toronto, Ontario
M5G 2E9

1 2 3 4 5    04 03 02 01 00

*for*
*Lynn Belsey*

# CONTENTS

# Preface

Events that really happened are often more fascinating than fiction, and in many cases wildly more dramatic than we could have imagined them. I stumbled onto the events in this story entirely by accident, and what astonished me in the first place was that they had actually occurred. Unearthing the story behind the events, and trying to make sense of it, took me on a long journey that eventually led to the writing of this book. In writing it, I have tried to record what happened exactly the way that it did. In a few cases, I have amended quotations for the sake of accuracy.

Many people over many years helped me in doing research for this book. While indebted to them all, I would like to pay special tribute to Joanne Frodsham of the National Archives of Canada in Ottawa, and Mitchell Yockelson of the National Archives and Records Administration in Washington, D. C.

I want to thank especially Alex Schultz of McClelland & Stewart for his guidance, his skills as an editor, and his telephone call upon first reading the manuscript.

For their encouragement, exactly when it was needed, I am profoundly grateful to Jack Batten, John Flood, Jim King, Greg Manson, Duncan McDowall, Peter Munsche, and the late J. J. Robinette.

The greatest debt I owe is to R. Craig Brown, now Professor Emeritus at the University of Toronto.

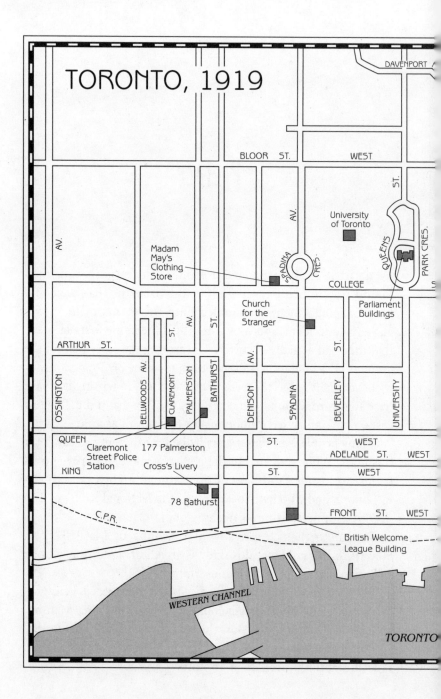

TORONTO, 1919

DAVENPORT

BLOOR ST. WEST

University of Toronto

Madam May's Clothing Store

SPADINA AV.

SPADINA CRES.

QUEENS ST.

PARK CRES.

COLLEGE

Parliament Buildings

Church for the Stranger

ARTHUR ST.

OSSINGTON AV.

BELLWOODS AV.

CLAREMONT ST.

PALMERSTON AV.

BATHURST ST.

DENISON AV.

SPADINA AV.

BEVERLEY ST.

UNIVERSITY

QUEEN ST. WEST

Claremont Street Police Station

177 Palmerston

Cross's Livery

ADELAIDE ST. WEST

KING ST. WEST

78 Bathurst

C.P.R.

FRONT ST. WEST

British Welcome League Building

WESTERN CHANNEL

TORONTO

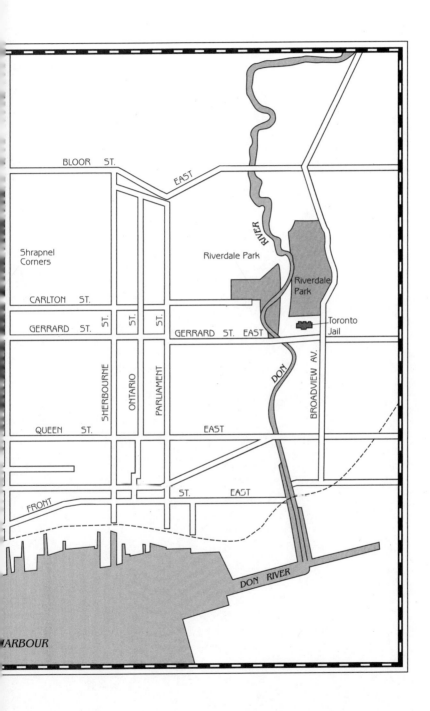

# I

# The Crime

It is no exaggeration to say that no case heretofore has aroused as much public interest as the events in the case of Frank McCullough.

— *Mail and Empire*, June 14, 1919

Under the law this is murder with the penalty prescribed. In these cases we are too prone to overlook the dead and sympathize with the living.

— Sir Thomas White, June 12, 1919

Acting Det. Frank Williams was shot dead in Toronto on November 19, 1918 – just eight days after the armistice had brought an end to the First World War.

He was the first policeman on the Toronto force to be killed in the line of duty,[1] and his death would put into motion what the *Evening Telegram* later called "the most sensational series of episodes that have ever gathered about a criminal in Toronto's history."[2]

We know little about Williams because public sympathy soon focused on his murderer. The acting detective had been a farm boy, born and raised near Clinton, Ontario, the youngest son of a large family that was "well and favourably known in this district," as the Clinton *New Era* reported. Williams "attended collegiate" at Clinton, worked in the local piano factory, and in October 1914, at the age of twenty, he joined the Toronto Police Force.

Williams had not enlisted for military service, at a time when it was patriotic to do so. Perhaps as a result, "he was a remarkably keen Constable," to quote his superior, Inspector of Detectives George Kennedy, who attended Williams's funeral at the family homestead outside Clinton with a contingent of fellow officers.[3] "He showed an aptitude for the work that is seldom exhibited in men joining the department."

"Noisy" Williams, as he was called on the force because of his laugh, spent the duration of the war at the Claremont Street police station in Toronto's west end. A week before the war ended, he was promoted to acting detective "owing to his initiative and detective ability."[4] At twenty-four, he was the youngest detective on the entire force.

On the day of the crime, Mr. George May, the owner of Madame May's clothing store on College Street,[5] became suspicious of two young men who arrived in a buggy and tried to sell coats and furs to him at greatly reduced prices. Excusing himself, May went to the rear of the store and telephoned the police station on Claremont Street.

Sergeant Philip Umbach took the call and dispatched Williams to the scene in the "emergency car." Williams had been looking for some men selling stolen articles of clothing, and the police had received a tip earlier in the day that two men in a rented buggy were attempting to sell furs.

It was 5:00 p.m. and getting dark.

When Williams and the driver of the emergency car, Constable McDermitt, arrived at 372 College, the buggy and its occupants had already left. May, a horseman all his life, said he recognized the vehicle as belonging to Cross's Livery Stable, located near the intersection of King and Bathurst streets.

Williams and McDermitt raced south down Bathurst, hoping to catch the suspects returning their rented buggy. McDermitt parked the car across from the entrance to Cross's Livery, and Williams went in alone.

Mr. William Cross was unhitching horses in a driveway that led down from King Street to a stable area in the back. He and Mrs. Cross lived in a house along one side of the driveway, and on the other side were two offices, front and back. These buildings, the house and offices, were joined by an arch above the entrance at the front, which supported a sign bearing the words "Cross' Livery."[6]

Yes, Mr. Cross told Williams, two men had rented a buggy. No, they had not returned. Williams telephoned May from the back office to compare descriptions, and then went out to McDermitt. "Mac – sorry to keep you waiting. It was here they got the rig all right. I'll stay until they come in. You can go back to the station."

When Williams returned to a darkened back office to wait, Cross told him that his suspects "were rather burly men for him to handle." Would he not need help? "If I do, I'll call you," replied Williams with his trademark laugh.

Why Williams made the fatal error of sending McDermitt away was asked only once in the inquest that followed. A juror put the question to Sergeant Umbach, who sheepishly replied that "it was just thought Williams had gone out to make an investigation." It may also be that the "remarkably keen" Williams, only two weeks into his new job as detective, was determined to make the arrests himself.

At 6:20 a horse and buggy with two occupants pulled in off King Street and stopped at the bottom of the driveway. Cross emerged from his stable, and while the three discussed payment, Williams crept from the back office and approached the two men quietly from behind. He grabbed both by the collar and announced, "I am from police headquarters, you are under arrest." All three men turned and walked towards the office. "They never made a move," Cross later said, "was as quiet as two children would go." Williams shoved one and pulled the other through the door into the darkness of the office.[7]

There were three deafening shots. One of the suspects "went right out through the front office door," running west along King Street, never to be seen again. His name was Albert Johnson. That night a streetcar driver found Johnson's coat and vest at the back of a King West car.

Williams and the other suspect, a young man, were left struggling in the back office and stumbled out through the door into the driveway. "They got out there," Cross reported, "and were scuffling around back and forward, both were hanging on to one another. I could see a gun flying around." Williams yelled to Cross, "Help me!" Cross ran over and reached his arm around the neck of the young man, pulling his head back, allowing Williams to pound him over the head with his baton.

There was another shot, and then another. With that fifth and final shot, the suspect let go and slipped to the ground. He had been beaten severely, and Cross thought he was shot. "He said, 'I'm all in,' and he went down to the ground on his hands and knees. I [Cross] was still kind of hanging on to him, and I heard a voice, I didn't look back, but it said, 'For God's sake, get a doctor, I'm shot.' " For a moment Cross and Williams stared at each other; then the detective collapsed against a wagon.

Cross later said he "could see a policeman on a bicycle and a whole lot of people standing outside, at the front, and I jumped up to telephone the doctor." Mrs. Cross had summoned the policeman by running down to the corner of King and Bathurst and yelling, "Everybody come! There is a fight!" Constable Henry Holmes, a traffic officer at the busy intersection, had leaped onto his bicycle and raced over to the livery with Mrs. Cross panting behind him. At the archway Holmes joined a group of workmen, who "seemed to be all dazed, did not know what was the matter, and everybody was hollering."

The moment Cross saw the constable and jumped up to

telephone the doctor, the suspect on the ground scrambled to his feet, shot out the entrance past Holmes, and ran east along King Street towards the intersection.

Cross shouted after him, "That man shot Williams, there he goes!" Holmes turned and made pursuit on foot. A newsboy at the intersection rushed across the street and managed to trip the suspect, who fell flat on his face. A military policeman also saw the commotion and ran over to the same corner: "I got there just about the time he dropped. There was no holding him, he never made any move at all. . . . He was all in."

Holmes handcuffed the young man and ushered him back to the livery. He left his charge in the hands of the military police-man, who had accompanied them down the driveway to the stable, then rushed back to see about Williams.

"There was four or five around," Cross later said, "and the wife, she came out with a pail of water and had his [Williams's] head on her knee. And they were bathing his head and opened his shirt, you could see blood coming out of him. They said he was dying. He never spoke."

Holmes telephoned the central police operator to report that a detective had been shot. He asked for an ambulance and a patrol wagon to be sent at once. When he returned from the office, Mrs. Cross was "hysterical and yelling." Williams was dead.

They carried the body into the kitchen, where Holmes pulled the detective's revolver, a Savage automatic, out of its holster. It was fully loaded. Cross brought in a second revolver that had been dropped in the driveway. There were five empty cartridges.

Holmes walked down to the stable, where his prisoner was sitting next to the military policeman on the front bumper of an automobile. He had his head in his hands and was plainly suffer-ing the effects of the beating received from Frank Williams's baton. "Why did you shoot him?" Holmes asked. The young man looked up and replied, "The bugger was going to shoot me!"

His name was also Frank – Frank McCullough. He was twenty-six years old.

# II

# Inquest and Investigation

I'm prepared to meet the consequences. I'll be a man. No
tears will go to the gallows with me.
                    – Frank McCullough, November 19, 1918

Remember, premeditation need not be a thing that is in a
man's mind for a day or week or month or year. Quick as a
flash a man determines to do a thing, that is premeditation.
                    – Dr. Arthur Jukes Johnson, November 20, 1918

The remains of Frank Williams were taken to the Lombard
Street morgue that night. Frank McCullough was taken to the
Claremont Street police station. He was held there (without
mishap) until the detective assigned to the case arrived and transported him to police headquarters.[1] That officer was Bartholomew
Cronin, the detective who first questioned McCullough, and who
would play a prominent part in the events that followed.

Originally from Niagara Falls, Ontario, Bart Cronin, forty-six,
was a Roman Catholic who joined the mainly Protestant Toronto
Police Force in 1900. In 1910, he was promoted to detective, and
twice had received citations for meritorious service. He was a
modest giant of a man, tall, husky, and fatherly. In spite of his

shyness, he was a highly regarded professional with a powerful presence on the force. Cronin would prove to be McCullough's most persistent adversary.

Curiously enough, however, an affectionate bond developed between the two. Although firm, Cronin had a paternal approach to young men in conflict with the law, while McCullough was daring and could endear himself to anyone. Neither underestimated the other's abilities. They could joke together in court, and come close to killing each other later. Cronin was the one person McCullough never deceived.

Earlier that evening, shortly after 6:30, Cronin was informed by the central police operator that Williams had been shot. He telephoned Inspector George Kennedy, was assigned the case, and made his way to the Claremont Street police station. Although a colleague of his had just been killed, Cronin showed impeccable restraint. After giving the terrible news to Williams's parents over the telephone, the detective encountered Frank McCullough for the first time.

> I was directed into the cell where they were, and I told him that my name was Cronin, that I was an officer from the Detective Department, and I cautioned him. I said, "You need not make no statement if you don't wish. If you make a statement it can and may be used against you."

Cronin asked McCullough point-blank whether he had shot Williams. McCullough replied, "I did." "I [Cronin] says, 'I understand that there is another party with you; did he have anything to do with it?' He [McCullough] said that the other party had nothing to do with the shooting. I says, 'What made you do it?' He says, 'Well, he was going to arrest me.' That was about all that took place at Claremont Street."[2]

Cronin and McCullough were then driven to police headquarters at City Hall, where McCullough was to be questioned further. Already there was a degree of intimacy between them. As they were transported along Queen Street in the dark, a trip they would make together more than once, McCullough confided to Cronin, "I'm prepared to meet the consequences. I'll be a man. No tears will go to the gallows with me."[3]

Cronin took notes at the questioning, which was conducted by Inspector Kennedy. He used these notes at the coroner's inquest the following evening,[4] and a portion of them is repeated below exactly as they were written.

Nov. 19.18

Cautioned by Insp. Kennedy in presence of Det Cronin:
- What is your name
- Frank McCullough
- what age are you
- 26
- where were you born
- Brooklin N.Y.
- How long have you been in Canada
- about 3 years
- where have you been employed
- I have not been employed. I have been out of Burwash since last April . . .
- what were you sent to Burwash for
- Housebreaking
- what was your sentence
- One year . . .
- why did you shoot the officer
- He arrested me and took me into the office at the livery and he started to hit or shoot me as he pulled something out of his pocket and hit me and then we started to fight and I pulled my gun out of my overcoat pocket and I fired 5 shots at him and we both fell and he fell on top of me and he said I am shot
- what did the other man do    had he a gun
- not that I know of, he ran away . . .

- where did you first meet him
- At the Durham house Cor Bathurst and King [now the Wheat Sheaf Tavern]
- were you the two men that were selling the fur coats
- I was     he wasn't
- where did you get them
- I will not say     You will find out in course of time
- what name did you know this man by
- He went by the name of Johnson . . .
- what age was he
- about 19     I do not know his first name . . .
- How do you justify your Conduct in shooting the officer
- I have no excuse to offer except temporary Insanity
- Where did you get the revolver
- I bought it from a trainman on a freight near parry sound and I got the bullets with the Revolver . . .

Revolver shown to McCullough

- Is that the revolver you did the shooting with
- Yes that is the Revolver
- Did you sell any coats today
- Yes Sir
- where did you sell them
- I won't say
- where have you been rooming since you came to Toronto last
- I won't tell
- were these goods stolen in the City or the Country
- I will not tell

So McCullough was an American. While this might be a matter of significance today, in 1918 it was not. During the entire length of the proceedings that followed, no one commented on the fact that McCullough was from the United States. It just didn't matter.

At this time, Canada – and in particular the City of Toronto – was wholly engrossed in the war and in the social upheaval that was a legacy of the conflict. Canada's sense of nationhood was only just emerging from its infancy, and the border with her ally to the south was virtually open. Throughout 1918–19, the period of this story, trains arrived daily at the North Toronto Station[5] to unload thousands of soldiers returning from the conflict overseas. Among their number were American soldiers who had hitched a ride and were passing through Toronto on their way home. In this context, at a time when millions had died and more were still dying, the fact that the main suspect in the killing of a Toronto policeman was an American was not even mentioned.

As for Burwash, a jail farm near Sudbury, Ontario, McCullough had indeed been sent there for a previous conviction of housebreaking. He had also smashed a whisky bottle over the head of the policeman who arrested him for this crime.[6] McCullough served ten months of his sentence at Burwash before being paroled on a "ticket of leave" in April 1918.[7]

Cronin and Kennedy suspected (wrongly) that McCullough belonged to a larger ring dealing in stolen property. Although the shooting of Williams was clearly the main issue, the detectives were also eager for information about the furs before McCullough's supposed accomplices vanished. But McCullough was, in reality, a loner, doing his best, nevertheless, to protect Albert Johnson. For there was indeed honour among thieves. If you got caught, you took the heat, and you didn't involve others.

McCullough was stalling to give Johnson time to get away: "I will not say. You will find out in course of time." Following the questioning in Inspector Kennedy's office, Cronin pressed McCullough again about his address, about Johnson, and about where the stolen articles were kept. McCullough replied, "I refuse to tell because I am in trouble now; I am done for and it is no use getting another party ten years. I am no snitcher."[8]

During this later conversation, McCullough also told Cronin that in the past he had been a boxer, but had quit the ring because he lost control when he was hit hard. "When a man comes to interfere with me I am not cool, I lose control of myself."

While McCullough was playing for time at City Hall to help his accomplice, Sergeant Umbach discovered McCullough's address while going through receipts he took from McCullough's pockets at Claremont Street police station. Umbach and two plainclothesmen proceeded that night to a small rooming house at 177 Palmerston Avenue and recovered "in the neighborhood of a couple of thousand dollars' worth of goods."

McCullough's landlady, Mrs. Gladys Mytton, was arrested on a charge of receiving stolen property. Her husband, Mr. Edward Mytton, a returned soldier "taking vocational training," would eventually move his entire family from Toronto owing to the shame of his wife's arrest, and to the behaviour of his daughter, Doris Mytton, sixteen, who had feelings for McCullough, as we shall see.

McCullough spent that first night in a cell at City Hall "without belt or braces." The Myttons were questioned until morning at the Claremont Street station. Cronin spent the night and most of the next day looking for Albert Johnson, who was never found.

Frank McCullough was five feet eleven inches and weighed 142 pounds. He had light brown hair, a fair complexion, and "protruding blue eyes." His forehead and cheekbones were prominent, and he bore a small scar on his upper lip. His photograph does not reveal a particularly handsome young man, but then his remarkable eyes could have made him strangely appealing.

It was McCullough's personality that was so subtly powerful and attractive. In the events that followed, he showed himself to be cocky but sensitive; reckless but thoughtful; brutal but polite; dangerous but affectionate. McCullough was funny and fun to be with. He was bright, and used surprisingly sophisticated language. Above all, McCullough had a boldly courageous spirit; or, to use the contemporary term, the man had "pluck."

Given these characteristics and McCullough's consummate ability to manipulate others, one is tempted to dismiss him today as a talented sociopath.[9] Yet in spite of his bravado, there was something in McCullough that was genuine, that even the most wary could not resist.

Although the post-armistice surrender of twenty German submarines was the most newsworthy item in the newspapers the next day, the death of Acting Det. Frank Williams received prominent coverage. Attention was given to details of the shooting based on interviews with Cross and others at the scene.

Exaggerated emphasis was placed on the bravery of Williams, the youngest detective on the force, who "proved himself to be a man, and with one bullet in his body [fought] one of the most courageous fights that a police officer was ever called upon to face." Herbert Jenkins, the newsboy at the intersection, received much praise for the "school boy trick" that brought McCullough to the ground. There were few details about McCullough himself, described erroneously as "a tall, husky man," but then at first no one seemed to know much of anything about him. Det. Sgt. George Guthrie "said last night that he had not obtained anything from the records of the Police Department regarding McCullough."[10]

In the morning, McCullough made a brief appearance in police court to be formally charged. Detective Cronin was present to make the official complaint that McCullough "did contrary to law murder one Frank Williams." As the charge was read, McCullough "lounged on the dock rail, but betrayed nothing of what his feelings may have been. He wore no collar." He was remanded, without plea, until November 27 so that further evidence could be gathered.

At noon at the morgue, Dr. Andrew Harrington cut open Frank Williams's body and found two bullets. According to Harrington's post-mortem, the fatal bullet entered to the side of the right nipple, passed through the lung and base of the heart, striking the spinal column, "then fell into the pleural cavity where it was loose.

I plucked it out afterwards." The bullet before this final shot had entered under the right arm and was found under the skin on Williams's back. Harrington then found a third bullet lodged inside Williams's pocketbook.[11] There had been five shots in total; the other two bullets had been found in the office ceiling.

Upon completing his examination, Harrington delivered his report, and the bullets, to the chief coroner for Toronto, Dr. Arthur Jukes Johnson. The principal means of gathering evidence supporting the charge of murder against McCullough was to be the coroner's inquest that evening.

The churlish Dr. Johnson had "officiated at more inquests than any other practitioner" in Toronto. He was initially a surgeon for whom "cases involving criminal aspects became a hobby," and as a coroner he became an acknowledged "expert on poisons." At the age of seventy, Johnson was "one of the oldest coroners in point of service in the province," and not an authority to be questioned.[12]

The inquest was held at the morgue before a jury of eight men exactly twenty-four hours after the shooting. McCullough sat immediately to the right of the witness box. Ten witnesses were called, most having been present at the scene of the crime. Also in attendance was Mr. William D. Williams, older brother of the deceased, who had come to town to identify the body and take it back to Clinton the next morning on the train. Most of the questioning was conducted by the Crown attorney for the County of York, Mr. R. H. Greer, a returned soldier who had organized the famous "Sportsmen's Battalion" (180th Battalion) during the war, and who went on to become "one of the leading figures of the Canadian bar."[13]

McCullough was on his own. He had no money, and so soon after the event had not found legal counsel, so he questioned witnesses himself. What the press found remarkable was that the "unknown McCullough did so with considerable ability."

The first witness McCullough challenged was Mr. William Cross, the owner of the livery.

Cross: They both got out this door [pointing to diagram] right into the yard and they were scuffling around there, I don't know how long, a minute or two, and he hollered for help.

Greer: That is, Williams?

Cross: Yes. He says, "Hit him with a club, do anything. . . ." There was a shot went off.

Greer: When was the fourth shot fired?

Cross: Out in the yard. . . . I jumped on to his back, I guess I kind of choked this man someway or other pulling him back and Detective got his baton out and he started pounding this man and he pounded him, seemed to be pounding him for a couple of minutes, and then there was a fifth one while that was going on. . . . The prisoner, he says, "You have done me, you have fixed me now," he says and went down like that. The other man he just seemed to be standing there kind of dazed and he says, "For God's sake, get a doctor, I am shot." I went to go to the telephone and this man jumped up . . . and then got out on to the street. I hollered, I says, "Get this man." . . . I went into the office and called up Dr. McCormick. I came out and my wife had him by the head and she said, "My God, this man is dead."

The Chief Coroner: (To Accused) Have you any questions to ask?

McCullough: One question I would like, that is: When the scuffle started in the office, did not Mr. Cross hear some words pass, and did he not see the Detective pull his billy[14] and hit me on the head?

Cross: No, I did not see that; I did not see the billy pulled until the fourth shot was fired.

McCullough: As regarding lighting of the inner office, there is no light there and it is very dark, and could this happen without Mr. Cross seeing it?

Cross: No, the light is not very bright there; it shines through from another place but it comes in the hallway there.

McCullough: It is like back in a closet with the door opened – you cannot see anything hardly.

Greer: When the fifth shot was fired, who fired it?

Cross: This man here.

Greer: Now, you spoke of the revolver. . . . Did you take the revolver from him finally?

Cross: I did. I kept it and I gave it to the policeman, that policeman down there [Constable Holmes]. And I think the baton too I gave him. . . .

McCullough: There is another point. Mr. Cross, I had no intention of shooting that man –

The Chief Coroner: Ask him questions.

McCullough: He had hold of my arm; I would like to ask Mr. Cross if he did not have hold of my arm, pinning both of my arms?

Cross: When was that?

McCullough: That was when the last shot was fired. You had hold of me?

Cross: I had hold of your arm right up here and you were trying to get the revolver up this way; I thought you were after me.

A Juryman: You did not see anybody else around at the time?

Cross: No, not a soul.

McCullough had his defence worked out already. He did not intend to shoot Williams. The detective began beating him in the office with his baton, even if it was too dark for Cross to see this. When the fifth shot went off in the driveway, McCullough was being pummelled on the head and Cross had hold of his arm.

Was the shooting a deliberate act? "Mr. Cross, I had no intention of shooting that man."

Williams's use of the baton was important to McCullough's version of events. Consequently, the moment Constable Holmes offered, in passing, some minor conflicting evidence over the baton, implying that it had not been used, McCullough went after him too.

Greer: Then the patrol came?

Holmes: Yes. Then we picked him up and carried him into Mrs. Cross' house and –

Greer: That is Williams?

Holmes: Yes. I took Williams' revolver out of the holster and I took his watch out and I had his baton and I went –

Greer: Where did you get his baton?

Holmes: Lying in his pocket, in his hip pocket. . . .

Greer: Then the revolver that has been produced by Detective Cronin, have you ever seen that before?

Holmes: Very much like the one that Mr. Cross gave me; no doubt it is the one.

The Chief Coroner: (To Accused) Have you any questions you want to ask this witness?

McCullough: You say you took the baton out of his pocket?

Holmes: Yes sir.

McCullough: What about the baton that Mr. Cross claimed to have given you?

Holmes: I beg your pardon?

McCullough: What about the baton that Mr. Cross said a few moments ago he gave you?

Holmes: Oh, I don't know –

McCullough: Mr. Cross stated that he gave you the revolver and also, he called it, a club?

Holmes: Well, I took the revolver from him to the best of my belief, to the best of my knowledge, when he was in the house.

Greer: But not the baton?

Holmes: I got the baton in the house. . . .

McCullough: In regard to that office I spoke about a while ago – did you take notice of how the lights were in the back part of the office – that there was no light?

Holmes: Well, it was kind of dim in there.

According to the *Evening Telegram*, the "feature of the inquest was the pertinent questions put to witnesses by McCullough, who, without counsel, sat in the right of the witness stand with bowed head."[15]

The strongest testimony against McCullough was delivered by his nemesis, Det. Bart Cronin, the final witness. Cronin had cautioned McCullough at Claremont Street ("You need not make no statement if you don't wish") and Inspector Kennedy had cautioned him again at City Hall. But in spite of these admonitions, McCullough had proceeded to answer their questions, had admitted to shooting Williams, and had offered information about Burwash that would now clearly influence the matter at hand.

Cronin: When we got down to City Hall, Inspector Kennedy cautioned him in my presence. He asked him his age and where he was from; how long he was in Canada and what his occupation was.

Greer: Do you remember his answers to these various questions?

Cronin: I do.

Greer: Let us have them.

[Cronin speaks from his notes]

Cronin: . . . Occupation, he said that he had not worked any lately. The Inspector asked him how long. "Well," he said, "not since I came out." Inspector says, "From out where?" He says, "From Burwash."

The Chief Coroner: Does the Jury know what that means or where that is?

Greer: It is a provincial prison. . . .

Cronin: The Inspector took the gun and he says, "Is that your gun?" And he took it quite coolly and looked at it and he says, "Yes, it is." . . . Appeared to be quite frank and cool. The Inspector asked him again what his reason was why he had done such a thing and he said, "I don't know. I have done it. . . ."

Greer: Did you find his address?

Cronin: Yes, 177 Palmerston Avenue, and also got a pretty good clue on the other man. I think we expect to get him, out all night and out all day; I have just come to the Detective Office and got the gun and come down here. . . .

The Chief Coroner: (To Accused) Have you any questions to ask?

McCullough: Was not the question, "Why did you do it?" and was not my answer, "Well, whenever I am hit on the head I seem to go crazy, something like that?"

Cronin: No, not to the best of my belief, McCullough, that was not the answer you gave.

McCullough: Did you hear any answer of that kind?

Cronin: Later on he gave an explanation, he says, "That is what made me quit the ring," he says. "When I get going I am not cool, I lose control of myself." That is later on, and he remembers it very well. That is the kind of explanation he gives.

The Chief Coroner: Any other questions?

There were none. Cronin's testimony settled the matter. McCullough had been in trouble with the law before. He had a record. He had spent time in jail. He admitted the revolver was his, that he shot Williams, and that he fired the revolver five times. The flimsy excuse of losing control when hit on the head was contrived afterwards. He had been "frank and cool" about it all.

For the veteran chief coroner, the whole story was "a perfectly straight one," and he made it clear to the jury what the finding should be: "Now, gentlemen, this is a case in which a man who has been convicted of housebreaking is found now carrying fire arms. I want rather to impress that upon your minds."

What, asked Dr. Johnson, was McCullough going to do with a loaded revolver? It had been "wisely said in the past" that anyone with a revolver "in his hand or in his pocket has murder in his heart, and any man who has served a term in a penitentiary and afterwards is found wandering about with a revolver in his pocket is, to say the least, under suspicion. . . . It is your duty now, gentlemen, to consider your verdict and let me have it at your earliest possible moment."[16]

The jury retired at 9:45 p.m. and returned shortly after with the following verdict:

> That Frank Williams came to his death in the City of Toronto on the nineteenth day of November 1918 from wounds caused by bullets fired from a revolver. That the said revolver was in the hands of and was fired by one Frank McCullough at the time the aforesaid bullets were fired therefrom; and that the said Frank McCullough did thereby wilfully and of his malice aforethought kill and slay the aforesaid Frank Williams against the peace of our Sovereign Lord the King, his crown and dignity.

# Mr. T. C. Robinette, K. C.

His opening syllables arrested the attention of usually immovable magistrates. Courts hung on his accents. . . . It is not mere rhetoric to say that tears flowed copiously and hearts melted noticeably during the passionate appeals he made to those bodies known as juries.

– Albert R. Hassard on Robinette, 1934

When Frank McCullough was returned to his cell at City Hall, he asked to speak to Bart Cronin.

McCullough told Cronin that he had lied about obtaining the revolver from a trainman near Parry Sound. He got it from a Toronto youth named Cowdrey, he said, and confessed that the week before he, Cowdrey, and Albert Johnson had burglarized Davies' Butcher Shop at St. Clair and Vaughan, where Cowdrey worked.[1] Cronin made investigations and arrested Hubert Cowdrey, seventeen, the next morning.

McCullough wanted to show Cronin that he was now willing to cooperate with the police. Perhaps he felt he had given Albert Johnson sufficient time to get away. Or perhaps the sombre verdict of the coroner's inquest had made an impression. Whatever the motivation, McCullough told Cronin that he was ready to identify both the places he had robbed and where he had unloaded stolen property.

Over the next few days, McCullough "had the unique experience of being motored around Toronto streets handcuffed, with county constables and city detectives as escort, to enable him to point out the places where he had unloaded stolen goods, the trips taking in Ossington Ave., Dundas, and several other thoroughfares."[2]

McCullough's reward for cooperating was to be promptly charged in police court for burglary. When he appeared before the magistrate, Maj. George Brunton, the police informed the court that McCullough, since his arrest for murder, had "done all in his power to enable the authorities to locate the stolen goods – most of which have been recovered." McCullough pleaded guilty to burglary. In view of the more serious charge against him, sentencing on the charge of burglary was postponed.

This minor incident is significant only for the faint note of sympathy we hear in the voices of the police before Brunton. After all, McCullough had killed a policeman, the first officer on the force to be killed in the line of duty. Yet here were Williams's fellow officers, having spent a few days in McCullough's company, pleading for consideration to be given on a minor charge of burglary. In spite of his crimes, there were few who came in contact with McCullough who did not grow to like him. Invariably they dropped the name McCullough and referred to him as *Frank*.

Take, for example, the statements made to the press by officers Forbes and Dunn of Claremont Street station. Plainclothesmen like "Noisy" Williams, they had all worked out of the same station for four years. Now, only two days after Williams's death, the two officers insisted to reporters that McCullough was "not a desperate gunman." He was "very well known to the constables and plainclothesmen of the division." McCullough had been convicted for three petty offences in the past and a charge of housebreaking. "We never had any trouble with him. We simply told Frank that he was wanted and he came with us."

Other than the telling reference to good old *Frank*, what may one infer from this statement? Either Forbes and Dunn thought the shooting a tragic accident, or perhaps they believed that Williams had provoked McCullough. Forbes added that McCullough had "resided in the vicinity of Spadina Avenue and Queen Street for a number of years, and was employed as a driver for various bakeries."[3]

→→    ←←

While detained at City Hall, awaiting his second appearance in police court, McCullough was visited for the first time by his lawyer, Mr. Thomas Cowper Robinette, K.C.

Robinette was one of the finest criminal lawyers in Ontario. "Such was his success that for many years there was hardly an important case in Ontario in which he did not figure, his reputation as a defence lawyer being unequalled."

He was born near Cooksville, Ontario, in 1863, a descendant of United Empire Loyalists from Pennsylvania. He attended the Strathroy Collegiate Institute in Toronto and was teaching school himself by the age of sixteen. He worked his way through the University of Toronto, earning a scholarship for general proficiency, and graduated B.A. in 1884 as an English prizeman with a medal in modern languages.

Success followed success. Robinette entered Osgoode Hall, from which he graduated LL.B. in 1887 with the highest distinction, the prized Governor General's Gold Medal. He was called to the bar that same year, and in 1897 entered and eventually became senior partner of the firm Robinette, Godfrey, Phelan & Lawson, with offices in the Bell Telephone Building on Adelaide Street. In 1902, he was created a King's Counsel (when the designation meant something)[4] and in 1911 and 1916 was elected a Bencher of the Law Society of Upper Canada.

Robinette was "a keen liberal and took a very considerable part in the Liberal Party's organization in Ontario," and although he failed in three attempts to enter the legislature (losing by one

hundred votes in 1908), "his influence on the party was consider-
able." Like many other provincial Liberals, Robinette was also a
Methodist. Typically for a generation known for its "muscular
Christianity," he was prominent in organized activities for young
men; at various times he was president of the Methodist Young
Men's Association, the (all-male) University of Toronto Literary
Society, and the National Sporting Association. He played lacrosse.
On occasion, he was a lay preacher, in demand on the church
circuit for a popular lecture entitled "The Boy: The National Asset
of Canada."

But the fifty-five-year-old Robinette was a young man's man
for more dramatic reasons. He was a dashing figure in the courts
who made his legal reputation as defence counsel in a number of
sensational murder trials. "He appeared in no less than one
hundred and fifty leading cases, but it was in the murder cases
that he made his name as a most powerful pleader for the defence
largely by reason of his oratorical gifts and his acute psychological
attacks on the feelings of the jury."[5]

He was tall and slim with coal-black hair. He had a rich, powerful voice that could be enchantingly delicate when required. He
was "a consummate actor, and there has been no other advocate
of recent years who was so frankly dramatic in his conduct of a
case, or who could influence the emotions of his auditors with
such ease and compelling eloquence."[6]

Part of the drama was his unpredictability. Once, while defend-
ing a Mr. Peter Hodges in the dock on a minor charge of illegal
distilling, Robinette suddenly turned to the magistrate and
announced, "I've got a conscience and I'm going to keep it. I will
not be led by the nose by my clients. I think it is my duty to retire
from the case."

Hodges appealed to the magistrate. "He did not see why he
should acknowledge himself guilty at the mere whim of his lawyer
when he believed himself as innocent as the Magistrate on the
bench. Nor did he see why his counsel should accept his money
and then refuse to defend him." Robinette promptly peeled off $25

and returned it to Hodges in the dock. "I'll keep $25 for my services so far," he said, and marched out of the courtroom.[7]

Like all the individuals in this story, Robinette was not without shortcomings. Prime among them was a full-blown case of self-righteousness that must have sorely tried the patience of his colleagues. Robinette could never be wrong. And when others remained opposed, he became frustrated, petulant, and ultimately capable of irresponsible behaviour. For this reason, he was never promoted to the bench. He was also a triple failure in gaining political office. As a result, he was prone to the suspicion that there was deviousness in high places.

How did Robinette come to defend McCullough? The *Star* claimed later that "Mr. Robinette took the case because he liked McCullough." The *Evening Telegram* observed that McCullough was well known along Spadina "as a driver of a bread wagon, and as one official expressed it yesterday, 'Why, perhaps 5,000 people knew Frank McCullough.'" Did McCullough deliver bread as far as the Robinette household up at 60 Spadina Road? It is more likely that Robinette took the case because it was a challenge; he liked to defend the underdog, and showed little hesitation in announcing that he took no fee in such cases.[8]

Robinette made his first appearance in the case when "a well groomed and much brighter" McCullough reappeared in police court on November 27 to be formally committed for trial. The evidence was heard again, although on this occasion before the notorious Col. George T. Denison, a seventy-nine-year-old magistrate and police commissioner.[9]

Robinette bore down hard on both Cross and Cronin. Under examination, Cross admitted McCullough "had received heavy blows on the head" and was "beaten up badly" in the scuffle. Robinette "questioned minutely" into the manner in which Cross grabbed McCullough's arms. "He left the court to infer that if he had not been grabbed at that particular moment, the revolver might not have gone off."

This line of questioning eventually tried the patience of an unimpressed Denison: "I would bring to your attention, Mr. Robinette, that three shots were fired before they left the office and that five shots were fired altogether. Three bullets were found on Williams, so one of the shots fired before the grabbing must have entered his body."[10]

As for the admirable Cronin, Robinette accused him of distorting the statements McCullough had made after his formal questioning at City Hall. He charged the detective with being determined to see McCullough convicted at all costs. Cronin was angered and explained that McCullough admitted after questioning that he had told a lie about how the revolver was obtained:

> First he said he had bought it on a train. Now he admitted buying it from a man at the present time in custody for selling it.
>
> "Think it all over before the trial," said Mr. Robinette.
>
> "I don't have to do any thinking," replied Cronin. "The man was a stranger to me. I had nothing against him. I'm telling the truth."
>
> "All right," said counsel, descending from treble to basso profundo.
>
> McCullough was then committed for trial.

Who was this stranger, Frank McCullough? From what shadows had he come?

IV

# The Firecracker

If you know Westville, you know it has its quiet weeks,
when every morning and every evening, everybody and
everything looks and seems exactly as they did before,
except that the children have grown a little in stature and
the old people a little more grey.

        – *Otsego Farmer*, June 16, 1893

No one in Toronto knew anything about Frank McCullough's
past. Not even T. C. Robinette came to know his full history. It
is important to keep this in mind as our story unfolds.

If the man's past had been known, it would have demolished
his chances for executive clemency. McCullough spoke of his
origins only when he gained some advantage from doing so, and
when he mentioned his past he invariably lied. The following
information has been pieced together by tracing the few isolated
statements McCullough made about his past. We know more
about the truth of his life today than anyone did in 1918–19.

To begin with, "Frank McCullough" was not his real name. His
real name was an unbecoming Leroy Ward Fay Swart, and he was
born in the tiny hamlet of Westville, New York, in 1892.

One cannot imagine a more beautiful place. Westville is secluded within the luxuriant hills of the Cherry Valley in Otsego County, less than five miles over the Cornish Hill from Cooperstown, New York. The tranquil village lines the road going north to Middlefield, merely a stone's throw from the gentle Cherry Valley Creek.

The place is little changed from the 1890s: it was, and still is, stunningly beautiful farm country. Dairy cattle, sheep, horses, hops, hay, oats, corn, buckwheat, potatoes, all manner of vegetables, and apples, apples, apples. To go to Westville today is to walk back in time to the place that McCullough knew as a boy. The only change is modest evidence now of "city folk" who spend leisurely summers in refurbished farmhouses concealed in the forests and meadows above Westville.

How did McCullough come to leave this paradise?

His grandfather was Chauncey Ward, a talented builder and contractor described as an "architect from Sidney, Delaware County." Ward and his brother, Gaius, a skilled carpenter, were drawn to Westville in the late 1880s by the promise of work in the region.

It would not be fair to say that Westville was "booming" or "thriving" at this time – Westville never boomed or thrived – but it was an attractive location where most farmers could earn an adequate living, and newcomers needed houses and barns.

It was also a place where the demon of alcoholism had a greater chance of being endured. Chauncey Ward was a drinker. He was moderately successful as a builder, but for reasons unknown – and with the progression of the disease itself – he gradually drank himself to death.

Ward married twice. His second wife, Minnie Ward, left him temporarily during an extended binge in 1898. In the words of the discreet *Otsego Farmer*, "Mrs. Minnie Ward left the bed and board of Chauncey Ward last week, removing her household property to the home of her daughter, but on Sunday she came back. Mr. Ward has been in feeble health all the summer, scarcely able to do any work."[1]

The daughter was Myrtle Ward, born in 1874, who married a Mr. Fay, thus becoming Myrtle Ward Fay.[2] Who Mr. Fay was or what became of him remains a mystery; he either died or left Westville for good (or bad). Some months before this unfortunate event, in February 1892, Myrtle bore a son named Leroy. When the boy was four, Myrtle was remarried to an Emory Swart, and the boy's full name became Leroy Ward Fay Swart.

His stepfather, Emory Swart, was from Sidney, like his grandfather. Emory met Myrtle while visiting the Ward family in Westville in 1895. At the age of twenty-seven, Swart was looking to settle, and Westville looked promising. He used all of his resources and borrowed some money to purchase a small farm close to the village where the three settled into a new life together. Swart's total investment was $1,700, but the choice of property did not reveal good judgment.[3]

Though an adequate living could be had in Westville, one soon gave up any ambition of becoming wealthy. Most farmers made sufficient and were thankful. It was an agreeable life, in a congenial place, unless there was misfortune.

Swart's first misfortune was to have invested in an odd and unproductive piece of property. In fact there were two parcels of land: a modest parcel fronting a road known as Norton's Cross where the ramshackle farmhouse sat; and the other, a small meadow concealed on top of a hill across the road, still known ignominiously today as the "Swart lot." Swart couldn't make a go of it, and within a year was ready to sell at a loss. But at the last minute he changed his mind. He would not admit failure.[4]

What about little Leroy? In spite of his parents' troubles, there was much to enjoy in Westville: swimming in the creek, raspberry-picking, picnics at "Hubbel Hollow," and the annual Oneonta Fair. There were Thanksgiving, Christmas, and Easter festivals, oyster suppers at the Grange, and theatrical performances by the Independent Order of Good Templars, including in 1899 the temperance play *Dot the Miner's Daughter*.

Much of the communal life revolved around Westville's two churches, Methodist and Baptist, which diffused their rivalry through the children at "combined" Sunday School picnics and "ice-cream festivals" on the church lawns.

The Swarts subscribed to the leisurely Baptist ministry of the Reverend G. D. Grant, invariably absent attending ministerial conferences or visiting his wife's affluent family. Pulpit substitutions were made by dramatic missionary luminaries, such as the "thrilling" Rev. George Rockwell, the "sailor-preacher" who miraculously survived a "fatal voyage to Patagonia." There was a steady stream of Baptists recovering from Christian adventure in exotic places such as Japan, Africa, China, and India, who left their farming audience spellbound with lectures and lantern shows in the church. And there were the semi-annual "Revival Meetings," also conducted by dynamic outsiders, during which an impressionable Leroy Swart heard the message – and the vocabulary – of commitment to the Saviour.

For a small village such as Westville, there was a surprising range of activities to spark the imagination of a young boy. This was complemented by the daily efforts of Miss Nettie Ellett of Schenevus who taught in the schoolhouse a mere ten-minute walk from the Swarts. Young Leroy was an avid reader with an unusual talent for drawing. He did well in school.[5]

But life was not always pleasant. The Swarts were poor, and there is a sense that they weren't entirely accepted in Westville. Did this have something to do with Leroy's real father, Mr. Fay? And there were minor tribulations. According to the *Oneonta Herald* of 1902, "Leroy, son of Emory Swart, was severely bitten in the cheek by a horse last week. Dr. Blakely of Milford dressed the wound, and the lad is doing well."[6] This may explain the scar on McCullough's upper lip that can be seen in his photograph.

Then in May 1902, tragedy struck. The succinct note in the *Otsego Farmer* masks the horror of it, especially for ten-year-old Leroy:

The house owned and occupied by Emory Swart was burned last Wednesday. The fire was started by a firecracker.

*Who* was playing with firecrackers? It isn't hard to guess. The house burned to the ground and the family lost everything. And with the loss of the farmhouse, the value of the property declined even further. Swart's $1,700 investment was virtually wiped out. A few weeks after the fire, he sold the property for $250 to the Green family, who lived nearby.[7]

The Swarts left Westville for good. There was no farewell gathering.

They moved to New Jersey, where Emory found work in Jersey City as a carpenter for the Pennsylvania Railroad. Leroy attended school there for three years until, in 1905, the family moved to a tenement across the river in the teeming heart of Brooklyn.[8] And at the age of fourteen, during his final year of school in Brooklyn, Leroy ran away from home.

Why? Perhaps there was trouble at home. His parents, and in particular his stepfather, never forgave him for the firecracker and the drastic change it brought to their lives. Moreover, there were now two new members of the family – Harriet and Elsie – both daughters of Myrtle and Emory Swart. As a stepchild, did Leroy feel unwanted in the Swart household? And could there be a more perfect place than Brooklyn, in 1905, for an angry young man to go astray?[9] McCullough later gave his own description of leaving home:

I enjoyed reading very much, and, as many young boys of that age, read what are termed dime novels a great deal, and when I was a few months over fourteen I became imbued with the glamour of the life of some of these fictitious heroes, and ran away from home.

But all delinquents gave an explanation of that sort, with a toothpick dangling from their mouths. McCullough also claimed later that his parents' house had burned to the ground "mysteriously."[10]

The young Leroy Swart travelled by boat up the Hudson River, disembarking at Albany.[11] He worked as a waterboy at the construction site for a new State Education Building, and then for a time in the railway yards. In 1907, he made his way to Erie, Pennsylvania, where, he said later, "I was taken in charge by a couple of real tramps, and they in a few weeks initiated me to the duties of a 'look-out' while they performed various burglaries and robberies."[12]

The next four years are unaccounted for. Where Swart went and what he did remain a mystery. It is unlikely that his time was spent entirely in criminal activity or he would surely have been caught sooner. But caught he finally was. On January 13, 1911, in Kansas City, Missouri, a Leroy Swart was charged with burglary and grand larceny. "'We will teach these Brooklyn burglars to remain at home,' Judge Latshaw said."[13]

He was sentenced to ten years in the state penitentiary at Jefferson City. He was nineteen years old. When he arrived at the penitentiary, he was registered as a steamfitter by trade. Under "Habits of Life," he was categorized as "intemperate" (the alcoholic genes of Chauncey Ward?). While incarcerated, he continued with his schooling, learned to box, and, all in all, seems to have behaved. As a reward, he was released on October 15, 1914, having completed less than half his sentence.[14]

What next? The following is McCullough's own account:

Being ashamed to go home then, I went to Joplin, Mo., and enlisted in the United States army. The Mexican trouble was raging at the time and I was shot in the right leg. I was in the army for two years and three months. After my discharge I came to Canada and received work at Banfield's munition plant, with the intention of joining an overseas battalion, as that was before the United States had entered the war, and as I had studied hard during my incarceration, and having had previous field experience, I thought I might be able to pass for a commission in one of the Canadian units.

These were barefaced lies. Swart was never wounded, nor did he ever serve in Mexico. He was a private in the less glamorous U.S. Army Coastal Artillery Corps, 4th Company, stationed at the inactive but imposing Fort Adams at Newport, Rhode Island.[15] But Swart did achieve notoriety of a sort – he was even mentioned in army dispatches – for on March 24, 1917, he deserted.

Perhaps our hero had been reading the newspapers. Perhaps he knew that with the imminent involvement of the United States in the war he would be on his way to France.[16] Perhaps he thought that the artillery would be too close to the front for his liking. Whatever the reason, he and another private (from the Bronx) deserted Fort Adams and a reward was issued by the adjutant general of the army in Washington "for the arrest and delivery of Leroy W. Swart."[17]

He headed straight for the Canadian border and made it across.

Leroy Swart arrived in Toronto in early April 1917. At first he used the name Frank Stanton but soon settled on Frank McCullough. This was to prevent either his criminal or military record from surfacing if checked with American authorities.

Having just deserted from one army that was not yet in the war, McCullough was not inclined to turn around and enlist in another that was: a Canadian Army massively engaged, bloodied, and desperate for men. Instead, he opted for the safe monotony of Banfield's Munitions Factory, until he "happened on one of my fellow-prisoners from Missouri" and returned to his old habits again.

The two drank and stole. Within a few days, McCullough was arrested by Constable Ewing at the corner of Ontario and Queen streets, where the whisky bottle was smashed over Ewing's head. Judge Emerson Coatsworth sentenced McCullough to a year at Burwash for housebreaking only, where he became a "trusty," a prisoner with special privileges. He was released early in June 1918, again for doing good time.

McCullough returned to Toronto and quickly went through

four more jobs, including work for the Dominion Steamship Company and Firstbrook's Box Factory, before Barker's Bread Bakery employed him as a deliveryman in the Spadina area.

But the friendly Barker's breadman was not what he seemed. In short order, McCullough cleaned out Sam Robinson's Cigar Store in West Toronto. He burgled the home and office of Dr. Naismith of Toronto, selling glass from this robbery right off his breadwagon on Yonge Street. He boarded a moving train at night and, with the use of a rope ladder, broke the seal on the freight car door and heaved out a quantity of "China silk" at a crossing in Port Credit where he had a wagon parked by the tracks, then hauled the silk back to Toronto. And, as if that weren't enough, he stole a motor launch on the Etobicoke River and crossed Lake Ontario to discard stolen property in New York State, returning the same night.[18]

It was his recklessness that finally did him in. McCullough's "friend from Missouri" introduced him to an Albert Johnson of Ottawa. In early November 1918, McCullough and Johnson travelled to Ottawa, where they broke into a clothing store and stole a large quantity of furs and coats. They shipped the merchandise by train to Mrs. Gladys Mytton, McCullough's landlady at 177 Palmerston in Toronto,[19] returning themselves the following Sunday. They then began to sell the stolen furs wherever they could, and on November 18 pulled up to Madame May's clothing store on College Street.

At the time of McCullough's trial, no one in Toronto knew anything about Leroy Swart, about Westville, about the Missouri penitentiary, or Swart's desertion from the U.S. army. No one knew that McCullough had another name. During his trial for murder, McCullough's past was revealed only as far back as the incident with the whisky bottle. His life before that remained unknown.

# V

# The Trial - Day One

I attach no weight to the evidence of the witness Cross. . . .
I have never been thoroughly convinced in my own mind
that the prisoner did, at any time, intend to shoot Williams.
. . . His act in its moral, as distinguished from its legal,
aspect resembled the act which is usually treated as
manslaughter.

– Hon. Justice Mr. Hugh Edward Rose, April 2, 1919

The trial of *The King v. Frank McCullough* was held in the criminal assize court hearings at City Hall on January 21 and 22, 1919.

On the first day, the trial was less important to the newspapers
than the jubilant arrival of the largest single party of returning
soldiers Toronto had yet welcomed from overseas.[1] By the second
day, however, all of the Toronto papers gave extensive coverage to
McCullough and the dramatic outcome of the trial.

The proceedings attracted a considerable number of spectators, "many of whom were women." There was much interest in
McCullough's physical appearance and demeanour. He "seemed
to show no evidence of weakness . . . and his 'not guilty' rang out
without a tremor through the crowded court room." He was
dressed in "a neat suit of dark green serge" purchased for him. In

the opinion of the press, except for a defiant show of emotion at the end of his testimony, McCullough maintained a controlled "indifference" to the proceedings.

The judge was the Honourable Hugh Edward Rose, who had been a justice of the Supreme Court of Ontario for three years. Like Robinette, he was a graduate of the University of Toronto, where he continued to examine students in law and served for many years on the board of governors. Rose was a bachelor who lived with his mother in Rosedale, a golfer, and known "as one of the most retiring judges of the Supreme Court."[2] But he had nerves of steel.

Both the Crown and the defence retired a number of candidates for the jury, but in the end they agreed on seven farmers, a gardener, a shoemaker, a carpenter, and a confectioner.[3] The foreman of the jury, whose involvement in the case did not end with the trial, was Mr. Arthur Hill, who owned a real-estate firm on Danforth Avenue.

The proceedings opened with an "animated" description of the shooting at Cross's Livery, delivered by the Crown attorney, Mr. Peter White, K.C. White was "prominent as a Crown counsel and defence lawyer in various murder trials." He was a former mayor of Pembroke, Ontario, and, like Robinette, a defeated candidate in the provincial election of 1902.[4]

Robinette objected vigorously and frequently during White's opening summary, but was overruled by Mr. Justice Rose in every instance. Throughout most of the proceedings as the Crown built its case, Robinette's objective was to sow as much doubt as he could in the minds of the jurors. He was obstreperous, on his feet protesting at every turn in the testimony, objecting, questioning the credibility of witnesses, and doing whatever he could to thwart the Crown's evidence.

White's posture, however, was one of dignified calm. The law was the law, and the law was fair. "Reasonable men" frankly presented with the evidence, said White, "would do their duty, although it is as disagreeable as it can be for everybody concerned."[5] He refused to be ruffled by Robinette's antics, and quietly goaded his energetic opponent.

After the evidence of Dr. Harrington, who had performed the autopsy on Williams's body (Harrington: "He would go down practically at once – there was no chance of recovery after that bullet went through his heart"), White called Mr. George May, the owner of Madame May's clothing store on College Street. White began to question May about his telephone call from the store to Sergeant Umbach at the police station.

The jury knew nothing about the attempt to sell stolen furs on College Street. There was no reason for them to know about it unless, during the course of questioning on the specific charge of murder, information about the stolen furs became pertinent under established rules of jurisprudence. In fact, the Crown never did call May – or, later, Umbach – to question him specifically about stolen furs. He and Umbach were called to establish that the information first relayed to Umbach over the telephone was sufficient to justify Williams's arrest of McCullough at the livery stable later. The issue was the legality of the arrest.

Here we must enter into the legal terminology of the Criminal Code. According to the wording of the code that applied in 1919, an act of homicide was unquestionably murder if, for the purpose of "resisting lawful apprehension," an offender "means to inflict grievous bodily injury" whether the offender "means or not death to ensue."[6] In other words, if you managed to kill a policeman who was legally trying to arrest you, this was murder – and nothing but murder – whether you actually intended to kill the policeman or not.

The legality of the arrest was crucial in establishing the case for murder. It was essential for the Crown to show that the information May relayed to Sergeant Umbach over the telephone, and which May told Williams himself on College Street, justified the acting detective's attempt to arrest McCullough at the livery.

But there was another reason why the legality of the arrest

was important. White suspected Robinette would argue that McCullough should be convicted of manslaughter instead. Murder carried the penalty of death; manslaughter did not.

According to the code at the time, homicide was manslaughter, not murder, "if the person who causes death does so in the heat of passion caused by sudden provocation." The code stipulated, however, that "no one shall be held to give provocation to another by doing that which he had a legal right to do."

White suspected Robinette would argue that by bashing McCullough over the head with his baton, Williams caused a "sudden provocation" resulting in McCullough reacting in a "heat of passion" causing Williams's death. He would claim that McCullough's crime fit the category of manslaughter more than murder, and that the charge should be reduced accordingly.

However, the code stipulated that a policeman, or anyone "doing that which he had a legal right to do" – such as attempting to make a legal arrest – could not be deemed to have caused the kind of "provocation" required by the category of manslaughter. If White could firmly establish that Williams was making a legal arrest, he could derail the argument that the use of the baton was a provocation sufficient to reduce the charge to manslaughter.

For these reasons, Robinette objected vigorously to any part of May's testimony being heard or accepted by the court as evidence. He wanted all discussion of a legal arrest out of the proceedings. In his view, what had happened or had been said on College Street had nothing to do with the charge of murder facing McCullough. If Robinette could keep the jury clear of anything to do with stolen furs and a legal arrest, he could focus entirely on Williams's "violent" use of the baton as a "severe provocation."

Robinette objected to May's testimony for another reason as well. The matter of selling stolen furs on College simply made McCullough look bad; it fixed in the minds of the jurors that he was a criminal. The case at hand was that of murder, but if the jury became aware of McCullough's previous criminal activity, it could prejudice them against him. McCullough's past, or what little was known of it, could seriously damage his case, just as Burwash had harmed him earlier at the coroner's inquest.

After a lengthy argument (with the jury absent), Robinette managed to secure restricted testimony from May, who was not allowed to mention anything about furs. When White then asked Umbach to describe in full what he had heard from May over the telephone, Robinette was on his feet again:

Robinette: I object as to what information came.

White: Perhaps my learned friend does not appreciate why I want to give this evidence, and on what principle it is admissible. It may not have occurred to him.

Robinette: The jury should retire. It is quite irregular and quite unheard of.

His Lordship: There is no evidence in yet that is irregular and there is not going to be, if I can avoid it. . . . Mr. White is endeavouring to prove, as part of his case, it was a legal arrest.

Robinette: It is going far afield. The question is murder or no murder of Williams. My learned friend cannot anticipate my defence. What was telephoned to this gentleman [Umbach], even if he is a police constable, cannot be evidence against prisoner in a case of murder. . . . My learned friend starts in to prove that the detective was making a legal arrest. How can he do that? The question is, did McCullough kill Williams or not.

His Lordship: That is not the only question.

Robinette: Supposing McCullough had assaulted May that day upon College Street. How could evidence of that be given in a case of this kind where McCullough is charged with the murder of Williams. We cannot give character evidence. . . .

His Lordship: It is not character evidence at all.

Robinette: It goes in as that. That is the difficulty with the

jury, it proves at once that something was wrong and has
an influence on the jury.

His Lordship: It has no influence at all. . . . I think what this
witness heard may be given in evidence.

This ruling effectively demolished Robinette's efforts to keep the
jury unaware of stolen property. Now the only weapon Robinette
had to counter the negative impression of McCullough as an
offender was the personality of McCullough himself. Although not
required, Robinette could put McCullough on the stand.

But there was great danger in doing this, for if McCullough
took the stand, he could be cross-examined by White. And under
the guise of establishing whether McCullough was a credible
witness, White would be free to question McCullough about his
past. The door would be opened and the jury would hear all about
a whisky bottle smashed over a policeman's head, Burwash, and
McCullough's career as a burglar in Toronto.

What Robinette needed was a glaring weakness in the Crown's
evidence that would shift attention from McCullough and cast
serious doubt on the case presented by the prosecution.

The witness who suddenly gave it to him was William Cross.

Cross, the owner of the livery where the killing had taken place,
was the Crown's most important witness. Other than McCullough,
he was the only person present when Williams was shot, and the
only one who could comment on how the incident had begun.
His testimony and Robinette's cross-examination took up most of
the afternoon on the first day. During Cross's testimony, an otherwise "indifferent" McCullough "leaned intently forward in the
dock, his left hand gripping the railing."[7]

Cross's testimony was also the most perplexing heard by the
court. Quite apart from what he had to say, his manner, as Justice
Rose reported after the trial, "did not impress me favourably."
Indeed, wrote Rose, "as between the two men – if neither had
little interest in the result – I should have had little hesitation in
saying that McCullough's manner of giving evidence was so much

better than Cross's that he was the man who ought to be believed."[8]

The surprise came as White led Cross through his version of events to the point where Williams arrested McCullough and Johnson and took them into the back office.

White: Where were you when that happened?
Cross: I was right close behind them. . . . They got in the office and there was some scuffling and the other man broke away, and there was a shot fired. . . .
White: Did you hear anything?
Cross: I didn't hear any words. . . . I could hear a racket. They knocked over a clipping machine that was standing there and Williams had McCullough against the wall and there was three shots fired.
White: Yes, when those three shots were fired were you inside of the back office or outside?
Cross: I was inside.
White: Who fired them?
Cross: I can't just say who fired them three shots.

There was consternation in the courtroom. How could Cross be inside the office and not be able to say whether Johnson or McCullough, or for that matter even Williams, started the shooting? If Johnson was gone, why couldn't Cross say McCullough fired the shots? This confusion prompted the direct intervention of Justice Rose:

His Lordship: Mr. Cross, where were you when those first three shots were fired?
Cross: In the back office.
His Lordship: Where were Williams and McCullough?
Cross: In the same room.
His Lordship: Not a very big room?
Cross: No.
His Lordship: And not very much furniture in it?

Cross: No furniture.

His Lordship: You were in there, and those two men, and the shots were fired?

Cross: Three shots.

His Lordship: Fired in there; didn't you see them fired?

Cross: There wasn't much light, it was a little dark, the lamp wasn't on.

His Lordship: You didn't see them?

Cross: I seen fire flying from one of them.

His Lordship: You didn't see who it was that shot?

Cross: No, I didn't see who had the gun or anything like that there. I did not know who was doing the shooting.

The impression this left on the jury can be imagined. It is conceivable that in the struggle over the revolver, Cross couldn't tell whether Williams or McCullough was pulling the trigger. What frustrated everyone, however, was that Cross claimed to have been there but was unable to describe how the shooting began or who did what. Justice Rose wrote after the trial that "I could not understand, and cannot understand yet, how if Cross got into the room as soon as he said he did, he failed to know who had the revolver in the commencement of the struggle and failed to observe more accurately than he did the circumstances that led up to Johnson's escape."

Was it possible that Cross had not been in the office when he said he was, and that Johnson had begun the shooting?

Robinette saw his opening and was merciless in cross-examination:

Robinette: You don't know who fired those three shots, do you.

Cross: I don't.

Robinette: You said so at the inquest, that you didn't know who fired the three shots?

Cross: I don't know yet who fired them three shots.

Robinette: Those three shots, as far as you are concerned,
    may have been fired by either Johnson or McCullough?
Cross: Johnson wasn't there at that time.
Robinette: You say Johnson went through the door?
Cross: He did, went through the door.
Robinette: And will you swear that Johnson wasn't there
    when the three shots were fired inside?
Cross: Not when the whole three were fired.
Robinette: He might have been there when two were fired?
Cross: He might have been there when two was fired or one
    fired.

So Johnson had been there when the shooting began, yet Cross couldn't say for certain who started the shooting. Reserving the right to examine Cross again, Robinette called on twelve-year-old Ernest Stanley, who had been parking a rig in the driveway on the evening of the crime and fled as soon as the first shot was fired.

Robinette: You went off down the lane?
Stanley: Yes, sir. I just heard one shot.
Robinette: That was the shot inside?
Stanley: The first shot.
Robinette: And where was Mr. Cross then? Was he down
    the lane with you?
Stanley: He was in the lane, that is all I know.

Here was evidence that Cross was not in the back office at all. It was logical to presume that Cross would be dealing with the horse and buggy as Williams took his two prisoners into the office. It was logical to presume that the shots would bring him running to the office and that he was not present when the trouble first began. No wonder he couldn't say who started the shooting. Robinette called Cross to the stand again.

Robinette: You put that horse away?

Cross: I didn't. I was helping to unhitch the horse.

Robinette: Did you help to unhitch the horse?

Cross: We didn't get the horse unhitched.

Robinette: Did you help to get the horse unhitched?

Cross: We partly unhitched the horse.

Robinette: Answer yes or no.

Cross: The horse wasn't unhitched altogether.

Robinette: Did you help to unhitch the horse?

Cross: As far as was done.

Robinette: Did you help to unhitch the horse?

Cross: Partly.

But how could Cross even partly unhitch the horse and at the same time be following the three back to the office? As Robinette pointed out later, if the first shot drew him from unhitching the horse, Cross would have to travel seventy-five feet to the office before seeing anything of the scuffle inside. There was now serious doubt about whether anyone could claim for certain how the shooting actually began. Robinette dispensed with the witness:

Robinette: You served seven days yourself in gaol, across the Don, for receiving stolen property?

Cross: Yes, sir.

Robinette: For buying buffalo robes from boys?

Cross: Yes, sir.

It was late afternoon and the question arose whether the testimony could be finished that evening. White believed his final witness, Det. Bart Cronin, would "take up some time," while Robinette offered the assurance that his principal witness, Frank McCullough, would extend the proceedings further. This was the first intimation that McCullough would be called to testify.

With a warning to the jury not to permit "any outside influence of any sort reach you until you have discharged your duty," Justice Rose adjourned the court until ten the following morning. McCullough was taken out "with just the same display of indifference as shown since entering the court room."

The second day of the trial would have its share of surprises too.

# VI

# The Trial – Day Two

If I am correct in that opinion, you are not concerned in finding whether there was murder or manslaughter. . . . You are concerned in finding whether the crime is murder or nothing.

— Justice Rose to the jury, January 22, 1919

It was a pity that I could not see my way clear to give to the jury such instructions as would have justified them in convicting of manslaughter only, which I dare say they would have been glad to do.

— Justice Rose to J. D. Clarke, April 2, 1919

The trial resumed at 10:00 a.m.

The court was "crammed with onlookers, and reporters were much in evidence." When Robinette arrived, he was "greeted and congratulated by spectators," while McCullough showed "the same dignified aloofness" as he had the day before. There was some jovial banter before Justice Rose arrived, but the mood was tense. Everyone knew the trial would likely end that day.[1]

It was not an easy day for Peter White, the Crown attorney. After the setback of Cross's confusing testimony, White began the proceedings by once more methodically building his case. Everything was going smoothly as he led Det. Bart Cronin through his written notes on the questioning at City Hall, during which McCullough had openly admitted to shooting Williams. Asked if he had coerced McCullough into this confession, Cronin replied, "No, I did not. It is a serious charge and I would far sooner have no admissions at all. It is a serious charge, a man on trial for his life, and I want to play the game fair."

Suddenly Cronin dropped a bombshell. As White drew his questioning to a close, he casually asked his witness, "Is there anything else?" and Cronin let loose.

> Cronin: Well, there is. On the night of the inquest the prisoner asked me if I would come and see him, he had something to tell me.
> His Lordship: Do not tell what it is.
> Cronin: It is in direct connection with the shooting.
> White: Did you go and see him?
> Cronin: Yes. He told me, "Last night," he said, "up in the office I told you some things that wasn't true, I told you that I got that gun on a train coming from Parry Sound, from the trainman." He said, "I didn't get it from that man at all." . . . He said, "*Johnson* bought the gun from Cowdrey."[2]

Cronin had not reported this before! At McCullough's appearance in police court, Cronin had said that McCullough admitted he had not got the gun from a trainman but had bought it from Cowdrey. Now it was Johnson who bought the gun. Why the change in Cronin's testimony? Did he somehow believe that the proceedings weren't being conducted fairly enough for McCullough? ("It is a serious charge . . . and I want to play the game fair.") Or had McCullough's winning personality had its affect on Cronin too?[3]

Robinette was desperately in need of evidence that McCullough didn't intend to shoot Williams, and here was Cronin tossing it straight into his lap. For if Johnson owned the gun, might it not have been Johnson who started the shooting in the office?

> Robinette: Mr. Cronin, he said Johnson bought the revolver?
> Cronin: He did.
> Robinette: And he said that Johnson had the revolver in his possession that night, the day and night of the shooting?
> Cronin: No, but he said Johnson was in the habit of taking a drink and (if you want the exact expression) he said, "Sometimes he is a crazy damned fool."
> Robinette: At any rate, this revolver belonged to Johnson?
> Cronin: Yes, according to Frank's story.
> Robinette: And you investigated and found that Johnson bought the gun from Cowdrey?
> Cronin: Yes.

Notice that Cronin had also taken to calling McCullough "Frank."

Cronin's testimony brought an end to the evidence presented by the Crown. The trial now turned to the case for the defence. Robinette called only one witness – Frank McCullough.

McCullough's testimony and White's relentless cross-examination occupied the remainder of the afternoon. By all accounts, McCullough made a favourable impression. "The unfortunate man was quite self-possessed during the time he was in the witness-box, and only once did he show any sign of nervousness."[4] His description of the events at the livery was straightforward and was delivered without a hitch.

Robinette asked McCullough to explain in his own words what happened. McCullough said that as the three walked slowly back towards the office, Cross took the horse "and led him toward the rear of the barn." Williams pushed Johnson through the door ahead of himself, and then was followed by McCullough.

> McCullough: . . . I went last. He had hold of both of us as we went in. Johnson turned and said, "Why are we

arrested?" and the detective started to answer, and
Johnson reached and pulled out the gun like that, and
says, "Keep back." Of course the detective had to let go
when he pulled out the gun. And the detective reached
into his pocket, and as he did so, Johnson fired a shot,
and the detective pulled out of his front pocket a billy
. . . it looked to me it was a gun he pulled. It was dark
and clammy in there, couldn't see very well, hardly ten
feet away, and as he did that, Johnson fired another shot.

Then, according to McCullough, he yelled at Johnson: "Quit
that, you damn fool!" He seized Johnson's arm and tried to grab
the gun from him. "As I grabbed, he shot again, and when he
shot the gun the powder burned my fingers." McCullough held up
his hand for the entire court to see: "I have some remnants of the
powder burn on my knuckles yet." When this third shot went off,
Johnson let go of the gun and bolted out the front door just as
Williams hit McCullough on the head with his baton.

McCullough: . . . And the detective grasped me with one
    hand and hit me on the head, and backed me up against
    the wall and Cross came running down and looked in
    there, he spoke and said, "Quit that, you fools" or words
    to that effect. He stood there by the door for a minute
    and turned – I don't know where he went from there.
    Well, we fought for a minute in there, I didn't want to
    shoot or didn't try to shoot, and that man was beating
    me on the head and shoulders.

Justice Rose asked McCullough to repeat what he had just said,
and McCullough went through it again, emphasizing that it was
Johnson who had fired the first three shots and that Cross had
arrived too late to see how the shooting began. The *Toronto World*
observed that "this was the first time that McCullough had made

these accusations, and Peter White, K.C., who acted for the Crown, was frankly skeptical."[5]

McCullough described the struggle in the yard. The following testimony begins when Cross jumped on McCullough's back and put his arms around his neck.

> McCullough: . . . When he did that the [fourth] shot went off. I didn't intentionally pull the trigger, that man had his arms around my neck and the man in front was beating me on the head, that is when the fourth shot went off. I didn't intentionally pull the trigger. I remember hearing the shot. Well Cross continued to hold me and the man continued to beat me on the head with the billy, and the fifth shot went off. I didn't do it on purpose, I wouldn't have done anything like that on purpose.

All that remained was to account for McCullough's City Hall confession to Kennedy and Cronin that he fired all five shots. He now said that as a result of the blows to his head, he was "semiconscious, dazed like" when questioned.

> Robinette: You were afterwards taken to Inspector Kennedy's office and Detective Cronin was there. What condition were you in then?
>
> McCullough: Why I was in a dazed condition. I was worried, and also my head was hurting me and I worried about my partner, and matters like that.
>
> Robinette: Do you remember clearly what you said to Inspector Kennedy there?
>
> McCullough: No, sir. I remember some of the things, I don't remember the exact words or what I said.
>
> Robinette: Do you remember telling Inspector Kennedy that your partner had nothing to do with it?

McCullough: Yes, sir. I did it to protect him. I felt it was on me, it would be called a crime. I felt it was on me and I thought there was no use of getting my partner time for something that I could take on myself.

Robinette: You had no intention of exploding that revolver?

McCullough: No, sir, I always refused to have anything to do with firearms.

Robinette: Did you ever carry a revolver?

McCullough: No, sir.

Robinette: And it was under these conditions you describe that the revolver exploded?

McCullough: Yes, sir.

Robinette: You having no intention to injure him?

McCullough: Good God no, I no more pulled that trigger than –

McCullough didn't finish this last sentence.

It was a flawless performance, with McCullough losing his composure at exactly the right moment. Reporters noted that as he gave a broken answer to Robinette's final question, he "leaned forward on the box unable to find an expression strong enough."[6]

Was McCullough truly innocent of murder, or was his story too neat to be true?

Now White had his opportunity. He immediately began to question McCullough about his past to undermine his credibility: "You were arrested before on a charge for which you served a term in Burwash? You hit that officer, who arrested you, on the head with a bottle, didn't you?"

Robinette didn't object and Rose didn't intervene. It was permissible to examine McCullough about his past, provided it had a bearing on the testimony given, just as Robinette had been allowed to question Cross about his time in the Toronto Jail. But as soon as White was permitted to touch on Burwash with impunity, he was free to roam through McCullough's life of crime since then.

The skill with which White manipulated this line of questioning left Rose feeling uneasy. He wrote after the trial that "I thought, and still think that it [White's questioning] was justified upon the authorities." Rose had in fact explained to the jury in his summation that this evidence was admissible "only in so far as it bore upon the credibility of the prisoner as a witness." "But," he continued after the trial, "it must have been well nigh impossible" for the jury to avoid considering White's questions "as bearing upon the question whether the prisoner was the kind of man who would be likely to shoot if he found himself in a tight place."

In short, although the judge believed the evidence concerning McCullough's past was properly admitted, he feared that "it may have had an effect which it ought not to have had, and may have been used for a purpose for which it could not have been admitted."[7]

White was relentless.

White: You backed up to a cigar store in West Toronto and practically cleaned the store out, even the clock on the wall?

McCullough: Yes, sir.

White: Didn't you steal a large quantity of glass and copper from Dr. Naismith's place? Took the glass right out of his conservatory, loaded it on to a wagon, and sold it out on Yonge Street?

McCullough: Yes, sir.

White: In other words, you and Johnson had been systematically living a life of burglars since you came out of Burwash, practically?

McCullough: Yes, sir.

White: Now, you told Cronin that Johnson had nothing to do with this shooting?

McCullough: Yes, sir.

White: You also told Inspector Kennedy that you fired the five shots?

McCullough: I say I don't remember saying in those words,
    I may have said it. I was dazed at the time.

White then moved to establish just how dazed McCullough
was when he was questioned. He painstakingly took McCullough
through virtually every question Kennedy asked him at City Hall
as recorded in Cronin's notes. Had he said yes to this question, or
no to that, and why? It was a cunning manoeuvre. McCullough
was fooled into thinking that White was challenging the accuracy
of his answers in Kennedy's office. As McCullough started to
explain the logic of his answers to Kennedy, he began to reveal
that he had not been dazed at all. Suddenly, McCullough realized
what was happening:

White: Were you asked, "Were these goods stolen in the city
    or the country?"
McCullough: Yes, sir.
White: What did you reply?
McCullough: I have forgotten the answer to that. I was in a
    dazed condition. I don't remember exactly.
White: I see you have at last found out the object of my
    questions.

This was a major setback for McCullough. He had been tricked
into revealing that when he admitted to firing all five shots, he
wasn't as dazed as he claimed to be, and that he had sufficient
wits about him to take evasive action under questioning to protect
his partner. McCullough's demeanour in the prisoner's box began
to change.

White: In respect to all of your answers, you say there was
    present at that time in your mind the object of saving
    Johnson?
McCullough: Yes, sir.

White: And today your object is otherwise, you don't care about Johnson, as long as you save yourself?

McCullough: It is a different matter now, sir.

White: You knew, and had the consciousness in your mind that you were leading a life of crime and that society was organized against you?

McCullough: Yes, sir.

White: You realized that?

McCullough: Yes, sir.

White: And nothing to protect yourself?

McCullough: [displaying his two fists] That is all, sir.

McCullough's final words were spoken in defiance. He lost his composure. He was angry at himself for being tricked, angry at White, angry about his whole predicament. White had him, and declared that he had no more questions for the witness.

This ended the testimony, and for the next hour and a half Robinette and White addressed the jury in summation. The arguments presented were much the same as those put forward during their questioning of witnesses, with one predictable exception: although the charge against McCullough was murder, Robinette made a passionate appeal for a charge of manslaughter. "This is not murder, get that into your heads at once," he began.[8]

For his part, White reminded the jury that the charge was "nothing but" murder; or, as he slyly put the matter, recounting McCullough's sins: "You are not trying him for burglary or for selling stolen goods or for lying," let alone a fictitious charge of manslaughter. He concluded with an appeal to law and order: "Are you going to say to policemen, 'do your duty, but if you are killed in the discharge of your duty we will let the man off because of weakness or a sentimental feeling we have for him?'"

Justice Rose concluded: "Gentlemen of the Jury – a good deal has been said about the law in this case, and I should take a little extra time so I may consider carefully what I have to say to you about the law. I think we will adjourn until ten minutes after three."

The judge had a thankless task to perform. As we shall see, he was not convinced completely that McCullough intended to shoot Williams, but his duty as a judge was to direct the jury precisely in the charge before the court. And he knew exactly where a proper interpretation of the Criminal Code would lead. When court resumed, Rose began by saying, "Gentlemen of the Jury – I am responsible for your proceeding upon a correct view of the law and you have no responsibility whatsoever as regards the law. You accept the law as I may state it to be."

He spoke for one hour, reviewing the intricacies of the Criminal Code as they related to the evidence, and concluded by making it abundantly clear that the jury's choice was between complete acquittal or a conviction of murder.

Rose explained that for the jury to consider McCullough guilty of manslaughter, they would have to satisfy at least one of two conditions: that Williams's arrest of McCullough was unlawful and McCullough knew it to be unlawful during the event, or that Williams used an "unreasonable amount of force" altogether. If they could not find one of these conditions, then manslaughter was out of the question. "If I am correct in that opinion you are not concerned in finding whether there was murder or man-slaughter . . . you are concerned in finding whether the crime is murder or nothing."

McCullough's statement was that he did not consciously pull the trigger, that the shooting was involuntary, or a reflex action during the struggle. "If you accept that statement," concluded Rose, "then there is no crime at all." But the jury had to accept McCullough's statement in its entirety or reject it. "You cannot give effect to his statement by reducing the charge from murder to manslaughter." It was all or nothing: "You are confronted with the alternative of deciding between murder and acquittal; not between murder and manslaughter."

The jury retired at 4:15 p.m.

As soon as they were out, Robinette complained to Rose that

in his charge to the jury the judge had not stressed sufficiently how badly McCullough had been beaten while the fourth and fifth shots were fired. White complained that Robinette was complaining. White added that if Rose were to say anything more to the jury about the last shots, he should also mention a point that hadn't come up in the testimony: that McCullough could have thrown away the revolver at any time.

> His Lordship: I think it is fair, if they are going to be spoken to about it at all. If I am going to talk to the jury about the 4th and 5th shots I think I ought to say: after the revolver had exploded at the 4th shot, why did he not throw it away?
>
> Robinette: No, I do not think your Lordship should. I do not think that should be commented upon. I am willing to withdraw my request for the other matter. I think it is clearly enough before the jury.
>
> His Lordship: I think it is.

They waited. The atmosphere in the courtroom was tense, although the *Star* observed that the "spectators and the bench showed the strain more than the prisoner." McCullough "continually talked to the guards. At times he laughed and joked with Detective Cronin, and the strain under which he was suffering did not seem to make as much of an impression as might be expected."[9]

An hour and a half later, the jury sent in word it was returning. There was a scramble as spectators and reporters outside returned to their places. Arthur Hill, the foreman, explained that they had returned "to go over the evidence of Cross with regard to the time when the first three shots were fired, as to his position and where he was at that time." Cross's testimony was read to the jury and they retired again.

It took another hour and a half for the jury to reach its decision. They returned at 8:30 p.m. "This was the tense moment for everyone present." McCullough "sat there straight, looking at the foreman of the jury, calmly awaiting the verdict. The only signs of nervousness were the swallowing in his throat and his heavy breathing."

Clerk: (Calls the jury and twelve men respond.)

Foreman: We find the prisoner guilty.

His Lordship: Mr. Robinette, have you anything to say?

Robinette: I have nothing to say at the present time except that in imposing sentence, as your lordship must do, I would ask for a reasonable time in which to make application to the Minister of Justice, and perhaps take other steps by way of appeal, after I look into the evidence.

His Lordship: What about the 2nd of May?

Robinette: Satisfactory.

Clerk: Frank McCullough, have you anything to say why the sentence of the Court should not be pronounced against you?

McCullough: No.

His Lordship: Mr. White, do you move for the sentence of the Court?

White: I move for the sentence of the Court.

His Lordship: The sentence of the Court upon you, Frank McCullough, for the crime of which you have been found guilty is, that you now be taken hence to the place from which you came, that you there be detained in close confinement until Friday, the second day of May, 1919, and that you then be taken to the place appointed for your execution and there be hanged by the neck until you are dead. May God have mercy upon your soul.

McCullough was handcuffed to the arm of Bart Cronin and escorted by a guard out of the courtroom. "He walked steadily with head up toward the door."

As he walked through the corridors of the City Hall to the elevator, McCullough appeared cool. He smoked a cigarette and glanced about at the oil paintings on the walls. Last night he was placed under his death watch, a guard of three men, and put in the death cell which Hassan Neby occupied before his execution.

## VII

# Albanian Mohammedan

All that night you could hear him all over the gaol; then he
started to pray.

– Guard Harry Denning, April 22, 1919

Before Frank McCullough's trial, while he was being held in the
Toronto Jail, an event took place that left a deep impression
upon him.

Hassan Neby, described in the Toronto newspapers as an
"Albanian Mohammedan," was hanged at the jail on January 3,
1919, for the violent murder of a Canadian Pacific railwayman.

The difficulty was that Neby neither spoke nor understood
English. The few words he could utter, which he repeated often,
were, "I never see that man, I never did nothing." It appears,
moreover, that Neby didn't understand the outcome of his trial
and had no idea he was to be hanged. He was under the impression that, in due course, he would be sent to the penitentiary at
Kingston, and that the matter of final punishment hadn't been
finally decided.

It was suddenly realized – the very day before the hanging –
that Neby had not been given a spiritual adviser. At the last
minute, the adviser so assigned to this "Albanian Mohammedan"

was the young Rev. C. M. Carew, assistant minister of the Jarvis Street Baptist Church.

The inexperienced Carew had officiated at weddings and funerals but had never attended at a hanging. When he realized, to his astonishment, that Neby had no idea what was about to happen, Carew complained to the guards. He was received with complete indifference. And so it fell to the young minister to explain somehow to Neby that the end was nigh. This unwelcome duty, no doubt involving unclerical sign language, was accomplished at 10:30 on the evening before the scheduled hanging.

When Neby realized his fate, "his Oriental stoicism deserted him," in the words of the *Evening Telegram*. He became hysterical, and kept the guards and inmates up the whole night. "All that night you could hear him all over the gaol; then he started to pray." The *Globe* observed blankly that "the offices of the church were tendered by Rev. C. M. Carew but were declined, the condemned man embracing the faith of his fathers." Kneeling on some pillowcases that he had arranged on the floor, Neby "faced towards Mecca . . . and performed the customary ablutions and prostrations of the Islamic faith. These devotional acts he kept up for a long time."

The day before, hangman Arthur Ellis had arrived in Toronto to perform what he described as his "public duty." Ellis was known for his "coolness and efficiency." Over a twenty-year career in England, the Middle East, and Canada, he had dispatched over six hundred souls.[1] On his arrival, Ellis announced to reporters that "it's too bad it is not William Hohenzollern [meaning the Kaiser] that's to be executed."[2] He explained that "when that event takes place it is my right to officiate as the oldest official in this line of duty in the British Empire." Ellis was prone to using the word "official."

In the morning, "a deathlike stillness pervaded the whole building as all the inmates of the institution knew that the hanging was to take place." Shortly before seven, guards abruptly entered Neby's cell and bound his hands behind him. He was then swiftly ushered the forty steps to the death chamber with the deputy sheriff and the chief turnkey, Mr. Henry Addy, leading the way. Neby was flanked by two guards followed by Reverend Carew and Arthur Ellis.

A visibly distraught Neby, "his face streaming with perspiration," yelled repeatedly, "I never see that man, I never did nothing!" As Ellis yanked the black hood and noose over Neby's head, an agitated Carew began to recite the Lord's Prayer. When he reached "Give us this day our daily bread," Neby fainted and collapsed to one side. Ellis, "the coolest man" throughout the ordeal, shouted to the guards, "Pick him up!"

When Carew reached "Deliver us . . .," Ellis "sprang the trap and Neby launched into a drop of seven feet six inches." He hung suspended for seventeen minutes, after which Dr. T. Owen Parry declared life extinct. "Although the post-mortem showed that Neby's neck was broken, he lived longer than any man that had been hanged in Toronto, according to the jail physician."

Ellis remained to chat with reporters while Addy "walked away and was seen to wipe tears from his eyes. 'I am glad it is over, I hope I won't have to see another.'" Carew was observed to be "bordering on the state of collapse."[3]

Neby left a wife and three children in Albania.

Frank McCullough was in the jail throughout this ordeal.

# The Death Watch

When Doris was home and Frank was there, they were
together. He seemed more like a friend than anything else.
He was always gentlemanly. . . . I think he must have been
fond of her but he seemed to have so many [women]. I
think now that he was playing everybody and everywhere.
. . . He always appeared to be so manly.
 – Mrs. Gladys Mytton, April 22, 1919

The jail was sloppy about Frank McCullough from the start.
His detention, after his trial in January 1919, coincided with a
low point in the administration of the Toronto Jail. But to make
matters worse, the jail staff soon showed themselves unequal to a
man of McCullough's cunning.

The Toronto Jail, designed in the 1840s by architect William
Thomas, was not officially opened until 1865. From the beginning,
the facility was overcrowded and repeatedly condemned for its
appalling conditions. It was constructed of cold grey stone and
black iron, with row upon row of small square cells containing
barred windows set above the line of sight.

The jail was near the intersection of Gerrard Street and
Broadview Avenue, which in the 1860s was on the eastern-most

fringe of the city. It sat on the edge of a valley containing the Don River, which separated the jail from central Toronto, and on its north side extended Riverdale Park. Because of its location, the Toronto Jail was often called the "Don Jail," or, at times, the "Riverdale Bastille." And because of its clientele and poor conditions, and persistently inept management, the place was widely known for its venality.[1]

In 1907, the governor of the jail, a Mr. G. R. Van Zant, was found "guilty of improper conduct, incompetencies and irregularities, favouritism and lack of discipline." About the only charge that didn't stick was that Van Zant profited from "certain financial transactions with prisoners," a matter found to be "unsubstantiated." Van Zant was fired.[2]

His replacement was a "soldier of the Cross," a "most kindly man" of sixty-six years, the Reverend Dr. Andrew B. Chambers. Chambers' chief qualification for the demanding job of governor was not administrative experience (he was vice-president of the Upper Canada Bible Society) but that, unlike many of his Methodist ministerial peers, he was "a sturdy adherent of the Conservative Party."[3]

The Reverend Doctor served as governor for ten long years "without losing the purity and dignity of his ministerial standing." In the words of his faithful deputy, the governor's "regime was characterized by the use of kindness" with his prisoners. Chambers "simply wanted to be a friend to everyone, especially those in trouble."[4]

Consequently, although there were no reports of the impure practices that had characterized the Van Zant period, the jail was virtually without leadership for a decade. Indeed, Chambers was so ineffectual that when, at the height of the war effort in 1917, the cry went up that the jail was overstaffed, the two positions declared redundant were those of the governor himself and his deputy. "Special monetary provision was made for the two officials to justify their removal, which was done without their being consulted."[5]

The position of governor was not refilled. Instead, the jail's administration was left in the hands of two men: one, the frustrated chief turnkey, Mr. Henry Addy, who knew by experience how the jail worked, and who reported to the other, the incompetent sheriff of the city, Mr. Frederick Mowat, whose office was at City Hall. Mowat had been appointed sheriff in 1888, when his father, Sir Oliver Mowat, was premier of the province.

During the winter of 1919, morale at the jail was poor. After his trial at the end of January, McCullough was moved from a regular cell to the "death cell" previously occupied by Hassan Neby.[6]

A prisoner condemned to death required special arrangements.[7] It was necessary to employ three additional guards to supervise the prisoner around the clock. Those hired for this purpose were known collectively as the "death watch," and their task, quite simply, was to prevent the prisoner from escaping or committing suicide. The work was anything but congenial.

When Addy applied to Sheriff Mowat for men to watch McCullough, Mowat assigned two men who were already working for him at City Hall: Sam Follis, a driver, and Alfred Amory, a former constable. Both had been on the death watch for Hassan Neby, knew the routine, and, because they had seniority, snatched the two day shifts.

It was always difficult to find someone to take the night shift. Mowat discussed candidates with an assistant at Osgoode Hall, who made the brilliant suggestion that a returned soldier would be good for public relations.

One of the major grievances of the returned soldiers in 1918–19 was that suitable employment remained closed to them. In their view, many jobs were filled by "slackers" who had cowered at home making money while the soldiers lost limbs in the trenches. It would certainly be good for the sheriff's office to be seen doing its part for the veterans, and so Mowat did something that for him was uncharacteristic – he made a decision. He was going to hire a returned soldier, and a needy one at that.

He contacted the Reverend Peter Bryce, widely known for his pastoral ministrations with veterans. For Bryce, the telephone call was evidence of providence at work. He had the perfect candidate: a "pitiable" case by the name of Ernest Currell. Admittedly, Currell had all of his limbs, but he was sick, had a starving family, and was desperate for work.

Mowat had a conversation with Currell and "found that he had been at the Front and apparently had done his duty there. Having these recommendations, I thought there was no question but that he was a suitable man."[8] Suitable or not, Currell was certainly needy.

The thirty-four-year-old Currell had joined the Canadian Expeditionary Force in November 1915. An unemployed tinsmith, he and his wife and three small children had been living in poverty. Currell was assigned to the 95th Overseas Battalion and reached the Somme in October 1916. Eleven days later, he was struck by a bullet in the right hand.

Much later, when McCullough got him into trouble, Currell relished being described as a former "wounded soldier." But his service record indicates that after the hand wound, and a spell of convalescence in Boulogne, Currell was sent right back to the field.[9] Three months later, he was admitted with back pain to the Canadian Hospital at Etaples.[10] It was sciatica, not a combat wound, that brought the mighty hero down. In September 1917, he was dispatched from Buxton back to Canada, his "services being no longer required." He was discharged in December at Exhibition Camp, Toronto,[11] suffering from "myalgia" and "hoarseness."

For the next two years, Currell's back kept him out of work. The Pension Board added to his suffering by questioning his application for disability. The family moved to a small house at 4 Hanson Road in Earlscourt, for which Currell hoped to make payments. Soon there were visits by the bailiff. His youngest child became seriously ill, but there was no money for medicine. There was no money for coal either, although small amounts were supplied on occasion by sympathetic neighbours. "It was stated that a child was expected in the household, and that the mother, who is very sick, needs immediate attention."[12]

Mowat hired the short, soft-spoken "wounded" soldier on the spot. He was to receive three dollars a shift, which led to much rejoicing on Hanson Road. Because Currell took the night watch, hardly anyone at the jail got to know him; except Frank McCullough, who could be a real friend.

Two days after the trial, the *Daily Star* reported that McCullough was showing "signs of worry and breakdown." He was "not eating very well, and smokes cigarettes incessantly. The brave spirit that he showed during the two days of the trial has vanished."[13] The article left the impression that McCullough's difficulty was guilt as well as fear, and that he had already lost hope.

His attorney, T. C. Robinette, knew that the press would be crucial in shaping public opinion over the matter of executive clemency. Other than an appeal (which was abandoned), McCullough's only hope was sufficient pressure on Ottawa to commute the sentence to life imprisonment. Consequently, Robinette called reporters to his Adelaide Street offices to announce his intention of "going to Ottawa in the near future to appeal for executive clemency."

He said that he and Det. Bart Cronin were at the jail only the day before and, contrary to newspaper reports, found McCullough to be far from dejected. "He greeted us with a smile and shook hands. During the brief stay he chatted freely, joked now and then, and listened eagerly. I told him of my contemplated trip to Ottawa to see the acting Minister of Justice. His eyes lit up and shone."

Then Robinette launched into the well-rehearsed recitation he delivered whenever he spoke to reporters about the case: there was "doubt" about the Crown's evidence, "doubt" in the verdict of the jury, "doubt in the case, whether or not McCullough really fired the first three shots . . . that it was done on the impulse of the moment followed by the pounding and striking he received on the head."

Invariably, as he did in this first interview, Robinette concluded with an appeal to sentiment: "McCullough broke down once when we talked of his mother. The tears streamed down his cheeks." He said that his "greatest sorrow was for his mother: 'One of the grandest mothers in the world,' as he put it, and here McCullough's big shoulders shook, and the tears flowed like a child until he recovered himself."

This was a deliberate effort to renew public interest in the case, and what would attract greater attention than a sentimental interview in the death cell between mother and son? The *Star* took the bait: "Mr. Robinette has sent a letter to McCullough's mother in Youngstown, Ohio, notifying her of the fate of her son." As a nice touch, the paper added that McCullough had himself "written a letter to Mr. Justice Rose, the trial judge, thanking him for the fair trial."[14]

The trouble was, McCullough's mother refused to play the part assigned to her. Myrtle Swart, "one of the grandest mothers in the world," had moved to Youngstown after her husband, Emory Swart, had died a broken man in Long Island. Myrtle wouldn't have anything to do with Leroy, who now it seemed was calling himself Frank McCullough.

Leroy burned their house down. He ran away from home. He hadn't contacted them for thirteen years. He deserted the army. He murdered a policeman. And now he wanted her to come crying to Toronto for the newspapers and goodness knows what else?

Her reply to Robinette was long in coming. When the "strange letter, a very cold one," did arrive, it said that she could not afford the trip to Toronto and would prefer if Robinette did not write to her again. She added that if McCullough's connection with the family became known in Youngstown, his sister Elsie would lose her job.[15]

Robinette kept the contents of this letter to himself and never disclosed the outcome of an associate's visit to Youngstown to appeal directly to Myrtle Swart. Throughout the remainder of the case, however, he left the impression that there was continuing anguish in Youngstown.

Arthur Hill, the guilt-ridden foreman of the jury, was not as discreet about McCullough's mother or the personal appeal to her in Youngstown. Later in the case, he let slip in a letter to officials in Ottawa that when McCullough's mother "was recently appealed to in her home at Youngstown, Ohio, to take an interest in her son, and try to have his sentence commuted, she refused to have anything further to do with him."

Mothers never seem to get a fair shake. To explain Myrtle Swart's indifference, Hill went on to claim that "McCullough's lawlessness was to a considerable extent the result of the negligence of his parents in his upbringing. It has been ascertained . . . that McCullough was turned adrift from his home, by his mother, when he was fifteen years old, as she had taken a dislike to him."[16]

The difficulty with Justice Rose, who did indeed receive a letter of gratitude from McCullough, was that he was too proper a judge to acknowledge in writing that he had his own reservations about the trial. This was a source of great frustration for Robinette. It was an open secret that everyone involved in the case was disconcerted by the outcome of the trial, but only Rose had the authority to recommend clemency to Ottawa.

According to Hill, the jury did not believe that McCullough was guilty of murder, but neither were they convinced that he was entirely innocent. Behind closed doors, some said they wanted to acquit, but others could not agree.[17] Manslaughter was the answer; but Rose had denied the jury this convenience with the lucidity of his charge to them. The Criminal Code had everyone boxed in.

Although it will never be known for certain, Arthur Hill seems to have used his position as foreman (and his forceful personality) to convince his reluctant fellow jurors to find a verdict of guilty, in the belief that, given the circumstances of the case, executive clemency would likely be shown. This may explain, in part, why Hill was so active in the effort to commute the sentence afterwards.

But executive clemency was a realistic possibility only if the judge in the case, in his formal report after the trial, made a recommendation accordingly. What worried Robinette was that he knew Rose and what Rose was likely to do. The man was utterly orthodox when it came to the holy writ of the Criminal Code. No matter how strong Rose's personal misgivings about the verdict might be, he would allow nothing to interfere with a dispassionate interpretation of the law.

Robinette's assessment was correct. On February 7, Rose filed his trial report with the secretary of state in Ottawa. The report was succinct and as cold as ice. Rose said he had explained to the jury that, if the arrest had been unlawful or Williams had used unreasonable force, the charge might be reduced to manslaughter; "but that unless the charge was upon that ground reduced, the only question was whether there was an act amounting to murder, or merely an involuntary movement which was not a juristic act at all." The report said nothing about executive clemency.[18]

Rose's report was acknowledged by the secretary of state and copied as a matter of course to Mr. J. D. Clarke, acting head of the Remission Branch in the Department of Justice.

Clarke was the faceless bureaucrat in Ottawa who exercised more power than anyone else in this case. He had two responsibilities. The first was not to trouble his minister, unless by not troubling him, more trouble would ensue. The second was to coordinate all requests for the reduction of criminal sentences in the Dominion of Canada that were within the jurisdiction of the federal government to decide.

This meant that the dutiful Clarke could be a dangerous man. He had the power of persuasion without responsibility for the final decision. After Clarke kissed his wife upon leaving for the office each morning, his work determined whether others lived or died.

➻ ➻

No visitors were allowed. By law only a doctor, the prisoner's lawyer, or a "Minister of Religion" was permitted access to a prisoner under sentence of death. All other visits were to be forbidden, unless exceptional circumstances justified the sheriff in providing written permission.

But Doris Mytton, sixteen, got in to see McCullough only two days after the trial.

"Little" Doris, "yet in short dresses,"[19] was the innocently alluring daughter of Gladys Mytton, McCullough's landlady on Palmerston who had been charged with receiving stolen property. Young Doris simply appeared at the front door of the jail, alone, and asked to see McCullough.

The chief turnkey, Henry Addy, denied her access. There were to be no visitors. She wasn't even a relative. And the Toronto Jail was no place for a sixteen-year-old schoolgirl to be flitting about the corridors. Doris was persistent, and Addy finally referred the "little girl" to the sheriff, Frederick Mowat, whom Addy assumed would also deny the interview.

But Mowat could be aroused from a narrow-minded view of the law. Doris returned shortly after, waving a signed permit granting her permission to see the prisoner. Addy was appalled by this flagrant breach of the regulations. "I went up to McCullough and said, 'There is a girl coming to see you Frank [note "Frank"], the Sheriff has permitted her to come, but there must be no embracing or anything like that.'"[20]

Doris was escorted by the chief guard, Harry Denning, to McCullough's cell.

When he opened the door Frank was standing about the end of the room. I just stood inside the door. I had made up my mind coming down to try and cheer Frank up, but when I got inside the door I just couldn't say a word. I was only there a minute, but it seemed like a long time. I guess I said, "Hello, Frank," and he just said, "Hello." I felt that I was going to cry or laugh out loud. I guess I was feeling pretty bad, for I said, "What a funny little bed!" I felt so foolish after I had said it. Even after I got outside I was the same way. I guess I am nervous.

Doris's visit was significant, quite apart from the revealing reference to the bed.[21] Henceforth, McCullough was a source of conflict between Addy and Mowat.

The issue was who was in charge of the jail. Addy felt that if Mowat wanted to break the regulations by allowing Doris's visit, that was his business. But who would be responsible if something went wrong? Addy knew the answer to that. He also believed he had been right not to let her in, and that Mowat had undermined his authority by reversing that decision. But without a governor, who could Addy complain to about Mowat other than Mowat?

The tension between the two men created friction, in turn, between the regular jail guards and the three men on the death watch. As chief turnkey, Addy was responsible for everyone inside the jail; but the three men on the death watch – employed directly by Mowat – viewed themselves as employees of the sheriff, answerable only to the sheriff. The resulting conflict over how McCullough was to be handled was, in reality, a fight for control of the jail.

McCullough was soon to gain unwarranted privileges due to Mowat's incompetence. All he had to do was wait.

Henceforth, Addy refused to inform potential visitors turned away at the door that they could appeal to the good offices of the sheriff. Thus, when another young woman (described later by Addy as "mysterious") quietly applied for entry one morning, shortly after Doris's visit, she was given no assistance. "She had a little parcel and I did not let her in; she wanted to know if she could see Frank and I said No, so she went away. She was well dressed, wore dark clothes, plainly made, was of dark complexion, rather French looking I thought."[22]

This is the first appearance of a character whose role is central to McCullough's story.

# IX

# The Church for the Stranger

I have no apology to make for what I did in connection
with McCullough. Some criticism, not all of it mild, has
been passed upon me, but the church is for such cases. The
church is not confined to the home.

         – Rev. R. Bertram Nelles, May 8, 1919

When Doris Mytton visited Frank McCullough at the jail, she
recognized Alfred Amory, one of the three men on the death
watch. Like Doris and her parents, Amory attended the Western
Congregational Church at 327 Spadina Avenue, where the
Reverend R. Bertram Nelles was pastor.

The following Sunday morning, Doris approached Amory at
the back of the church and asked if he would take a letter to
McCullough. "It was kind of a love letter," Amory said later. "In
one part of the letter it said, 'I want you to pray Frank as I am going
to pray for you.' That was the reason I brought in the letter because
I thought it might have a big influence on him to pray and that it
might help him."[1] Amory clearly broke a jail regulation by delivering this letter without the knowledge of the chief turnkey.

Doris suggested in her letter that McCullough request a visit
from Reverend Nelles. This McCullough did, and after a first

interview on January 29, at which McCullough presented himself
as humbly in need of spiritual guidance, Nelles undertook to visit
the jail daily and was designated McCullough's "spiritual adviser."

Nelles was forty when providence permitted him to stumble
upon McCullough. Although Nelles had no way of knowing at the
time, McCullough would be his most dramatic conversion in a
lengthy ministerial career that would never again achieve such
public notoriety.

Nelles was a Presbyterian who had studied at the University of
Toronto and Edinburgh University. In 1916, he was invited to
Western Congregational, because the drive for church union
among Congregationalists, Methodists, and Presbyterians was
already underway,[2] and because the spiritual language of Nelles's
ministry transcended denominational boundaries. The other
reason for the call was that the previous minister, the garrulous
Dr. J. W. Pedley, had had a falling out with church elders and quit.

Pedley was a practical man who had nurtured Western
Congregational since his arrival in 1899, when the church carried
a burdensome mortgage of $23,000. With noisy determination,
Pedley retired the debt ("with the satisfaction of burning the
mortgage in the pulpit while the choir sang the Doxology")[3] only
to face pressures of an entirely different kind.

Well before the outbreak of war, the Congregational saints at
327 Spadina woke to find themselves surrounded by a thriving
Jewish community.[4] By the time the war arrived, Pedley could
gather no more than a small Sunday-morning meeting. The
church was in decline, and what was worse, leaders of the Jewish
community had made attractive offers to purchase the property
and transform the building into a synagogue.

Pedley's businesslike advice to his elders was to hold out "to
the Jews" for $70,000 and then locate elsewhere in the city. But
the elders feared this "would seem to be sounding a retreat, whereupon Pedley presented his resignation." Nelles was hired to keep
the Christian cause afloat upon a rising tide of Judaism, and
during his pastorate, the church became a classic example of the

community-based "institutional" church typical of a weakened, early-twentieth-century urban Protestantism.

Nelles transformed the self-preoccupied, denominational "Western Congregational" into an outward-looking, non-denominational "Church for the Stranger," as it came to be known in the city.

The watchword was "organization," and the drive was for membership. The Church for the Stranger opened its doors to anyone in need. It was a "home for the unknown," of whom there were many in wartime Toronto. Clubs were organized for every member of the family. There was a daycare. And Nelles marshalled the young people into an extensive program of "district visitation" that ventured beyond the Spadina region to draw in new members.

At the Church for the Stranger, a mix of organizational bustle during the week, combined with Nelles's vaudevillian[5] (but "spiritually focused") services on Sunday, revitalized the congregation and proved for a time to halt decline.[6]

Could there be a more sensational triumph than the conversion of a young man facing the gallows? After their initial interview at the jail, McCullough became a frequent subject of Nelles's sermon illustrations. In time, there were special prayer services and "letter-bees" organized in support of executive clemency. Mrs. Bell's "Non-Denominational Young Women's Bible Class" took a special interest, and soon Alfred Amory was taking in cookies and fresh eggs to the jail (another breach of the regulations). It was Nelles's young "district visitors" who first circulated petitions on McCullough's behalf throughout the streets of Toronto. The petitioning campaign soon spread to other churches and beyond, eventually assaulting Ottawa with more than 20,000 names.[7]

McCullough's alliance with the church was at first purely self-serving. The man knew how to use others. He knew that a personal demonstration of religious transformation could have a persuasive effect on public opinion in a churchified city such as Toronto in a Protestantized province such as Ontario. And he played his part to the hilt.

McCullough sat (and kneeled) with Nelles day after day, expressing sorrow for what had happened, and "sorrow for his poor dear mother." They studied the Bible together, prayed fervently, and soon the effort began to produce results. By February 17, the *Star* (which had reported earlier that the prisoner was demoralized) declared that McCullough was "more concerned now about his soul. His whole attitude has changed wonderfully in the last two weeks. Mr. Nelles visits the condemned man daily, coming in the morning and spending two hours in Bible reading and prayer."

Descriptions of rejuvenation and peace replaced previous reports about depression and anxiety. "In fact he doesn't seem to worry at all. He is in splendid condition, eating and sleeping well, and is a model prisoner. He is gaining weight and exercises daily, with Swedish stunts in his death cell, using his towel rack as an exercise bar."

The newspapers' coverage progressed from McCullough's state of mind to his talents, considered unusual for a man convicted of murder. It was recalled that McCullough had demonstrated "remarkable cleverness" in his questioning of witnesses at the coroner's inquest, and his passion for drawing received considerable attention. "He spends his time reading the Bible and in drawing and painting pictures and portraits. His work, according to art critics, shows a great deal of talent. . . . His counsel are straining every effort to obtain executive clemency, and petitions are being largely signed."[8]

The March 26 edition of the *Evening Telegram* ran McCullough's portrait of a British battleship steaming towards an engagement – on the front page!

→→   ←←

T. C. Robinette's appeal for a commutation of the sentence began with a letter to the Honourable Hugh Guthrie, the acting minister of justice.[9] The letter reviewed the evidence in favour of manslaughter, included a note from foreman Arthur Hill, claiming that the jury "now feel executive clemency should be extended," and enclosed a sample of petitions. Robinette concluded by playing a political card, for in 1919 executive clemency was very much a political game:

> I may say personally that I have discussed this matter at the National Club with my friends, all well known business men as you know, and I find that there is almost a universal opinion on their part that if the Government commuted his sentence it would be the right thing, and they as representative business men of the community represent very well the rest of the citizens of Canada.

The reply came from the ubiquitous J. D. Clarke, giving Robinette an assurance that his letter "will be given every weight possible and will be laid before His Excellency the Governor General in Council."[10]

Robinette knew what that meant. It meant the letter would be given no weight. It would go into a file and wouldn't be seen until the Justice Department finally got around to dealing with the matter in its own time – which was usually at the last minute.

This was exactly the kind of response that could unnerve Robinette. When he knew he was right and was met with indifference, he felt justified in taking another course of action. After all, a man's life depended on it.

He wrote another letter to the acting minister, marked it "Personal," and opened with the salutation "My dear Guthrie." Robinette reported he had "had a long interview with Judge Hugh Rose yesterday at Osgoode Hall." He intimated that Rose had his own doubts about the case, and said that the judge was "*expecting a request from your Department*" for a second report on the trial. "I understand he has already made one, as is customary, but if you will ask him for the second report now, he tells me he will be in Toronto at the non-jury sittings the next three weeks."

It is doubtful Rose would have played such a game. As the judge in the case, he could submit any number of reports any time he wished. He didn't need Robinette to manipulate a request for one. Having thrown caution to the wind, however, Robinette went further: "I am writing you this letter personally because the Judge intimated to me that he would *like* a request from your Department."[11]

It worked. On March 30 a no doubt surprised Justice Rose received a letter from Clarke stating that the acting minister "would be glad to receive any additional statement that you may see fit to make in elucidation of the facts of the case. As the time is short an early reply will be appreciated."[12]

The hanging was scheduled for May 2, only a month away.

A standard issue of prisoner's clothing and a daily issue of paper for letter-writing (all letters to be read by the chief turnkey) were all that McCullough was to receive in jail. According to the regulations, he wasn't to receive food or utensils or amenities of any kind that weren't either inspected and approved beforehand or prepared for him in the jail kitchen.[13]

The cookies and fresh eggs tenderly packaged by Mrs. Bell's Young Women's Bible Class, and concealed by Alfred Amory, weren't the only indiscretions. McCullough also had a glass bottle of jam in his cell that could have been used as a weapon. He received on one occasion an uninspected roast chicken that, while it may not have been suitable as a weapon, could well have concealed a weapon. There were other items too.

On various occasions McCullough received oranges, boxes of chocolates, loaves of bread, pies, sandwiches, fish and chips, buns, candies, a "French stick," strawberries, "paris greens," and a side of bacon, among other supplies.

This prisoner – who was to have no utensils – had a kettle, a teapot, a coffeepot with an ample supply of coffee, and a toaster.

He also had a frying pan in there for his bacon and eggs. He had playing cards, pencils, watercolours, drawing paper, frames for his paintings, and a stock of writing paper and envelopes that could have supplied half the jail.

Indeed, McCullough possessed so many illicit supplies that Sam Follis, one of the three men on the death watch, brought in a cupboard from home to conceal their presence from the regular guards. How were these things getting in? The answer is that McCullough had all three men on the death watch supplying him: Amory, Follis, and especially Currell. Later, at an inquiry, all three denied responsibility, pointed fingers at each other, and irreverently tried to implicate Reverend Nelles (who owned up to some candies and the strawberries but nothing more).

Since the days of the kind-hearted Governor Chambers, the guards were permitted to bring their own food to work in substitution for the matron's fare. The head matron and cook, Miss Tanny Soady, was much loved, but all agreed she deserved the death chamber herself for the concoctions that came from the kitchen. The guards carried their own food to work in satchels that, because of a curious code of ethics that prevailed at the Toronto Jail, were not inspected upon entry. The inspection of a guard's belongings, or the area under his supervision while he was "on duty," was considered a grave insult to his character and professional standing, and was not undertaken lightly. Thus it was relatively easy for the men on the death watch to supply McCullough without interference. Furthermore, because responsibility for the jail was held jointly by Sheriff Mowat and Henry Addy, there was confusion over who was actually accountable for these men.

The men on the death watch were considered a lower species than the regular guards, but the jail's code of ethics extended to them just the same. Alexander Davidson, the regular night watch, "did not like the appearance of Currell in the first place and said so to several of the guards." But he never openly questioned or interfered with Currell's work, "because I did not think it was my duty."[14]

Whose duty was it? Logically, it was the duty of the chief turnkey, who was responsible to the sheriff. But in these matters, Addy's experience with Mowat had been far from satisfactory. When chief guard Harry Denning was alarmed by the sudden appearance of a coffeepot in McCullough's cell, he went to see the chief turnkey about it. It turned out that Addy himself had been concerned about the coffeepot and promised he would speak to the sheriff about the conduct of "his men." But the sheriff's response was similar to his decision about Doris Mytton. "I [Addy] spoke to the Sheriff on the matter and he said he did not see what harm it would do to have a coffee pot in there." The coffeepot remained.

Denning was also concerned about other reports. He had heard that during the night, Currell was "free and easy" with McCullough. It was reported that scuttles of coal and a short poker were left unattended in the cell. Although McCullough's "Swedish stunts" had been permitted, it was reported that Amory was "wrestling and fooling around" with McCullough on his shift. Follis was known to taunt the other guards with the luxuries enjoyed on the death watch. He "would sometimes say, 'Here Denning, have a chocolate or have a cigar.'" Denning was appalled. "When I began to see bottles of stuff and packages, and knew what he was getting in there, it just seemed not right – more like a playhouse than anything else."

Again we see the winning personality of Frank McCullough. The death watch had become more like a gang of schoolboy chums. There were hoots of laughter down the corridors. Then Denning saw McCullough had "a frying pan and was putting a piece of bacon in it and had a couple of eggs ready to fry." He complained to Addy again, but again nothing changed.

Then I [Denning] saw a deck of cards in there and that is something we don't allow in the gaol. I reported that and asked who brought them in. It turned out it was the night man who brought in the cards. Right along from one time to another things were taken in. Sometimes there would be five scuttles of coal in there. I never saw anything like the way this fellow was treated.

Otherwise, however, McCullough seemed a model prisoner. Referring to McCullough's newfound faith, Addy commented to Reverend Nelles one day that "McCullough is truly a reformed man or one of the greatest scoundrels I ever ran across." McCullough spent his time in Bible reading, exercising, and drawing. "He was always drawing or painting, or tinting those pictures." The only minor indiscretion he committed was to be found occupied at one of the barred windows standing on a chair. When ordered to get down, he would complain, "Can't I get some fresh air?" or he would say that he was looking down at the graves in "murderers' row" in the yard. Nelles reported that McCullough asked him once "to get up on the back of the bed and look out the window and he showed me where the last fellow [Neby] was buried and said, 'You see my place is right next.'"

But McCullough was not so thoroughly reformed or as innocent or as much a model prisoner as he appeared to be. As one investigator described him later, McCullough "would pray to the Lord God Himself when he was planning to drive a knife through your back." Although he seemed to be quietly absorbed in his painting and reading, and oblivious to the tension around him, he was all the while subtly pushing the conflict among the guards to a breaking point.

Inevitably, Denning would make his move. One day, while Amory was called downstairs to the telephone, the chief guard entered the death cell and inspected the cupboard. McCullough made a point of telling each of the men on his death watch afterwards that Denning had inspected their territory. Amory was livid: "If he wants to look into the cupboard I invite inspection." Follis was "quite hostile because it was private property." That evening, the conflict erupted when Follis ordered up a scuttle of coal and Denning delivered it in person.

> When I [Denning] went up I said, "Why here is a scuttle of coal already." Follis said, "Oh, I did not know it was there." I said, "What! You have been in here since 12 o'clock and did not know that scuttle of coal was there?" He got mad and said, "Denning, you have been picking on me ever since I have been in this place." I said, "I have not been picking on you; I am very seldom here when you are here." Then he said I had no business to look in the cupboard and had better not do it any more. I said, "Who will stop me?" He said, "I will."

Denning went straight to Addy and demanded that the death watch be dismissed. Addy went straight to the sheriff, but Mowat declined to take any action. He said that they "had better not quarrel with them too much as it is so hard to get anyone to take that kind of work." He asked Addy "to be a little lenient."[15]

The arrival of spring seemed to raise everyone's spirits. By the beginning of April, Robinette was saying he was "fully confident of clemency" in the case. According to the *Globe*, the "city at large" was discussing the question, "and generally there seems to be a feeling that McCullough does not deserve as bitter a fate as hanging." During April, thousands of names poured into Ottawa on petitions circulated by Nelles's battalions and by members of other churches.

Even Justice Rose joined the cause in his own way. On April 2, he penned his second report, in which he confessed that "I have never been thoroughly convinced in my own mind that the prisoner did, at any time, intend to shoot Williams." Although the charge was murder, the act was "in its moral aspect, manslaughter only." Thus, while he and the jury were right to have been concerned solely with the "legal" quality of the act, "the moral aspect is considered by the Acting Minister in dealing with an application for the exercise of executive clemency."[16]

At the jail, tensions seemed to abate as the focus turned on news from Ottawa. About the only excitement during the wait had to do with the unpredictable appearances of "a woman out in Riverdale Park waving her hand and throwing kisses to Frank McCullough." There was a scramble to question her whenever she appeared, but she was too fast for the guards. "I never saw it," said Addy, "and the first I heard of that was from Detective Cronin. He said that she used to be out there throwing high balls to Frank and him to her."[17]

This is the second appearance of the "mysterious" woman who is so important to our story.

At the Church for the Stranger, McCullough's "definite decision for Christianity" brought much rejoicing. On a Sunday morning "at a special communion," the congregation "accepted the doomed man to membership with them." Nelles and two members proceeded from the service to the jail, "and formally performed the ceremony of membership." "Brother McCullough" was now a full member of the church. "It was a thing we thought was best to do," commented Nelles to reporters. "McCullough has fully repented of his sins, and has placed his trust in a Higher Power."[18]

McCullough's transformation touched Nelles deeply. He could now "love McCullough as a brother in Christ," and there was a warm intimacy between them.

I had a little pig skin testament that I have carried for I guess fifteen years. I said, "Frank, if you would like to use this little testament you can have it." He said he would like to use it and he kept it at the head of his bed. One night he got this little book and brought it over and said, "I would like to keep this book. I would like to carry it all the years of my life." I thought that was rather a strange thing for a man to say who had only a few days to live.

But McCullough had not forgotten he had only a few days to live. In the early-morning hours of April 16, 1919, during the course of a violent thunderstorm, he escaped from the Toronto Jail.

# X

# Miss Vera de Lavelle

Windsor Hotel
Montreal
April 17/19

Dear Sir [Arthur Meighen],

I am glad to hear that McCullough has escaped from Jail. He never should have been convicted of murder. If you offered Ten Thousand dollars for him I would throw your dirty money in your face. The Police Courts are rotten and make a mountain out of petty offenses. Look at the Yellow police in Toronto and Ottawa. How many went to War? Precious few of them. When all these soldiers get back there is going to be a great change in this country and you narrow minded old Wind Jammers will get what is coming to you all! All your Police Courts are good for is to kick people down and keep them down. I say to hell with the whole lot of you. I hope McCullough never gets caught.

"Tom Fairplay"

The alarm above the death-cell door began to ring at 5:00 a.m. When the night guards entered, they found a sheepish Ernest Currell, alone, without pants or shirt, holding a piece of paper in his hand. Discovered also were two iron bars sawn through, top and bottom, and placed carefully on the windowsill. Frank McCullough was gone.

"Chief Turnkey Henry Addy was notified and hurried to the jail." Sheriff Mowat, Det. Bart Cronin, and Mr. W. W. Dunlop, provincial inspector of prisons and public charities, were also contacted and came as soon as they could.

Amid the confusion, Addy discerned how McCullough had done it. Having squeezed through the opening he had made in the bars, he managed to drop to the surface of a retaining wall located dangerously far below his cell window. "Marks were left on the wall [of the jail building] where he climbed through the window and let himself down, his boots scraping the wall." From here, McCullough crawled along the top of the retaining wall that eventually joined the main wall surrounding the jail. Once there, he jumped down some eighteen feet to freedom.

Currell announced he had been drugged. He explained later that he "went to the cell, about twenty minutes to ten, and McCullough appeared the same as usual. He said, 'Are we going to have some coffee?' to which I agreed and Frank made the coffee which we drank." By eleven, according to Currell, he fell into a "deep sleep" and did not wake up until five in the morning when, "finding McCullough gone and the bars cut, I rang the alarm bell and the other guards came running."

As proof of his story, Currell handed Addy a letter left by McCullough, which read:

Currell, old man,

I am sorry, but it had to be done. Now do not you be scared, for it isn't your fault, for I doped your coffee with a sleeping powder of Veronal and so you see kid they cannot blame you. I am leaving the paper wrapper in which I had

Frank Williams (right), outside Claremont Street police station not long before his death. Promoted to acting detective, he did not wear a uniform like the constables with him here. Williams looks old for his age; he was only twenty-four. (*Toronto Police Museum*)

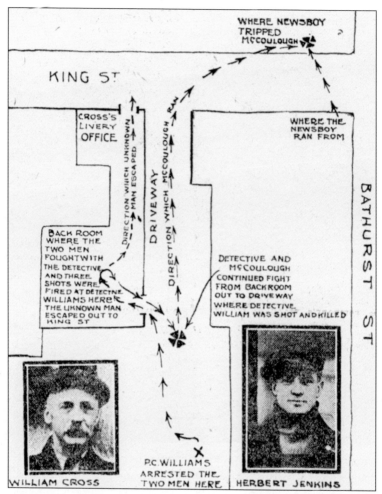

The scene of Frank McCullough's arrest, as depicted in the *Evening Telegram*. Pictured here are the livery owner, William Cross, and the newsboy who foiled McCullough's escape, Herbert Jenkins.
(Evening Telegram, *Nov. 20, 1918; courtesy Toronto Public Library*)

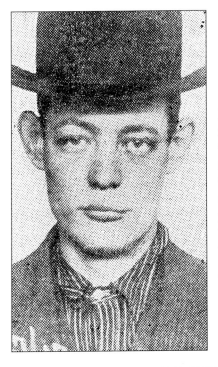

Frank McCullough, probably in 1917 when he was charged with housebreaking. He smashed a whisky bottle over the head of the constable who arrested him. McCullough's personality was more attractive than his physical appearance; the bowler hat only adds to his charming air of impudence. Note also the slight evidence of a scar on his upper lip. (Daily Star, *Nov. 20, 1918; courtesy Toronto Public Library*)

Detective Bartholomew Cronin in 1920, a year after McCullough's case. Cronin was greatly respected in Toronto and a favourite with the newspapers. He and McCullough liked each other, even though McCullough had killed a policeman and Cronin almost had to shoot McCullough. (*City of Toronto Archives; James Collection, sc244-1040*)

Thomas Cowper Robinette in 1905. He had made his reputation in a number of sensational murder trials and was a dashing figure in the courts. The more difficult the case, the more likely Robinette would be there to offer his services, free of charge, if necessary. McCullough was Robinette's last famous case. (*from* Bench and Bar in Ontario, *1905; courtesy the Law Society of Upper Canada*)

The Honourable Mr. Justice Hugh Edward Rose. Although he lived with his mother, and was known as one of the most retiring judges in Ontario's legal system, Rose had nerves of steel and was utterly orthodox when it came to the holy writ of the Criminal Code. (*The Law Society of Upper Canada Archives; "Hugh Rose" photograph collection, p. 141*)

Finger-print classification: $\frac{9 \quad U \quad 0}{25 \ aU \ 00}$ 17

# $50.00 REWARD

FOR THE ARREST AND DELIVERY OF

## LEROY W. SWART,

CHARGED WITH BEING A

## DESERTER FROM THE ARMY.

LEROY W. SWART, private, Coast Artillery Corps, 4th Company, Fort Adams, who was enlisted December 12, 1914, for seven years, is reported to have deserted at Fort Adams, R. I., March 24, 1917. A enlistment he gave his residence as Brooklyn, N. Y., and the name and address of person to be notified in his behalf in case of emergency as Mrs. E. U. Swart (mother), 1617 Summerfield Street, Brooklyn, N. Y.

DESCRIPTION (at date of enlistment): White; born in Westville, N. Y.; age, 21½ years; occupation photographer; eyes, blue; hair, dark brown; complexion, medium fair; height, 5 feet 11 inches. Promi nent scars and marks: Front view—scar on left cheek, lower right forearm, each palm, each index finger right ring finger, right knee, lower right leg, and left foot; two scars on left knee. Back view—scar on uppe right arm, left elbow, each hand, and right heel.

A REWARD of $50.00 is payable for the apprehension of this man, and for his delivery to the military authorities, at any time within three years from date of desertion. The reward is payable at any United States Army post to any civil officer or other civilian who delivers the man there. If he is apprehended he should be delivered at, and the reward claimed at, the nearest Army post.

The act of Congress approved August 29, 1916, provides that "It shall be lawful for any civil officer having authority under the laws of the United States, or of any State, Territory, District, or possession of the United States, to arrest offenders, summarily to arrest a deserter from the military service of the United States and deliver him into the custody of the military authorities of the United States."

Any information that may be secured as to the whereabouts of this man should be communicated to

THE ADJUTANT GENERAL OF THE ARMY,

WASHINGTON, D. C.

April 17, 1917.                    32769

The reward notice issued for Leroy Swart (Frank McCullough) after his desertion from the U.S. Army. The photograph was probably taken upon his enlistment in 1914, having been released from the state penitentiary at Jefferson City, Missouri. Our hero is younger here, looks healthier, and his facial scar is more in evidence. (*National Archives and Records Administration; Office of the Adjutant General, Doc. File No. 2565389*)

The Toronto Jail from the side. This photograph, taken in 1907, gives one a sense of Riverdale Park behind the jail. From a gradual rise in the park, crowds could see McCullough over the top of the jail wall, waving from his cell window. An inspector described the institution in 1914 as "the worst jail on the American continent." (*Archives of Ontario, Acc 9258-S14378*)

The entrance to the death cell at the Toronto Jail. In the decade before McCullough, five men were executed here: a Macedonian, an Italian, a Russian Pole, an American described as "coloured," and Hassan Neby, the "Albanian Mohammedan." When it came to hanging, Toronto displayed an early adherence to multi-culturalism. (*Nir Bareket*)

Henry Addy, the chief turnkey of the Toronto Jail. Addy emigrated from Ireland in 1876 and began his working career at the bottom as a regular guard in the jail. When the position of jail governor was vacated in 1917, Addy reported directly to the sheriff, Frederick Mowat. (Toronto Telegram, *Apr. 4, 1925; courtesy Toronto Public Library*)

Frederick Mowat, appointed sheriff of the city – a provincial position – when his father was premier of the province. Mowat lived at the opposite end of the social spectrum from his subordinate at the jail, Henry Addy, and his social standing prevented him from being fired over McCullough. (Toronto Telegram, *Apr. 12, 1924; courtesy Toronto Public Library*)

Toronto's popular mayor, "Tommy" Church, in his straw hat, waiting
to address a recruitment rally outside City Hall in 1916. Exactly two
years later, on the same spot, he threatened to read the Riot Act against
returned soldiers and their civilian supporters. He blamed the provincial
government for McCullough's escape. (*City of Toronto Archives; James
Collection, SC244-721A*)

the stuff so that you can have the evidence if necessary. If you do not want this note shown to them, why lay the paper [wrapper] on the floor and some where where you will be able to accidentally find it. You understand, I got the stuff I am using from a friend who came here as a prisoner on purpose and managed to slip it to me.

Wish me luck. I am sorry but you know life is sweet, old man.

So long,
Frank

The powder is harmless and is called Veronal and I will send your clothes back or the money for them at the very earliest opportunity. Maybe the authorities will let you have the ones I have downstairs. So sorry, friend Currell. Good luck to you and forgive me.

Addy showed the letter to Cronin, whereupon Cronin arrested Currell and took him to City Hall for questioning. When Currell emerged from this experience, he appeared to be "in a somewhat dazed condition." The next morning, he was charged in police court before Col. George Denison with "aiding and abetting the escape of one Frank McCullough."

Counsel: He is a returned soldier with a good character.
Crown Attorney: If he had done this at the Front he would have been shot.

Currell pleaded not guilty and was remanded for eight days. He found himself a prisoner of the jail in which he had been a guard.

The police hastened to give chase. "Police autos carrying detectives and plainclothesmen" were dispatched immediately to all railway stations and points of departure, "and soon all the railway officials were keeping a sharp lookout for the medium-sized, fair, clean-shaven man." The central terminal in the city, Union Station, "was suddenly set agog this morning" by news of the break. "Word came by telephone from the City Hall, and almost simultaneously several plainclothesmen were on the spot making thorough search and inquiries."

At police headquarters, "all the telegraph instruments were tapping away, the news being flashed to every Canadian centre and every border town." A detailed description of McCullough was "sent broadcast from the Atlantic to the Pacific, and the border is being vigilantly watched by the Canadian and American immigration officials."

By two that afternoon, arrangements were completed for the announcement "at the Parliament Buildings that a reward of $1,000 had been offered for information leading to the arrest of the murderer, Frank McCullough." By late afternoon, the *Star* gave expression to the day's excitement with the unqualified assertion that "McCullough's escape is the most sensational in the history of the police." It was "the first escape of its kind in Dominion Police annals."[1]

Every Toronto newspaper gave front-page coverage to McCullough's escape. Indeed, from the day of his departure in mid-April until well into June, almost every daily newspaper carried one or more articles pertaining to his case. It was his escape (and the dramatic events following his escape) more than his trial or the death of Williams that drew the full attention of the press and made McCullough a subject of intense public interest. He refused to submit to authority. The man had pluck.

This didn't mean the papers were accurate. Without a shred of evidence, the *Toronto World*, the *Mail and Empire*, and even the *Globe* reported that McCullough had been assisted from the outside by "an organized gang of crooks." "There is not a shadow of doubt in the minds of detectives that plans have been carefully made by colleagues of McCullough's to furnish money and assistance to have him make good his escape from the gallows."

This theory led to the conclusion, again without evidence, that a car had been waiting outside the jail, "and boarding the waiting motor car, he changed his clothing, and in the opinion of police has a six-hour lead over them." According to the *Globe* (which went as far as to claim "the bars were sawn from the *outside*"), McCullough joined his confederates "under cover of the storm which was raging all that night, and in a powerful car, headed for the border by way of Niagara Falls, a trip which could be made with little trouble in a few hours."[2]

The *Star* and the *Telegram* were more suspicious. Both thought it unlikely that McCullough or an associate could saw the iron bars in four places in the time Currell claimed he had been drugged. They got a bar and tried it themselves. "A test of sawing one of the iron window bars was made and it took 72 minutes to make each of the four cuts. With one saw it would take nearly five hours or two hours with half a dozen good steel saws."[3] There must have been collusion on Currell's part. It was noted that black-stained "chewing gum, butter and soap" were found on the bars, which were likely used to conceal several days of cutting from the other men on the death watch. According to these newspapers, it was definitely an inside job, and Addy agreed: "Speaking to The Star, Mr. Addy said that it must have been done from the inside and alleges collusion. . . . 'He is a daisy,' continued the chief turnkey."[4]

Another reason to suspect conspiracy was that both papers had received a signed letter claiming the opposite from the one individual who couldn't be trusted in the matter: Frank McCullough. The letters were post-marked on the morning of the escape, suggesting to some that McCullough had managed to catch the Grand Trunk to Montreal before the police arrived at Union Station.

I will explain part of my escape to you [the Editor] so that you may find out the truth and not put the blame for it on any of these men who were my keepers, for it is not their fault. The Veronal sleeping powder which I introduced into the night guard's coffee was given to me by a prisoner who came to the jail for that very purpose, and after the guard had gone to sleep I pulled the saw up through the window by means of a string, and was able to cut the bars in about one hour and 40 minutes.

Hoping you will find it possible to publish this, I thank you in advance, and remain, yours respectfully,

Frank McCullough

These letters, similar to the one shown to Det. Bart Cronin, were so obviously an effort to absolve Currell of complicity that the opposite conclusion was drawn. They reveal an intriguing side to McCullough's character; for once gone, why should he care at all about Currell? Was friendship that important to him? Was this another manifestation of that loyalty among thieves that made McCullough honour-bound to protect Albert Johnson after the shooting? The irony is that McCullough tried so hard to protect Currell that he helped to condemn him. "So sorry, friend Currell."

There was another purpose to these and other letters received from McCullough and published in the newspapers. By the time of his escape, a great many people, and not all members of the Church for the Stranger, had worked on McCullough's behalf. According to Robinette, one omnibus petition alone contained "about 4,000 names asking for the commutation of the sentence, Toronto, Winnipeg, Montreal and Owen Sound each subscribing many names."[5]

Now that he had escaped, what word did McCullough have for his supporters in the matter of his innocence? The letters sent to the newspapers, and a similar letter received by Reverend Nelles, were written to maintain the spirits of the faithful. Their purpose was to explain how the escape was justified, thereby maintaining McCullough's innocence.

My Dear Friends:

Do not lose faith in me through this last step I have taken, for I will not break my word to you nor to the glorious Father

I have come to recognize. My friends, in my heart I believe this [the escape] is a miraculous answer of your own and my prayers for mercy, and I believe it such from the manner in which it was perpetrated[6] without injury to anyone, and that is but one reason for believing in God's handiwork.

McCullough's use of religious language, absorbed as a child in Westville's Baptist Church and later from Rev. Nelles, suggests that he knew precisely how to appeal to this sizeable portion of his constituency. He was speaking to churchgoers, of whom there were many in Toronto in 1918–19. He was speaking to those tireless church workers, mostly female, who belonged to denominational versions of Mrs. Bell's Young Women's Bible Class at the Church for the Stranger. Many of McCullough's sympathizers were religious people swayed by his sentimental claim to youthful innocence, and captivated by the drama of saving a belated disciple from the noose. They found confirmation of the power of their own religious convictions in McCullough's "decision for Christianity." McCullough was now one of them, a believing child of God who had repented of his sins. Did such a one as this deserve to die?

For his part, McCullough had no qualms about presenting himself "through this last step" as Jesus-like, and he had a theological argument for them, too:

Which is the larger sin in the eyes of God, to escape, without injuring no man, or to stay to be executed? If the latter is not suicide, what is? And what does the Good Book say regarding that?

He claimed he had received a fair trial "excepting for one thing, and that was the perjury of one of the witnesses for the Prosecution." If William Cross had not perjured himself, McCullough would have "received my just deserts cheerfully" and would have accepted whatever prison sentence was assigned, "for I am a man and can take my medicine like one. Thank God." But he didn't receive justice, because Cross had lied. Thus McCullough viewed the chance to escape as "a miraculous answer to my prayers."

> I am not the desperate criminal which people first believed me to be, but a boy who has come to man's estate, and never had a chance. But I will, with the help of God, make good somewhere on this funny old planet of ours, now that a miracle has intervened. . . .
>
> I have not time to write more – I should be on my way now, but I had to write this little bit. God grant that his purpose may be fulfilled.
>
> I am your unfortunate friend,
>
> Frank McCullough
> Toronto, April 16th, 10:30 a.m.

What is so intriguing is that McCullough's voice had a strain of honesty to it. There seems something genuine about him, and there was also some truth to what he said. He *was* a boy who came to man's estate without having had a chance. And with time he *did* appear to find his own peculiar faith in God. But could he be believed? Or was he at heart a consummate charlatan – "one of the greatest scoundrels I ever ran across"?

McCullough's escape exasperated Robinette: "If he had but waited, I am practically certain that next week McCullough's death sentence would have been commuted to life imprisonment." Robinette had arranged for Nelles to go to Ottawa the following Sunday "at the head of a deputation," and there was "reason to believe that the judge's reports to the Department of Justice were not averse to a commutation of the sentence."

Nelles was confounded by McCullough's duplicity. "I got to like the fellow. As a matter of fact everybody around the jail liked him. It may sound foolish, but he had a very human side. He was athletic and clean looking. If you had seen him in Muskoka in flannels, you would have admired him."

For his part, Henry Addy knew that "on this funny old planet of ours" someone would have to pay. He knew there would likely be an inquiry, and he came out swinging. Addy claimed that all along "complaints had been made to Sheriff Mowat" about the death watch. Then he exaggerated the merit of his own conduct:

I saw the Sheriff, and stated that I would refuse to relax my vigilance, for I considered the prisoner to be a dangerous man. And I did consider McCullough a dangerous man. I have handled men here for over thirty years, and I picked McCullough out for a clever, cunning man, and he has proved it. Why, I have lined up the men here and particularly cautioned them all twice about always exerting the greatest care.

Addy flatly denied "remarks made around the Police Court yesterday" that he allowed parcels to enter McCullough's cell. "I refused to allow him to have any. I have never taken chances, and with this man none whatever."

Mowat was not as comprehending as Addy, and had no idea he was in peril. But he was smart enough to remain tight-lipped: "There will be an investigation and until that takes place I have nothing to say. The jail is under the Provincial Secretary's Department, but in this case it is possible that the investigation will be conducted by the Attorney-General's Department."

One ambitious reporter for the *Star* went to Earlscourt later that day to interview Currell's wife, Katherine. His effort in doing so was unsuccessful.

The Currell house at 4 Hanson Road was locked up. Inside were the dog and the three children, aged about ten, eight and four respectively. Sly smiles through the front window were all the encouragement the reporter could get, and any attempt at conversation was drowned out by the loud barking of the dog inside.

Such were the developments of April 16, 1919, the first day of McCullough's freedom. "He will never be taken alive," commented a more reflective Robinette that evening. Was Robinette beginning to fathom the mettle of his man?[7]

On the second day, Ernest Currell was questioned closely by Mr. W. W. Dunlop, provincial inspector of prisons and public charities. Dunlop was responsible to the provincial secretary for all of the "common gaols" in Ontario. He didn't like escapes.

That same morning, Kate Currell received an envelope in the mail from McCullough enclosing Currell's service buttons, a discharge button, and his veteran's association badge.[8] Thinking the buttons might somehow have a bearing on her husband's innocence, she left Hanson Road for the jail to see Addy.

While she was at the jail, the *Globe* published a report of her husband's questioning by Dunlop and "revealed the startling fact" that Currell had been acting as a "go-between" for McCullough and a "mysterious young woman on the outside." Currell had been carrying letters and packages back and forth without inspection.

> Currell told the Chief Inspector how he carried a letter of introduction from McCullough to the woman, whose name was given as Miss Vera de Lavelle, and of his subsequently carrying boxes of chocolates to the man in his cell, and of delivering letters from him to the woman. Other guards in the institution tell of seeing the girl waving and blowing kisses to the prisoner, who could easily see her from his window, as she stood in Riverdale Park.

Not only did Currell make this woman's acquaintance, "he took her to his home, where he introduced her to his wife as a friend, and several times lunched with her."[9]

*Who was Vera de Lavelle?* This was precisely the question put to Kate Currell by the *Star* reporter waiting at Hanson Road on her return from the jail.

> I treated her as a friend, as she appeared to me quite honest and straightforward. She brought on one occasion several petitions which she said she had received from a local man, and that these petitions were to be sent to Ottawa. She told me she lived at 9 Trinity Square and was employed as a book-keeper at $10 a week. She said she had been brought up in Canada since she was three years of age and was of French parentage. Her mother was living down east and was shortly going back to France. Miss Lavelle said she was also considering returning to France.

Vera de Lavelle was twenty-four, short, slim, "neatly dressed" and "of fairly good features." She had a "bright smile," blue eyes, and was usually described as dark in appearance: "dark complexion," "luxuriant black hair," "dark apparel." Addy saw her only once, when she tried to visit McCullough at the jail: "She was well dressed, wore dark clothes, was of dark complexion, rather French looking I thought."[10]

> "When was she last at your [the Currell] house?"
> "She was here last Sunday and stayed for dinner, leaving in the afternoon. I had asked her to come on Good Friday, if she was not otherwise engaged."
> "Did she ever bring anything to your house?"
> "Yes, she used to bring chocolates for the children about every time she came."

The newspapers shifted their attention immediately to the "mysterious Miss Vera de Lavelle," partly because they had no information about McCullough himself. He had vanished completely. "It is the consensus of opinion in both provincial and local police circles that McCullough managed to cross the border."

American authorities had been contacted. It was believed McCullough was "either still heading south, or is in concealment in Chicago, Buffalo, or some other large American city." It was to the fugitive's advantage that the American authorities had no record of a Frank McCullough, and no one in Canada knew his real name was Leroy Swart.

A bewildered landlady at 9 Trinity Square was besieged by detectives followed by an even larger contingent of reporters. Yes, she had a boarder who "went by the name of Miss Vera." "Miss Vera is of quiet demeanor and dress. She always wore a dark suit and never used any 'make-up' on her face." She was seen leaving on Tuesday evening, the night of McCullough's escape. "Miss Vera" had not returned and her room contained all of her belongings.

> Among the articles in the room was a folder card bearing the inscription: "Your Heavenly Father Knoweth." Further down on the card was another inscription bearing the words: "Keep a Brave Heart." It was signed "Yours in sympathy, Emma Thompson."

Did Vera de Lavelle flee Toronto with McCullough? Was she outside the jail when he jumped to freedom? Did she drive the car? Did she pack saws in those boxes of chocolates? And how did she come to know McCullough in the first place? These were among the questions asked once the gorgeous and endearingly pretentious name of Miss Vera de Lavelle surfaced in the case. It was the additional conjecture of the *Evening Telegram* that "the importance to her connection in the affair may have been intended as a blind, which has been successful in accomplishing its purpose."[11]

Ernest Currell was released on $2,000 bail. The money was raised by the Earlscourt chapter of the Great War Veterans Association (GWVA), which also retained Mr. C. E. MacDonald as his legal counsel.

Currell was a mixed blessing for the GWVA. His "pitiable con-dition" was a useful example of the poverty facing returned sol-diers who couldn't find employment. "A friend of the family told The Star that there is not a penny in the household." On the other hand, Currell's bumbling complicity in the escape and his egre-gious dependence on the GWVA were something of an embarrass-ment. But the Earlscourt chapter could not abandon their brother. He was, after all, a "wounded soldier." If they were going to support him, Currell simply had to be innocent of the charges facing him, and thus his vindication became an issue of principle for the GWVA. MacDonald was not retained by Currell; he was retained by the veterans association to act on Currell's behalf.

When Currell finally returned to his home on Hanson Road, in the company of GWVA officials, a more extensive interview took place with reporters. Kate Currell, "her eyes filled with tears," pleaded it was "for love of his family" that Currell worked at all while suffering such ill health. "Ernest insisted that to get ahead we needed the three dollars a night he was earning." Currell, "visibly exhausted," claimed he was innocent, although he admit-ted he had "foolishly taken letters and on two occasions chocolates to McCullough." He did this "only to help others out," and was "only doing what other guards had done. Another guard had carried letters from a Mrs. Bell" (of the Young Women's Bible Class).[12]

The *Star* completed its version of this interview with the Currells by noting that:

> During Miss Vera Lavelle's visits to the Currell home she played the piano and when there on Sunday sang various hymns. She also attended Earlscourt Methodist Church with Mrs. Currell on various occasions, and was given the freedom of their home.

Miss Vera de Lavelle was certainly a most interesting young woman.

# XI

# In the Matter of the Prisons

Dear Sir,

I'm just a little girl seven years old. And just want to plead with you to please change Frank McCullough's sentence to life imprisonment. I don't know the man personally but I feel so sorry for him because he has never had a fair chance in this old world. I've been praying for him and I don't want to see him die. Just think Dear Sir if he was our brother how we would feel. Please do excuse me for troubling you but I just wanted to write you regarding this matter. Trusting you will grant this request and thanking you very kindly.

I remain
yours very truly,
Viola M. Wilson

Miss Viola M. Wilson,
79 1/2 Anderson Street,
Ottawa, Ontario.


Dear Madam,

I beg to acknowledge receipt of your letter, dated the 4th. inst., urging that the sentence of death imposed upon

Frank McCullough, detained in the Gaol at Toronto, be commuted to life imprisonment.

Your request will be given due attention.

Yours truly,
J. D. Clarke
For the Deputy Minister of Justice

B y the Monday following his escape, the police had concluded that McCullough was no longer in Toronto. It was thought that he was too well known to avoid detection easily; his picture had been published in the newspapers, and "as a driver of a bread wagon he possibly knew several hundred people [on Spadina alone]." McCullough must have managed to cross the border, most likely at Buffalo, and, according to the newspapers, "the police have little hope in capturing him."

Indeed, it was reported that during the night of the escape, "a closed limousine whizzed westward" along Lakeshore Road at an estimated speed of sixty-five miles per hour.

> It was 5:30 in the morning when the motor attracted the attention of a workman out at Stop 16. He did not know that a murderer had escaped, and although the reckless speed of the machine commanded his attention he made no attempt to get the number. He is able, however, to give a fairly accurate description of the car.

The police pointed out further that on the evening of the escape, "a woman in the case made several long-distance calls to Buffalo to a man who is thought to have been registered at a hotel there."

The Buffalo theory had the greatest currency, despite the fact that over the weekend the detective department, the newspapers, the chief of police, and the Currells each received an Easter greeting card post-marked in Sudbury and signed by McCullough.

My Easter greeting isn't new,
I've used it almost yearly,
And yet it's just what's in my heart,
I mean it most sincerely.

A happy Easter to you and yours,
Frank McCullough

The police concluded the cards were either "the insane effort of a practical joker" who had accurately copied McCullough's signature, or were written in Toronto "and given to someone to post for him in order to mislead his pursuers." "The man must be cracked!" exclaimed Henry Grasett, chief of police.[1]

A rival theory was promoted by a dispatch from Sarnia, Ontario. A man fitting McCullough's description had been spotted, "and there is no doubt in the minds of officers that the man seen is McCullough." Claiming Sarnia to be "the nearest point to the American border" from Toronto – a matter of boosterism rather than fact – the dispatch reported that McCullough was observed "on the bayshore front yesterday trying to hire a boat to ferry himself over to the American side. The immigration officers and police of down-river ports have been warned."

A second dispatch from Sarnia claimed that McCullough had tried to get a job on the steamship *Naronic*. When "the applicant learned that the Naronic plied up the lakes, and not to Montreal," he dropped the matter and was seen making his way downriver. "Stag Island is being closely watched, and if it be that McCullough is in the district, he may be taken into custody shortly."[2]

On that same day, Tuesday, the inquiry into the escape commenced at the jail. The proceedings were conducted by W. W. Dunlop, provincial inspector of prisons and public charities, under the jurisdiction of the provincial secretary, Mr. W. D. MacPherson MPP, an elected official to whom Dunlop was accountable.

It had not occurred to Frederick Mowat that, in his capacity as sheriff, he was responsible when things went wrong. He considered himself beyond reproach and remained oblivious to the possibility that he too might be culpable. Mowat showed up at the inquiry, actually took a seat next to Dunlop, and interrupted the proceedings with his own questions. It was in keeping with his limitations that he considered himself an official inquisitor rather than a potential witness. He was to have a rude awakening.

The inquiry was a closed hearing. Reporters were not allowed. They were told that once the provincial secretary received Dunlop's final report it "would be given to the press,"[3] but it never was. Further developments in the case diverted the attention of reporters, and the report itself remained buried in the voluminous files of the provincial secretary's office for seventy-five years, filed under the off-putting title "In the Matter of the Prisons and Public Charities Act and Inquiry Pursuant to Section 9."

The report was buried, in part, for political reasons. The Conservative government of Sir William Hearst was fast approaching an election. All signs indicated they were in trouble, and the government did not want a last-minute scandal to erupt over the Toronto Jail.[4] Neither would it be helpful to have another battle over the jail's management with Toronto's popular mayor, the tenacious T. L. "Tommy" Church.[5]

The tension between the provincial government and the City over the jail was caused by the same jurisdictional confusion that strained relations between Addy and Mowat. As a "Common Gaol" in the province of Ontario, the Toronto Jail came under the jurisdiction of the provincial government. But most of the funding was supplied by the City, and almost all of the jail employees were municipal employees.[6]

As chief turnkey, Addy was an officer of the City of Toronto, and the guards under him worked for the City. However, as sheriff "of the City of Toronto," Mowat actually held a provincial position. He was responsible to the provincial secretary through the provincial inspector of prisons, and consequently "Mowat's men" on the death watch were technically provincial employees. Currell was a government man.

The inevitable problems under these perplexing administrative arrangements were left to underlings to sort out – unless there was a public scandal or a request for more money. McCullough's escape prompted both. Mayor Church, who frequently accused the provincial government of making "political appointments" to the jail, announced that responsibility for McCullough's escape "was not in any way attributable to jail guards [that is, City employees]." It was "the failure of a special death watch [appointed by the province] which had nothing to do except to see that this one prisoner did not gain his liberty."

The day after the escape, Church also fired off a memorandum to the property commissioner, ordering him to report on "what guards you have at the Toronto Jail, and on securing additional guards thereafter at once. You can take your instructions to report to me." Noting that the law required sufficient staffing at the jail, Church made the surprising claim that "I have been continually urging the Board of Control that there should be additional guards provided for this institution."

In an editorial, the *Globe* agreed that the "hocus-pocus with regard to the Toronto Jail" was largely the fault of the government "and provincial authorities who have not held the progressive views which they might have been expected to entertain." This was a veiled reference to an earlier controversy over the need to maintain a jail at all in the city, or a "Don Bastille," when a more progressive facility, the Langstaff Jail Farm, had been established north of Toronto. More to the point, the *Globe* was not in favour of increased staffing at the Toronto Jail as much as the mayor apparently was. Speaking for the beleaguered taxpayer, it argued that "if the present inquiry is likely to result in the creation of a lot of new jobs the whole question of the jail's future will have to come under review again."

To Grasett, the veteran chief of police, the interminable bickering over responsibility for the jail obscured the main issue: "The escape is wholly due to laxity at the jail. No apparent difficulty about getting things in to prisoners. They could get a rhinoceros in there if the entrance was large enough."[7]

Because the public was excluded from the hearing held at the jail, reporters had to wait in a corridor outside, and witnesses entering the room were forced to run a gauntlet. Newspaper reports of the inquiry consisted of speculation based on the comments of each witness as they entered and exited through the corridor. Currell declared, "I have nothing to hide, and as God is above, I did not take in anything which would help McCullough to escape." Amory, who had playfully wrestled with McCullough, claimed that "beyond being, perhaps, too strict, he [Amory] had done nothing irregular." Follis, who had taunted the guards with cigars and chocolates, "said he did nothing out of the ordinary. He had never felt sure of McCullough, and had taken no chances."

With such a litany of innocence, reporters gave full attention to the arrival of a wide-eyed "Miss Mytton, who is a good looking girl in her 'teens.'" Mytton claimed, "I really never did care for Frank in the way you have probably been led to imagine. He had a room at our house, and he was very nice, and I was friendly with him. But to care for him in any other way – why I just never thought of it."[8]

About the only dependable information reporters gleaned that first day had to do with the properties of Veronal. Dr. T. Owen Parry, "Gaol Surgeon," freely offered his opinion outside the hearing that "Veronal is a mild sleeping drug, and is administered in the hospitals. There are no dangerous properties in the drug, and it contains no morphia." The most McCullough could have given to Currell without the presence of the drug being tasted would produce a sleep "as near natural as possible." "But," noted Parry further, "coffee counteracts the effects of Veronal."[9]

Seven days had passed since McCullough's escape, and the police weren't a step closer to finding him. "'The trouble is,' said one police official, 'that we get fifty people in a day "seeing" McCullough, and we can't afford to pass up any reports.'" With tongue in cheek, the *Globe* asked why the police were bothering to look in Toronto at all when McCullough had himself disclosed his whereabouts. The night before, the paper had received a picture postcard enclosed in an envelope.

> Just a note to let you know that I am in Kingston. This is surely some fine place for a rest. Will not stay long, however.
>
> Yours to a cinder,
> Frank McCullough

The *Globe* noted that the police "are beginning to think that some commercial traveler is having some fun out of the escape." "And where is Vera de Lavelle?" asked the *Evening Telegram.* "The police admit they know who she is, but her whereabouts is an unknown quantity."[10]

⇥ ⇤

Det. Bart Cronin arrested Vera de Lavelle on the evening of April 22. As she walked briskly along Queen Street near Bathurst, absorbed in thought, she was met with a casual "Hello, Vera," from Cronin as he emerged from a doorway.

She was taken to City Hall and questioned for three hours by Cronin and Assistant Inspector of Detectives William Wallace. "The girl admitted having sent letters and chocolates to the prisoner by Currell," said Wallace to reporters after midnight, "although she absolutely denied any participation in the escape. The girl has been living in empty houses in different parts of the city since she left her abode at Trinity Square."[11]

The police held Vera de Lavelle under the strictest security. "Hardly ever in its history has the Toronto Detective Department been so secretive about a prisoner." This did not prevent the newspapers from providing exaggerated details of her story, again without much evidence. She was arrested, apparently, "with less than one dollar in money in her pocket" and had slept "anywhere she could lay her head, in vacant houses, outside, anywhere, in fact, she thought safe from the prying eyes of the police." At night, "she nearly perished from the cold and want of food, but she continued in her efforts to avoid police detection as long as possible."[12]

Vera's potential for selling newspapers was enormous, and reporters exaggerated her story accordingly. Like McCullough, there was a reckless daring about her, softened in her case by a straightforward humility that proved irresistible. Either Frank or Vera alone would have made sensational copy. But Frank and Vera together were dynamite.

Vera de Lavelle, "slight and petite, attired tastefully in a large hat, flowing cloak and air of romance," appeared before Colonel Denison in "women's court" on the morning of April 23. She was "modest and neat, dark in color, and she wore a stole with chic effect."

Her attorney was T. C. Robinette, accompanied by his associate, Mr. W. B. Horkins. The appearance was brief, with Vera showing little emotion: "If she had worn a mask, the features could not have been under better control. But the face was colorless." It was charged that she "did aid and abet one Frank McCullough to escape from lawful custody," to which she quietly pleaded not guilty. She was remanded until May 1 – the day before McCullough was to have been hanged – and was taken to the Toronto Jail.

Robinette spoke to reporters afterwards:

> I won't likely get bail for her. She didn't give me the names of any friends. Since McCullough was convicted Miss Lavelle was in my office twice. She was doing all she could in McCullough's interests and obtained over one thousand names to a petition. . . . McCullough never mentioned Miss Lavelle to me either before he was convicted or after. She was always well-spoken, well-educated, and lady-like.[13]

Two days later, the "diminutive miss" was ushered secretly from her cell to the inquiry room, where Dunlop's investigation resumed specifically to hear evidence from her. She was heard in camera, like the others before her, but reporters were unable to interview her before or after her questioning. They were denied the hottest story in town.

The following is from her testimony behind closed doors at the jail:

Vera de Lavelle, Sworn.
Mr. W. W. Dunlop, Inspector, questioning:
How old are you?
24.
When did you come to this country?
Oh, when I was only about a year or two old; I was just a baby in arms when my mother came over. I have been in Toronto nearly 21 or 22 years. My mother lived here for a certain number of years, then she went back to France.
Where were you working?
At a place on Queen Street. There were two brothers; they had a wholesale store.
What number was it on Queen Street?
I don't know, I never took any notice.
You were the book-keeper?
Yes. I minded the store when they went out; then they broke up and went to the States.
Then what did you do?
I took up petitions for Frank McCullough.
Did you have success with the petitions?
Yes, everybody is in his favour, the majority of the people. . . .[14]

She explained that she first met McCullough at a society dance and that they planned to be married. She was horrified by news of his arrest but knew in her heart that he was innocent. While some of her friends attended his trial, she couldn't bear to. "I have never been in a court in my life until the other morning."

She wrote to McCullough at the jail but didn't receive a reply. She tried to visit him but was turned away by Addy. Then one day she received a letter from McCullough that had been posted outside the jail. It directed her to a house on Hanson Road, and explained that she could trust the man there – an Ernest Currell – and asked her to send her replies through him.

> I went up to see Mr. Currell and he gave me an intro-duction to his wife. They have three nice children and I am so fond of children, so I would go because they made it almost like my home. I had the little girl down staying with me for a few days. I usually went in the afternoon, or on Sunday morning and I would stay and go to church with them. I took a few boxes of candies and cakes to the Currell children when I went up there. They cost about 35c, like you get in Patterson's.

One morning she received a letter from McCullough saying, "Come up Tuesday night and look at the window and if I am not there you will know something has happened and that I am gone."

> You came up on the car to look at the window?
> I walked down Broadview into the park. It was rather dark and raining and I was afraid. I saw a figure coming across the park and he called my name and he took me in his arms and kissed me and said he was free.
> Did he tell you where he was going?
> No. I never asked him. He said never to ask him any questions.
> When did you next see Frank McCullough?
> That was the last time I saw him, in the park. He just kissed me and said, "I am going dear and when I arrive at my destination I will write to you." Then he turned and went

towards the north. I could not say anything else because I would not lie even to save myself. I have never been in any trouble and there is no use of lying.

She was lying. Her testimony was certainly touching, if not entirely believable. Vera had an endearing frankness that was persuasive; she looked you straight in the eye and said exactly what she thought. But if she "would not lie even to save myself," she would lie without reservation to save Frank McCullough.

> You knew that when you met him in the park he must have escaped. You knew that they did not allow him to walk out. Did you report that to the police?
>
> No, I was too afraid because I knew I would be implicated in the matter.
>
> Why should you be implicated?
>
> Because I was writing to him and probably they would think I had done something. You know the police think some very funny things sometimes.
>
> But this was a terrible thing. You met a condemned man in the park at midnight; you knew he must have escaped and yet you walked away and did not report the matter to the police?
>
> I was afraid. I knew nothing about it. I just put my trust in the Lord, that is all.

This testimony, like Dunlop's inquiry report itself, was never released. The public did not hear Vera's story until Harry Drew, veteran reporter for the *Evening Telegram*, published a sensational article about her the following day.

The day Vera was questioned at the inquiry, Harry Drew appeared at the front door of the jail and asked if he could speak to the head matron. The guard at the entrance, Charles Spanton, let the reporter in, explaining afterwards that "I did not think it was any of my business." This was typical of the attitude among the guards. It was only sensible to question a reporter who wanted access, but it was always somebody else's responsibility to do so. Dunlop exclaimed later, "Charlie . . . you knew he wanted copy for The Telegram! If you didn't know that a newspaperman didn't want to sell bananas or real estate or insurance around this jail, your degree of intelligence is not very great."

But "Charlie" allowed the reporter in (perhaps pocketing some money) and called down the head matron, who was also the infamous cook, Miss Tanny Soady. Soady assumed that the reporter had obtained an entrance pass from Addy's office, and besides, she knew why Drew was there. A week before, the resourceful reporter had asked her whether some day he could inspect the women's quarters. "He said he had heard that they were particularly nice and clean and he would like to see them and some day he would come in."

Now here he was, and Soady proceeded to show the reporter "around the hall, and the dining-room, and around the upstairs cells and all over the women's part." He said "that he did not think there were nicer quarters in Canada."

> And then we came on down the stairs. I think I had the women sewing there and he saw this girl and he said, "That is the girl, isn't it?" and I said, "Yes," and he said, "Might I speak to her for a minute?" I thought, and then said, "Well, I suppose there is no harm," so he stood back and I called the girl. I think they were going to sit down on the bench, then they went into the Matron's dining room.

Drew had over half an hour alone with Vera. At 4:00 p.m., Addy happened to see the reporter leaving. "I knew perfectly well that day when I found out that he had been up there that there was going to be a row; that is what I said in my own mind."[15]

Drew's sensational interview with Vera de Lavelle appeared the next morning in the Sunday edition of the *Evening Telegram*.[16] It opened as follows:

> "I AM GOING TO MAKE MY FLIGHT FOR LIBERTY. COME TO THE JAIL ON TUESDAY NIGHT AND SEE IF I AM HERE."
>
> — Frank McCullough, imprisoned murderer, to Vera de Lavelle

> She did not understand this letter, but she did go to Broadview Avenue and, standing alone in the dark around midnight, heard a voice say, "Vera." She knew it was Frank. He folded her in his arms for a very long time, perhaps ten minutes.
>
> "How did you get out? Where are you going? What am I to do?" were the questions that rose to her lips. She asked Frank, but he refused to tell her.
>
> He went out into the night and away. . . .

Emphasizing to his readers that he was the first reporter to interview her, Drew observed that up close "Vera de Lavelle is a neat bit of femininity . . . bright and vivacious at times, and inclined to be deliberate in her talk and actions."

The article was intended to establish that Vera's story was believable. She had a good memory, "replied immediately to questions without hesitation" and was "trusting," although, "like other women, is prone to take her 'imagination' of things as the only way[!]." Drew declared her story to be "convincing. It sounded strange at first, but as explained in her own way it seemed to be what did happen to McCullough."

She was innocent, didn't know anything about Veronal – "never heard of it" – never purchased saws, and didn't know where McCullough had gone. "He didn't tell me anything and I'm glad he didn't." She loved him, and they had planned "to marry and settle down for good and all" in the spring. "I want to say this about Frank. He is a clean fellow morally, and always treated me like a girl would wish to be treated. I think he did become converted, for it showed in his letters. I often used to pray for him."

Asked about Doris Mytton, Vera claimed she was "not at all jealous of her. Why she is only a young girl. . . . He often talked about her and I told him to take her out if he wanted to, that I wasn't jealous. He roomed at the Myttons you know."

> Another thing that I could put right is that I haven't the money I am thought to have. I worked six weeks as a book-keeper and had at one time $93. When Frank got away my funds had dwindled down to about nothing. I had but four dollars that week. I got my laundry and paid for a bath at a public place. I was dirty for staying in a vacant house on Spadina Avenue. I did not sleep for two nights, and now here I am in jail. I could get out of here on bail but I do not want to drag my friends in. I am treated well here, and it is nice and clean, but I have never been in jail before.

The article concluded as it began, with Vera's emotional account of meeting Frank in the dark: "He caught me in his arms and held me for perhaps ten minutes." For readers interested in fashion details, the following description was provided:

> Her clothing was inexpensive and refined – the general get-up of a downtown office woman – a bookkeeper. She was neatly, carefully attired in a smart business dress of blue cloth, etched with colored bead-work – her own decoration. Blue eyes, and luxuriant black hair neatly arranged over a high forehead, her face was slightly drawn, and she showed unmistakable signs of loss of sleep and worry.

The article caused a furor. Tanny Soady and Charles Spanton were immediately suspended without pay. The provincial secretary,

W. D. MacPherson, claimed that by gaining access, Drew had "broken the law" and should be charged.[17] W. W. Dunlop, enraged by another public demonstration of mismanagement at the jail, expanded his inquiry to include the Drew incident.

No public explanation was given for the suspensions of Soady and Spanton. Reporters naturally wondered whether Dunlop's inquiry had found them complicit in McCullough's escape, but they couldn't get a straight answer. "The Hon. Mr. MacPherson puts in to Mr. Dunlop who in turn passes it back to the Provincial Secretary. Meanwhile, the poor public would like to know whether the Riverdale Bastille is a jail or merely a resort where hide and seek is played at the expense of law and order."

Sheriff Mowat was equally unhelpful: "In jail matters Mr. Dunlop is my superior officer. Why not ask him? I feel that I cannot tell you anything about the matter. I must not say."[18]

> "We would like to know why Spanton and Soady were suspended?" The Star asked Inspector Dunlop. "Well, you cannot ask me," he answered.
>
> Can you tell us where we can apply for this information?
>
> "Ask the Kaiser. He's in Belgium at the present" was the official rejoinder, as he banged down the receiver. And so far as giving the public satisfaction or security as to the conditions at the Jail, the matter rests there.

Just before this angry exchange with reporters, Dunlop had received the following card in the mail:

> I see by reports in the Toronto papers that you are examining Currell, my guard. So you know by the note that I left that Currell was drugged. Don't be too hard on him. It was my fault.
>
> > Catch me if you can,
> > Frank McCullough

In the absence of any official explanation, the suspensions of Soady and Spanton suggested that city employees were responsible for McCullough's escape. This prompted Alderman Samuel McBride, rising on a question of privilege in city council, to make the following statement:

> I see by the morning papers that more irregularities have occurred at the Toronto Jail. In view of the fact that effort has been made to place the blame on this council and its employees, I think the matter should be cleared up by a public investigation. Not one behind closed doors like the present one. Later in the afternoon I am going to move for an open investigation. . . . I want to take the stigma off the members and employees of this council and place it where it belongs – on the Provincial Government.

Frank McCullough was beginning to fray nerves within "officialdom."[19]

# XII

# Administrative Incompetence

The Minister of Justice,
Ottawa, Ont.

Honorable Sir:

We, the undersigned members of the Toronto Bread and Cake Salesmen's Association, hereby subscribe our names to the attached petition earnestly imploring the Department of Justice to grant clemency in the case of Frank McCullough.

The fact that at one time the condemned man followed the same vocation as ourselves (and performed his duties faithfully) calls forth our sympathy. We are also of the unanimous opinion that the crime for which he is convicted was not of a premeditated nature, but rather of a sudden impulse.

Fervently trusting and praying that his life may yet be spared,

We have the honor to be, Sir,

> Very respectfully yours,
> W. L. Grigsby,
> President
> Bread and Cake Salesmen's
> Association of Toronto

On Tuesday evening, April 29, a dutiful clerk working late in the sheriff's office heard a knock at the door. The visitor was a government courier bearing a letter addressed to Frederick Mowat. The letter, marked "Urgent and Confidential," was from the provincial inspector of prisons and public charities, W. W. Dunlop.

The clerk delivered the letter personally to the sheriff at his home.[1] By doing so he ruined an otherwise pleasant evening.

The letter contained a two-page excerpt from Dunlop's final report to the provincial secretary. There was a covering note from Dunlop: "In all justice to yourself, I feel that you should have an opportunity of making a report to me in regard to this matter, so that the same may be submitted to the Honorable Minister at the same time that I deliver my report and recommendations to him."[2]

The inspector requested that Mowat submit his report the following day.

The attached excerpt concluded that in accordance with the Criminal Code, the Sheriff's Act, the Prisons and Public Charities Act, and the Official Rules and Regulations Governing the Common Jails of Ontario, "the prisoner, Frank McCullough was clearly under the absolute control of the Sheriff."

"The Sheriff," moreover, "engaged the men to act as special watches and must accept the responsibility of those appointments." Though he had hired the guards, he "did not administer the Oath of Office to these men, nor is it shown that any specific instructions were given the men as to what their duties comprised." Furthermore, despite receiving repeated reports from the chief turnkey concerning irregularities regarding food, cooking utensils, writing materials, and so on,

> The Sheriff did not correct them, and Mr. Mowat knows
> that if these irregularities did exist, it was only a matter of
> degree what other materials or implements could have been
> brought into the cell, and I [Dunlop] believe that the escape
> of Frank McCullough is due to the fact that Mr. Sheriff

Mowat did not correct these irregularities when they were reported to him.

Poor Mr. Sheriff Mowat!

Mowat dispatched a letter to Dunlop the next morning, saying that upon reading the excerpt, "I found that it would be impossible to make a sufficient answer without consideration in the short time before you wished to hand your report to the Minister." He asked for more time, but if Dunlop couldn't wait, "will you be good enough to hand this letter with your report?"

Mowat complained that he was entitled to a copy of Dunlop's full report and a complete transcript of the evidence, "this being a very serious matter." He asked that both be sent immediately by messenger. "I may also say that I considered that I was in the same position as yourself [at the inquiry], and that any report should be signed by me as well as by you. If I had known that you considered that I was on trial I should have taken a different course."[3]

Dunlop didn't wait. He sent his report to the provincial secretary that same day, along with a covering memorandum: "I sent to Mr. Sheriff Mowat a copy of that part having reference to himself and have received the attached letter from him." He had not supplied Mowat with a copy of the full report or a transcript, "as he was present and heard everything that was said."

Dunlop added that "if Mr. Mowat wishes to hold an investigation himself, he is no doubt qualified to do so. In the meantime, I do not think I have any alteration to make in the report as submitted."[4]

Two days later, Mowat sent the provincial secretary his response, entitled "Observations by the Sheriff of Toronto on the Memorandum Sent Him by the Inspector of Prisons and Public Charities." Mowat's "observations" were pitiful. First, he argued that prisoners condemned to death were not "in the absolute control of a sheriff" in that others, such as a spiritual adviser or medical officer, had access without the permission of the sheriff. Secondly, he had "a reference from a clergyman" in the appointment of Currell; and thirdly, there was "no form of oath of office" conveniently available to be given to temporary men. Further, how could he be held responsible for the escape when the inquiry did "not show how the escape actually took place?"

But the heart of Mowat's defence was a pathetic and embarrassing accusation of carelessness against his chief turnkey, Henry Addy.

> Mr. Addy only spoke once to the sheriff [this was not true] with regard to cooking utensils and writing paper being in the cell. When Mr. Addy directed the sheriff's attention to these things, the sheriff replied that he did not see that any harm could come from such being in the cell. This did not mean that in future the chief turnkey should be careless as to what went into the cell, and there is no evidence to show that he was, and the sheriff does believe that he was careless.[5]

What? Addy should not have been careless; there was no evidence that he *was* careless; but the sheriff nevertheless *believed* he was. Mowat clearly did not do well under pressure.

Dunlop's report recommended that the vacant position of jail governor be filled; that regular guards be assigned to the death watch; and that a new punch-clock alarm system be installed to ensure "that the man appointed to watch the prisoner is awake." Addy was just to be censured and subsequently reduced in authority only by virtue of the new governor's appointment. And on the subject of Mowat, Dunlop wrote, "No doubt you [the provincial secretary] will consider that something should be done in respect to the office of the Sheriff."[6]

These behind-the-scenes machinations explain the prickly behaviour of Dunlop and Mowat when pressed by reporters in public on other issues. The day after Dunlop submitted his report, the window McCullough had used to make his escape was sealed with bricks. When reporters asked for the source of the order, they got the runaround:

Inspector Dunlop states it was done by Sheriff Mowat. The Sheriff says it was done on Inspector Dunlop's authority. Property Commissioner Chisolm, whose men did the work, said he did it on the instruction of the steward at the jail.

"Who gave the order?" The Star asked Inspector Dunlop. "I did not know until yesterday that it had been done. I suppose Sheriff Mowat did that."

Sheriff Mowat, however, said: "That is a matter for the Inspector of Prisons. I gave no instructions about it."

The Star called up Inspector Dunlop later and told him what Sheriff Mowat said. "Tell him the Kaiser must have done it again. I don't know a ___ thing about it," was the reply.[7]

The day of this heated exchange with reporters – May 2 – was also the day McCullough had been scheduled to hang. Hangman Arthur Ellis was ordered to show up even though there was no prisoner. Should the authorities manage to recapture McCullough at the last minute, they didn't want to find there was no executioner to perform his "public duty." Ellis attended the jail, and promptly asked to be paid his fee.[8]

But what was to happen if McCullough was recaptured after the day officially appointed for his execution? Would there have to be another trial? Was he considered to be "dead," in the eyes of the law, after May 2?

The ever-efficient J. D. Clarke in Ottawa had already anticipated this problem. The plan was to postpone the execution by using an existing provision in the Criminal Code for a "reprieve."

Section 1063 of the code allowed for a reprieve in two instances: if time was required to examine a further point of law after a sentence of execution had already been handed down, or if further time was required to consider a formal recommendation for executive clemency. Authority to grant a reprieve was assigned by the code to the judge in a case; however, a reprieve could also be granted by the governor general acting for the Crown.

The code made no specific mention of a reprieve being used in the unusual case of an escaped prisoner under sentence of death, but conceivably, and with a loose interpretation of the law, an escaped prisoner could be reprieved (or the execution postponed) until he or she was once again in custody and the sentence could be carried out. While the prisoner remained at large, the end-date of the reprieve could theoretically be extended as the need arose so that a new trial would not be necessary once the prisoner was finally recaptured.

This was the strategy that Clarke proceeded to implement, though no one in Toronto or Ottawa had previously experienced the procedure of using a reprieve in the case of an escaped prisoner.

A week before the scheduled date of execution, Clarke had written to Mr. J. R. Cartwright, deputy attorney general of Ontario in Toronto, "to inquire if your Department has taken the necessary steps to have McCullough reprieved." Clarke asked for a reply "at the earliest opportunity," for if Toronto had not applied to Justice Rose for a reprieve, "it would be necessary for this Department to consider what action it should take."

The next day, Cartwright replied succinctly from Toronto that he had received Clarke's inquiry "and may say that no steps have been taken to have McCullough reprieved under section 1063 of the Criminal Code." That was it. Cartwright said nothing more.

Clarke fired off a telegram from Ottawa marked "IMMEDIATE":

AS QUESTION OF REPRIEVE OF THIS MAN ARISES BY REASON OF ESCAPE FROM PROVINCIAL INSTITUTION AND IN NO WAY CONNECTED WITH QUESTION OF CLEMENCY OR COMMUTATION IT SEEMS CLEAR TO ACTING MINISTER OF JUSTICE THAT SECURING OF REPRIEVE SHOULD BE BY ATTORNEY GENERAL OF PROVINCE PLEASE WIRE ME IMMEDIATELY VIEWS OF YOUR DEPARTMENT AS TO THIS.

Silence. There was no reply from Cartwright in Toronto. What were they doing up there? As we shall see, Cartwright's neglect in answering this single telegram would have momentous consequences.

In the meantime in Ottawa, Clarke became nervous. He quickly prepared a letter to the "Governor General in Council," signed by the acting minister of justice, Arthur Meighen, recommending that, in light of Toronto's silence "and as it is important that there should be no further delay," McCullough be reprieved for a month, until June 2, 1919.

Consequently, two days before the scheduled date of execution, Government House issued an order, signed by the clerk of the Privy Council stating: "THEREFORE the Governor General is pleased to Order and doth hereby Order that the said FRANK MCCULLOUGH be reprieved till Monday the Second day of June, 1919."

This was immediately telegraphed to Cartwright and Sheriff Mowat in Toronto with the instructions: "Repeat back this telegram immediately after receipt. Letter confirming same follows." Mowat obediently replied to his telegram and that looked to be the end of the matter. Clarke had once more saved the day. McCullough, if recaptured, would hang on June 2.

One can imagine Clarke's reaction when, the very next day, he received a letter from Cartwright stating "for your information" that Justice Rose had been approached in Toronto and had signed a reprieve postponing the execution "until the 13th day of June"!

Here was a fine state of affairs: two official dates for McCullough's execution, one signed by a justice of the Supreme Court of Ontario and the other authorized by the governor general of the Dominion of Canada! What would T. C. Robinette have to say about that?

In fact, Robinette was completely unaware of this development. But if he *were* to discover the existence of two differently dated reprieves, his "basso profundo" would be heard to the mountaintops until McCullough walked free. Perhaps this was the reason

Rose was curiously reticent when reporters questioned him about his reprieve. "When asked if he had issued a reprieve, Mr. Justice Rose refused to say. Asked if such was not the custom in similar cases, Mr. Rose said, 'I do not know. I never had one like it before.'"[9]

As soon as it dawned on the authorities in Toronto that there were now two dates set for McCullough's execution, there was a flurry of self-righteous communication with Ottawa. Cartwright wrapped himself in the Criminal Code, claiming that his actions were "utterly consistent," since the power of reprieve "was in the first instance that of the trial Judge." The solicitor for the provincial attorney general's office wrote that the Toronto reprieve "was made in pursuance of a letter and telegram from the Department of Justice itself suggesting that a reprieve be obtained." Even a bewildered Sheriff Mowat smelled trouble and wrote to Ottawa saying he "would be glad for any instructions that you might care to give me."

Finally, Cartwright had the nerve to suggest to Clarke that "it might be well if the Order of His Excellency [the governor general] was amended so as to conform with the order made by Mr. Justice Rose" to "prevent trouble hereafter."

Clarke put feelings aside and fixed the matter. Another recommendation was made to the governor general extending the date of Ottawa's reprieve to coincide with the date of Rose's, and another exchange of telegrams to confirm the matter took place. McCullough, if recaptured, would now hang on June 13, 1919. Luckily, the problem had been solved without Robinette ever becoming the wiser. And perhaps Rose's date was more suitable anyway, since the 13th of June fell on a Friday.[10]

While no one knew it at the time, this chain of events – prompted first by Cartwright's failure to answer Clarke's telegram – leading to a reprieve issued by the governor general which then had to be changed, was destined to alter McCullough's fate.

⤜   ⤛

A blue-eyed, "diminutive miss" Vera de Lavelle was tried before Judge Emerson Coatsworth on May 7. She elected against trial by jury and was defended by W. B. Horkins of Robinette's firm.

The trial was notable for the evidence of one witness. The Crown attorney, R. H. Greer,[11] called Harry Berman, a chauffeur who worked for the *Daily Star*. Berman testified that he had lived "out of wedlock" with Vera for four years. On Spadina Avenue (where the two had lived together, and McCullough delivered bread), she was known as "Mrs. Berman." Vera had left Berman several weeks before McCullough's escape.

Berman described how he ended up driving Vera to the jail to meet Currell on the evening of the escape. The lovesick chauffeur had not seen Vera for weeks when he suddenly spotted her from his car on Adelaide Street one day after work. Berman pulled over. Vera refused to get in, but she asked him "to make an engagement to meet her on Tuesday, April 15, at eight o'clock at the corner of Teraulay [Bay] and Dundas. I agreed to do so."

Berman was waiting in his car at the time and place appointed. Vera got in and "said she wished to go for a ride and I took her for one. It was raining. She told me she had to meet Currell at 9:30, but didn't say where until I started driving around. She then said I am supposed to meet Currell at the corner of Gerrard and Broadview." This was the main intersection outside the Toronto Jail. They waited in the car. Vera had a package. "It was thundering and raining heavily."

Currell alighted from a streetcar on Broadview. Vera left Berman's car and hastened with Currell to a store. "He was carrying a large bag." After "only two minutes," they emerged from the store and parted. Vera returned to the car. The last Berman saw of Currell, "he was going up Broadview toward the jail with the bag in his hand."

Vera had just given Currell a box of chocolates for McCullough. Hidden inside were the saws he would use later that night to escape from the jail.

Mr. Berman, what did Miss Lavelle say was her object in meeting Currell?

That she wished to tell him she was not feeling well and would not be able to see Mrs. Currell the next day.

When first did she mention Currell to you?

When she got petitions from Mr. Robinette in the middle of March. She had several petitions. She told me Mr. Currell was a guard.

You didn't know she ever saw Currell before?

Oh, yes. I know she saw Currell at his house.

Did you know McCullough?

I never saw him.

You didn't know she was acquainted with him prior to this trouble?

No, I did not.

What occurred on your motor drive? Did you ask her any questions?

No, I did not. I just asked her when I could see her again.

She had dumped him for McCullough. She had used him in helping McCullough to escape. Now, with his testimony, Berman had his revenge.

Greer called three more witnesses. Irene Marks, "well known to the police" and a prisoner at the jail ("for stealing a silk dress when I was 'stewed'"), said that while they were incarcerated together Vera had told her of buying the saws "at a Rice, Lewis Store for 65 cents." Florence Smith, a neighbour on Spadina, testified that Vera came to her after the escape and "said she wanted money for Frank to get away with and I told her I had none to give her."

Finally, before Judge Coatsworth reserved judgement until May 15, Mrs. Violet Smith, owner of a restaurant on Queen Street, testified that after the escape Vera came to the restaurant "and said she was in trouble as the police were after her." She said that rather than be taken "she would commit suicide. Pointing to a small parcel she carried she said that she had something which would put her to sleep for 150 years."[12]

# XIII

# The Toronto Riots

Over there in your Parliament buildings is where a great
deal of the trouble lies. Those big fat slobs in Government
positions should be put out and their places filled by
returned men. . .˙. Is it fair that these returned heroes, some
of them minus legs or arms, or otherwise mutilated for life,
should be placed in the position of being forced to beg for
work while these aliens are taking the best and living on
the fat of the land?
                                   – John Galbraith, protester in Queen's Park,
                                                                   August 6, 1918

The crowd was swearing and calling us offensive names.
Pte. Button shouted, "Are we going to allow these yellow-
backs to take our men? We fought the Huns and we can
fight the police." I did not see anybody hit Button. His head
struck the sidewalk as he fell and bounced.
                                   – Constable W. J. Tait, September 27, 1918

The police came around like a bunch of lunatics. . . . I saw
a man trip and fall, and then saw a policeman strike him
two blows with his baton while he was lying on the ground.
I said, "What are you trying to do, kill people?" I told the

policeman he should look after the man. He told me to go about my business, and he told my wife that if she did not go home he would beat her up. My wife told him to go home and beat up his own wife.

– Mr. S. G. Young, September 18, 1918

We need to step back for a moment.

Why did so many people support Frank McCullough? The answer takes us to the heart of popular sentiment in Toronto at the close of the First World War.

There were those who believed McCullough deserved mercy because of his religious conversion.[1] There were others who were opposed in principle to capital punishment.[2] Some were tired of all the killing and hoped the end of the war would bring a new world order.[3] Still others complained about the trial and thought the verdict unjust.[4] Indeed, there were many who subscribed to all of the above. But there was more to it than this.

Frank McCullough typified a valiant defiance of authority. His escape openly ridiculed government officials and the police who were the agents of an established order ("I say to hell with the whole lot of you. I hope McCullough never gets caught"[5]). In 1918–19, both at home and abroad, there were many who felt they were the victims of a war begun by politicians, generals, and the upper classes. There were many who had reason to hate "officialdom."

McCullough was seen as a victim too. Remember that no one in Toronto knew anything about his dubious past. The opinion on the street was that his punishment was just too severe. He was far from perfect, but didn't that make him all the more human? Sure, the man was a thief, but that policeman was bashing him over the head when the gun went off. The boy hadn't meant to kill Williams. Still, the officials and the courts made no distinction; they refused to admit the complicated circumstances of the case. They had simply labelled Frank a murderer and were dragging him off to be hanged. He was a nobody, had come from nowhere, and, like most, didn't get a fair chance in life. But unlike most, McCullough had the courage to fight back. He refused to submit and wore his defiance with flair. Frank McCullough fixed them; he made fools of them all. The man had pluck.

And then there was the matter of the baton. At that particular time, the image of a policeman wielding his baton was loaded with significance for the people of Toronto. When they read that Williams smashed his baton over McCullough's head, most knew what that was about. The baton had become a symbol of injustice brutally imposed upon the innocent – because of the Toronto Riots.

In August 1918, four months before McCullough shot Williams, thousands of returned soldiers, police, and civilians fought a bloody battle in the streets of Toronto. The outbreak, lasting several days, came to be known as the "Toronto Riots"; and the confrontation left seething resentments that were unleashed again by the case of Frank McCullough.[6]

Before the war had ended, a large number of returned soldiers were already in the city.[7] Most had been sent home early because they had fallen ill or were injured, and a high proportion of them were congregated in Toronto because of the city's many hospital facilities. All amputation and major orthopaedic cases, for example, were first concentrated in Toronto upon arrival from England.[8] In addition to those receiving medical treatment, there were thousands more attempting to readjust to civilian life; men such as Ernest Currell and Doris Mytton's father, who was "taking vocational training."

These men and their families were not a happy lot. First of all, there were the problems of unemployment, substandard housing, and inadequate pensions. In addition, many suffered the painful personal experience of having lost a limb, while others – "shell-shocked, gas-poisoned, disease-ridden" – faced a lifetime of illness. Most also felt that their sacrifice, made in unimaginable conditions, had not been sufficiently recognized or rewarded. And they were not alone in these sentiments, for among Canadian cities, Toronto had supplied the largest contingents of men for service overseas.[9] There were few residents in the city who did not have a son, a brother, a husband, or a father in uniform.[10] And as usual, it was left to the women to pick up the pieces.

Regrettably, in such times of hardship a scapegoat is often required. The soldiers and their suffering families found two.

The first were the "aliens," specifically the hated "enemy aliens," whose mysterious number and capacity for evil grew as large as public imagination could expand. "Enemy aliens" were residents of Canada who had emigrated from nations now at war with the Allies. These were the Germans, Austrians, Hungarians, and Bulgarians who had come to Canada before the war to begin a new life. In the confusion of wartime, preceded by decades of massive immigration, it wasn't always easy to keep track of who came from where, wherever that was, exactly. The suspicious "foreigners" were lumped together indiscriminately in the public mind as a mass of strangers from enemy places. The most convenient catch-all term for them was "Hun."

It didn't seem to matter that by law these people were forbidden to serve in the Canadian Forces.[11] A prevailing theory was that most were secret supporters of the "Boche." They were shifty-eyed shirkers, hiding in Canada to make huge profits off the war; "greasy-haired foreigners" conducting espionage in the back of smelly restaurants; "sheltered enemies" socking away their cash while their foreign brothers maimed the "real Canadians" now returning from overseas to find their jobs gone.

The second odious group were the "slackers," the men who should have, but didn't, join up; the "yellow-bellied milksops" who cowered at home making money, and were now hogging those precious jobs the suffering soldiers felt they deserved. And the slackers always seemed to be protecting the enemy aliens, for chief among the slackers were government officials and public employees ("public poltroons") in their "cushy" jobs. The worst slackers of all, however, were the police.

And Acting Det. Frank Williams fit the description of slacker perfectly.

There was a further reason to resent these particular slackers. The police and government officials were the agents of a larger civil authority that was also challenged and derided. Men who had faced death at the Front were capable of a rebellious disregard for authority at home (and abroad). They were the ones who had been shot up. They were the ones whose friends had died beside them. Now at home, struggling to find work and a place to live, they had to put up with "pettifogging," incompetent bureaucrats who would piss their pants at the first sound of a "Whiz Bang." And they weren't going to be pushed around any more, especially by some "lily-livered slacker," some pot-bellied cop who thought he could order them to "Move on!" Who the hell did he think he was?

There was a Greek restaurant at 433 Yonge Street called the White City Café. Soldiers found it convenient to take their "lady friends" there, even though the "alien" proprietor was known to be "a mighty rotter. . . . He would make insinuations reflecting upon the character of the young women."[12]

Pte. Cluderay, a returned soldier, took a young woman to the White City on the unbearably hot evening of August 1. Some "insinuations" were made, there was a fight, and Cluderay was soundly thrashed by one of the Greek waiters.[13]

The next evening, having gathered at a hospital parkette known as Shrapnel Corners (at College and Yonge),[14] a number of returned men, "many of them cripples," marched directly to the café. "Three of them entered the White City and attacked a waiter." A noisy crowd of civilians joined the soldiers outside. Constable Peacock of the Toronto police, alone on his section of

Yonge, rushed to the restaurant to stop the fight.[15] Outside, "women, who claimed to be soldiers' wives, urged the men on." A Pte. Brown yelled, "Let's smash up the bloody place." Bricks went through the plate glass, and "soldiers climbed through the windows to the cries of 'Over the top, boys.'"

Within a few minutes, the men demolished everything in sight. "The plate glass windows were smashed, as were 32 mirrors which lined the walls, expensive marble tops of tables were taken off and thrown on the ground and smashed. The counter came next, everything around it being a veritable wreck."

A truck pulled up loaded with military police. Constable Peacock called for them to go to the rear of the restaurant, "where the rioters had a Greek up against the fence." But the military police did not interfere; "they stayed in the truck in the middle of the road."[16]

The White City was only the beginning. Reinforced by some four hundred returned men and a larger number of civilians, "the angry mob, headed by soldiers in uniform and returned soldiers wearing their badges," proceeded "jubilantly on their way" to destroy eleven more restaurants along Yonge Street and at other locations in the city. "In many cases the alien keepers or waiters made a hurried exit by the rear doors and windows."[17]

After the White City, they hit the Colonial Café, "brilliantly lit up by the electric lights where a fight between three police officers and the mob took place." The police became "targets for bricks, broken glass, and other missiles," and were powerless in holding back the rioters. "Here the scene was unforgettable": while comrades demolished the restaurant, an amputee "standing on the counter swept down the chandeliers with his crutch" as "a constant stream of water played like a fountain behind the fight from the wreck of the coffee machine, which sent a stream up to the ceiling and fell in cascades back on to the fountain to the counter and to the floor."

The returned soldiers, "now growing into an ungovernable

mob, made their way in motor cars and street cars" to the Star Lunch at 441 Yonge.

> The same methods were used to gain entrance, by breaking the big plate glass windows at the front. . . . Traffic was held up both ways on Yonge Street by the crowd which had gathered to watch the scene. The air was filled with flying glass and fragments of wood. . . . Tables were broken and thrown to the cheering crowd outside. . . . Boxes of tea, sugar, biscuits and other edibles were tossed out of the upper windows, till the ground below was littered with food of every kind. The next stop was made at the Marathon Lunch, 822 Yonge. . . . After demolishing everything in sight, the parade started down Yonge Street once more. Several alien restaurant keepers on the way down were compelled to salute the flag, with the threat of dire results if they refused. "We took our chance in France and we'll take it here again," was the slogan of the parade.

All available police were called out, but they found themselves outnumbered and powerless to halt the escalating violence. While some attempted dashes "for some particular ringleader among the rioters . . . using their batons and even their revolvers as clubs," they were "pelted" by the crowds and "compelled to retire again without their prisoners." Consequently, the police "deemed it advisable to confine their interference to a watchful interest in the proceedings." That night few arrests were made.

Mayor Tommy Church blew a gasket.[18] He held an emergency meeting in his office the next morning and declared that "drastic action" would be taken to prevent any recurrence. "We don't need any Russian scenes in Toronto," he declared. "It is just such occurrences as last night that take away public support. If places employ enemy aliens and if there are grievances, there are lawful ways . . . of dealing with the situation."

The Great War Veterans' Association (GWVA), holding its national convention in Toronto at this time, also condemned the violence, although with greater sympathy for the rioters. "Returned soldiers are coming back from France in shiploads," commented an association vice-president, "and when they see foreigners making money hand over fist, there's bound to be trouble."

To the great frustration of the mayor, the commanding officer of Military District No. 2,[19] Col. H. S. Bickford, took a legalistic view of the situation. Bickford pointed out that by law he was responsible for men in uniform only. The "discharged men," without uniform, were the main culprits, and were clearly the mayor's responsibility under civil authority.[20] However, "immediately the Mayor or any police magistrate requisitions the military under the Riot Act," Bickford promised, "I shall proceed to clear the streets. . . . There is enough infantry and cavalry for three times as great a disturbance." But the difficulty was that if Church did read the Riot Act, Bickford would be compelled to "clear the streets using ball ammunition."

Thus it fell solely to the police to prevent further trouble the next evening, Saturday, August 3. During the afternoon, virtually the entire force was marshalled in the downtown core, Frank Williams among them. Acting Police Chief Samuel Dickson gave firm orders to "deal forcibly with those refusing arrest."

The police were under great pressure. Word went down the line that Mayor Church wanted "prompt steps" taken – whatever that meant. The mayor didn't want to have to rely on Bickford's "ball ammunition." Further, the mayor had heard a rumour – which turned out to be true – that the night before, some constables were seen standing idle smoking looted cigars during the destruction of a restaurant.[21] Any similar behaviour would be punished severely. All that afternoon the soldiers taunted the police. One returned man called them "yellow-backs and told the police to go to a warmer clime or he would put a bullet through them."

The trouble began at the Court Street police station that

evening. There, a "crowd of some thousands," including "a large number of women," gathered at 7:00 p.m. to demand the release of a soldier who had been arrested the night before. The police made a charge to clear the crowd, and in "the next few minutes a hundred civilians were laid out on the sidewalk bleeding and groaning. The officials used their batons mercilessly on everybody within reach."

The frightened mob raced to Adelaide and Victoria, where another group of veterans had gathered. Mounted police followed, and just as one of the veterans shouted for his companions to "fall in," the police charged among them. "One veteran received a crack on the head. . . . This incensed the veterans and a general uproar followed."

"Get bricks," shouted some; "Get the boys together," shouted others. There was a rush to Yonge Street to gather more men. "On went the returned men, on went the mob, and the police followed." The crowd, "now numbering several thousands, surged northward" up Yonge in the direction of Shrapnel Corners. A stand was attempted near an arcade where two rifles (one a "double-barreled weapon") were seized from the shooting gallery. "Go get the boys!" shouted a one-legged soldier. "We'll stand them here." Again batons were used, and the mob broke towards Carlton, where another crowd had gathered outside the Great War Veterans' Club. "A hail of bombs from some aerial invader could not have made a more general stampede."

As thousands arrived at the intersection of College and Yonge, the bugle call "Fall In!" rang out from the steps of the club. "Again the strident notes rent the air. Again and yet again." Outside the club, a soldier climbed on top of an automobile shouting, "Line up, fellows! I'll be back with more men." As the police pressed forward with their batons, the crowd turned and enveloped Shrapnel Corners. Here the veterans suffered a serious casualty: the popular Pte. Mason Buttons, an "Original First"[22] who had lost both legs, was seriously injured. "Crack went a policeman's baton over the head of a crippled veteran who fell with a groan to the sidewalk in a huddled heap. . . . Women screamed, veterans were seeing red now." The cry was heard: "Buttons has been laid out!"

> Then the trouble began. The civilian crowd shrank back. The police charged with batons right in amongst the crippled soldiers occupying the seats at the corner. In a second crutches were countering the blows of the police batons. It was a pitiful sight. Veteran after veteran went down. Men on one leg hopped backward with crutch poised ready to give blow for blow. . . . "We've killed better men than these Toronto policemen in France," said one. "Wait till we get our revolvers: we'll kill these ___ pigs."

While this battle continued at Shrapnel Corners, the police were charging other crowds that had congregated up and down Yonge Street. Mayor Church was frantically moving from scene to scene in his car "standing up and waving his stick": "Now, all you people, if you want to keep out of trouble, go home!" "Booh!" responded the crowd "with one voice. Fifty yards up the street he repeated the operation. The 'Boohs' were more pronounced than ever. The crowds remained."

The worst occurred at Queen and Yonge, where "upwards of ten thousand people" had gathered. At precisely the moment the police made a decision to clear the mob, "some 2,000 people came pouring out of Loew's Theatre." The police "apparently lost their heads and charged the crowd, which was nearly entirely made up of women and civilians, and not a few children."

> They charged the crowd using batons with utter disregard as to who they were striking. This resulted in a veritable panic. Many women and children received heavy blows, and screaming, attempted to turn back through the jam of people behind them. This move threw the whole crowd into a stampede, with the result that scores were trampled down

Western Congregational Church, at 327 Spadina, which Nelles transformed into the Church for the Stranger. He covered the organ pipes with a lantern screen, introduced topical sermons, organized clubs, and pushed district visitation to increase membership. Sunday *evening* attendance grew from twenty-five to seven hundred within two years of his arrival. (*Toronto Public Library,* T10840)

The Rev. R. Bertram Nelles, minister at the Church for the Stranger. He was "a big pastor with a big program and lots of push." Nelles rallied his congregation and other churches in support of McCullough, who would be his most dramatic conversion in a lengthy ministerial career. (Evening Telegram, *June 13, 1919; courtesy Toronto Public Library*)

The only known photograph of the "diminutive Miss Vera de Lavelle." She was dark in complexion, with flashing blue eyes, a radiant smile, and an "air of romance." In her own way, she was as fearless as the man for whom she risked everything to save. (Globe, *May 30, 1919; courtesy Toronto Public Library*)

Some of Toronto's newspaper reporters and photographers in 1919. It was in a vehicle such as this that reporters pursued the police in their final arrest of Vera de Lavelle, "all quite in the true spirit of the 'feature fillum.'" Newspapermen were crucial but mostly anonymous players in the case of Frank McCullough. (*City of Toronto Archives; James Collection, sc 244-3532*)

VERA LAVALLE
as she appeared in court.

An artist's sketch of Vera de Lavelle as she appeared in court before Judge Emerson Coatsworth. She was a "neat bit of femininity," who "wore a stole with chic effect." Vera claimed to be innocent of assisting McCullough in his escape. In fact, she supplied him with saws hidden in a box of chocolates. (Evening Telegram, *Apr. 23, 1919; courtesy Toronto Public Library*)

Outpatients awaiting their hospital appointments on College Street, some time in 1917-18. Shrapnel Corners is nearby. "Down with the slackers" can be faintly seen beneath the surface graffiti at the upper left. The man with the striking sunglasses reminds us that black Canadians played their part in the war effort. (*City of Toronto Archives; James Collection, SC244-736*)

Canadian soldiers, possibly 48th Highlanders, arriving at the North Toronto Station in 1919. Behind our field of vision are cheering crowds. These men look healthy and most look happy to be home; the men who preceded them, before the end of the conflict, were mostly sick, wounded, or diseased. (*City of Toronto Archives; James Collection, SC244-814*)

The British Welcome League Building, where McCullough hid with de Lavelle after his escape from jail, is seen here on the left at the corner of Front and Spadina. Stacked building materials in this 1926 photograph conceal the basement window from which McCullough saw Detective Cronin searching for him. (*City of Toronto Archives; RG8 58-56*)

The Honourable Arthur Meighen, acting minister of justice in 1919. Meighen had a reputation for "blood and iron," and McCullough could not have been given a more heartless politician to decide his fate, or a worse time for the decision to be made. At the time, Meighen was caught up in dealing with the Winnipeg General Strike. (*National Archives of Canada, C5799*)

McCullough's case provided opportunity to ridicule the incompetence of "officialdom." Inept management of the Toronto Jail was widely attributed to political interference in jail staffing. "All the Comforts of Jail" was the caption for this newspaper cartoon. Note that the jug of Veronal and the stepladder, used in McCullough and de Lavelle's escapes, stand side by side. (Evening Telegram, *May 31, 1919; courtesy Toronto Public Library*)

Arthur Ellis, the hangman, known for his coolness and efficiency, until he encountered McCullough. Ellis had dispatched over six hundred souls across the Middle East, England, and finally Canada. He married a Montreal woman in 1915 and managed to convince her for seven years that he was a travelling salesman. (*from Frank Anderson,* Hanging in Canada; *courtesy National Library of Canada,* NL22092)

in the mad scramble to escape the flying sticks. People who took refuge in the doorways were roughly pulled out, struck, and ran for safety. One little girl of ten years, who was standing in Woolworth's doorway, had her arm broken by a policeman's club when she attempted to ward off a blow. . . . Another policeman hit a girl on the head four times and she fell on the sidewalk. . . . Judging from various figures, the number of victims of police clubs here was well over the 500 mark.

During the appalling violence along Yonge Street that night, one veteran by the name of Hunter "saw them hit a young man who dropped into the gutter like an animal which had been pole-axed. I went over to help him." While leaning down, Hunter was hit over the head himself. There were four policemen. "I lay down on the pavement and covered my head with my hands until the wave had passed over. When I saw that it was clear I got into a restaurant."

While he was recovering inside the restaurant, three more policemen "running down the street came to the door. I was holding my hands over my head," reported Hunter, "and I said to them don't come in here, you have no business here." One police-man entered, and Hunter grabbed the policeman's arm as he raised his baton to strike. The other policemen claimed later that they thought Hunter "was assaulting a police officer." They too entered, "grabbed me by the leg and pulled me out into the street. They threw me on the pavement and hit me on the head and shoulders."

Hunter insisted on being formally charged. "The police put me in a car they had there. The car stopped twice and each time it stopped one of them in it said I had better get out and go. I told them that I wanted them to take me to the police station and enter a charge in the regular way."

He was bleeding profusely but was not given medical atten-tion. At the police station, "They did not know what charge to lay." He was asked for identification, and among the papers Hunter drew from his wallet was his GWVA membership card. "This seemed to enrage the officer, who struck the card violently to the floor." Hunter, covered with blood, remained in a locked cell for one and a half hours. When two associates – a colonel and a captain in uniform – arrived to take Hunter to the General Hospital, the police suddenly became cooperative.

Hunter was brought from his cell. Constable Scott described the scene later at an inquiry:

> When asked for his name, Hunter said, "Lieutenant," put that down; now "Colonel," put that down; then "A. T. Hunter, barrister," put that down, and you are making the biggest mistake in your life. (Laughter)

Lt.-Col. A. T. Hunter, K.C., barrister at law, veteran of the First Canadian Contingent, commanding officer of the York Rangers, had completed three years of military service, including action at St. Julien,[23] before being wounded and eventually discharged.[24] He was also a vice-president of the GWVA national executive, and an associate of the Honourable Hartley Dewart, leader of the Liberal opposition.

That night Hunter was admitted to hospital. He remained there for seven days.

The riots continued for another three days, after which there was a formal inquiry lasting well into October 1918.[25] To the bitter dismay of the soldiers and their outraged civilian sympathizers, the inquiry formally absolved the police of any wrongdoing.[26] Curiously, no policeman called before the inquiry could recall actually seeing another policeman strike a civilian or a returned soldier.

In the case of Lt.-Col. Hunter, no policeman could recall seeing him struck on the sidewalk, although "he might have hit his head on the bench" when he "stumbled" in the restaurant. The police could definitely recall, however, that Hunter "was under the influence of liquor, and there was a very objectionable odor of liquor upon him."

The police had rehearsed their stories and were lying to protect themselves. The descriptive term used by the soldiers was "platoon swearing." Hunter said he was the victim of a "police poison gas attack." "Talk about Prussianism," declared a civilian at the inquiry. "I never saw such Prussianism as I saw that night."[27]

Why did so many people support Frank McCullough?

The baton!

The Toronto Riots and the resulting inquiry took place shortly before McCullough shot Williams in November 1918. Is it any wonder that his case stirred up resentments towards the police and the authorities? Like the civilians outside Loew's Theatre, and the "crippled" soldiers at Shrapnel Corners, McCullough was a victim of brute force imposed by the police. If that "slacker" Williams had not used his baton, would the gun have gone off? Did McCullough deserve to hang?

Consider the following letter to Arthur Meighen:

Minister of Justice:

I think it is a rotten shame if you allow that young man McCullough to hang. . . . During that soldiers' riot on College Street policemen struck with their clubs people who had nothing to do with those riots. I saw a little boy cycling on Yonge Street struck over the head with a policeman's club! I don't believe in murder but if I'd had a club or a gun and that was my boy he struck I would have shot him. Take yourself . . . if you were struck over the head with a club, wouldn't you shoot on the spur of the moment from the pain inflicted? Yes I guess you would. . . . So just come down off your high pedestal and give that harmless boy McCullough who has had to shift for himself all these years a chance to make good.[28]

And then there was Vera. Many supported McCullough because Vera supported McCullough. Here was an ordinary young woman, a bookkeeper, trying to make something out of her little life, transformed by the heroic strength found within her when called upon to help her "sweetheart." Like all those anonymous women who stood courageously by their returned men when they were down, Vera risked all to save her man. And like the valiant Frank who defied the authorities, Vera could make fools of them too.

## XIV

# 78 Bathurst Street

A Bill of H. M. Mowat, M.P., to change the method of execution of a prisoner sentenced to death from hanging to electrocution was read a first time today in Ottawa. Mr. Mowat pointed out the condemned man would be kept at a penitentiary instead of a jail while awaiting the fulfillment of the death sentence, and would not be so likely to escape as Frank McCullough. . . .

– *Evening Telegram*, May 2, 1919

McCullough was in Toronto.

Information concerning his hiding place came to Det. Bart Cronin on the morning of May 8. Someone had "squealed" for the reward of $1,000.

Accompanied by detectives Tuft, Silverthorne, and Armstrong, Cronin proceeded immediately by motor car to a boarding house at 78 Bathurst Street. "The house itself is a tall, rather dingy two-and-a-half story structure, the front of which is red brick. McCullough's room, for which he paid $3 a week, was on the second floor at the back, immediately to the left of the head of the stairway which ascends directly from the front door."

Cronin was not surprised by McCullough's choice of hiding place. The boarding house was literally around the corner from Cross's Livery on King, where McCullough had shot Frank Williams. Cronin had combed the area several times. From the beginning he had suspected that, if McCullough were in the city at all, he would do the opposite of what was expected of him and hide as close as possible to the scene of the crime. Cronin was right.

The detectives left their car some distance away and approached the house swiftly on foot. Silverthorne and Armstrong slipped into a lane that ran behind the house and waited, while Cronin and Tuft entered by the front door, whispered to the elderly landlady, and quietly climbed the stairs, revolvers in hand.

McCullough heard them coming. He had enough time to grab his boots and raise a side window with a crash. As Cronin smashed open the door, McCullough "threw himself feet first out of the window," leaping "some twenty feet" to a driveway below and shattering the kitchen window with one foot on his way down. Silverthorne and Armstrong raced from the back and had McCullough covered with their revolvers before he could move. "I've got nothing on me" were McCullough's only words. "Cronin admitted that he was never so close to shooting a man before."[1]

We don't know what was said as Cronin and McCullough made their way along Queen Street towards City Hall. It was a trip they had made together six months before, when McCullough had said, "I'll be a man. No tears will go to the gallows with me."

McCullough was back in a jocular mood when the car arrived at City Hall. Ushered up the side steps in handcuffs, he "appeared almost happy," and shouted a friendly greeting to his lawyer's son, Mr. Robinette, Jr.,[2] as he was marched through the building and into the detectives' room on the first floor. On the way, McCullough "was recognized by several of the police, and word spread throughout the great Hall in a few seconds that McCullough was captured."

A crowd gathered round McCullough and Cronin before the prisoner was taken into Chief of Detectives George Guthrie's office for questioning. "He smiled considerably, but was very pale. . . . He talked and joked with detectives." After questioning behind closed doors, McCullough was taken to a large room at the rear of the detective office, where they could be seen through a glass-panelled partition. "Here he sat in the middle of the big room, Detective Cronin in front of him, and surrounded by quite a large crowd who were later removed."

Those who were removed, and several reporters who had arrived by this point, peered through the glass panels while Cronin spoke alone to McCullough. "One bracelet was undone by Detective Cronin while a small box lunch was brought in, which McCullough commenced to devour almost ravenously. A glass of water was also brought in, and from the way McCullough ate the two sandwiches, banana, and cake, it would appear that he had not had much to eat for some days. As he ate, Detective Cronin talked to him and frustrated all attempts from outsiders to hear what the murderer had to say."

When the two finally emerged, they were surrounded by the waiting crowd. "Hello 'Red'! exclaimed McCullough as he recognized one of the interpreters of the police court. He greeted everyone he recognized with smiles and was permitted to shake hands." Cigarettes were offered "and he smoked heartily."

In the meantime, outside the detective office quite a crowd had gathered and were eagerly craning their necks in an effort to see McCullough. . . . At 11:30 he was hand-cuffed by Detective Cronin and, guarded by five, he walked downstairs again to the side entrance of the Hall. Here the new police car was waiting, driven by one of the motorcycle police. McCullough was placed within, together with Detectives Cronin, Koster, and Mulholland, and was taken direct to the jail.

Frank McCullough and Vera de Lavelle were now both imprisoned behind the same grey walls.

Chief Detective Guthrie spoke to reporters after McCullough was taken away. "He had all his stuff, such as overcoats, collars, etc., packed up, and he had a new bicycle, as if he intended to get out of the city. He had $18 in the house. He made no statement to me when brought here, except that when I said, 'Well, McCullough, I'm glad we didn't have to shoot you,' his reply was: 'Well, I wish you had.' He then said, 'You just got me a day too soon, that's all.' The old lady who kept the house at 78 Bathurst Street was very deaf, and is evidently an innocent old body."

Robinette was defiant when interviewed. Now that McCullough was in custody again, Robinette insisted the escape should have no bearing whatsoever on the application for clemency:

> We have not given up the fight. I shall go down to Ottawa. I shall go myself, and with me probably will be McCullough's pastor. McCullough's escape was a bad thing for him. The commutation of his sentence was being considered in Ottawa. Petitions on his behalf were pouring in. It looked as if a life term would be substituted for the death sentence. Then he broke away. But so far as I am concerned the situation is unchanged. The arguments that applied when we were seeking to save his life before his escape are still true. I shall go on fighting for him.[3]

The Reverend Bertram Nelles's statement to the press was curiously defensive:

> I have no apology to make for what I did in connection with McCullough. Some criticism, not all of it mild, has been passed upon me, but the church is for such cases. The church is not confined to the home. Since his escape I have not been in touch with anything concerning McCullough. . . . Regarding my relations with him, I do not know that I have any. . . . When he escaped my connection with him

ended. . . . If McCullough again requests spiritual advice, the appointment of a minister will rest with the sheriff.

Why was Nelles so insistent that there had been no connection since the escape?

Kate Currell, whose husband, Ernest, had yet to be tried, was pleased that McCullough had been recaptured, although she made it clear she did "not wish McCullough any harm." "He will tell the truth, and that will show that my husband is innocent. It is everybody for himself in this world, and I want everybody to know that my husband is innocent. . . . I wonder how Miss de Lavelle is taking this. I believe the girl is innocent. I saw her several times here, and if she is not innocent, all I can say is, she deceived me. But she was very much in love with McCullough."[4]

These interviews, with individuals already prominent in the McCullough story, were to be expected upon news of his recapture. But now an entirely new person had been drawn reluctantly into the case, and reporters were eager to speak to her. Mrs. C. Kinsella, an Irish woman of eighty years, was the "innocent old body" who owned and operated the boarding house at 78 Bathurst.

The other occupants of the house were Mrs. Kinsella's son, a man of forty, "who is an invalid from paralysis of the brain," and two female boarders, none of whom the police connected with McCullough. It was Mrs. Kinsella who first revealed details to reporters concerning the period of McCullough's hiding.

The newspapers were delighted at this ironic twist in the story. That McCullough had been hiding within sight of the crime scene while the police had searched for him across the province and up and down the border was almost too good to be true. Their subtle mockery became open derision of "officialdom" as the case unfolded. McCullough, a convicted murderer, was anointed a popular hero.

As for Mrs. Kinsella, her first intimation that she was to have a new boarder occurred when "a dark young woman" using the name

Mrs. Vera Knight called at 78 Bathurst four days after McCullough's escape. She asked for a room for herself and her husband.

"What does your husband do?"
"He drives a coal wagon."
"Who for?"
"Conger Lehigh coal firm."
The room was rented to the young woman and her husband, the latter arriving for the first time at 9:30 that evening. His face was covered with coal dust and he apologized for it when the landlady caught sight of him.
"Dirty business driving coal," he said.
"It certainly is," she said.

The next day, a Monday, "Vera Knight" told the landlady her husband was ill and couldn't go to work. McCullough remained secluded in his room while his "wife" cooked meals for him in the kitchen. On Tuesday, according to Mrs. Kinsella, "the young woman left." This was the day Bart Cronin arrested her on Queen Street. A despairing McCullough read about Vera's capture in the newspapers.

Her husband remained constantly in his room. When questioned as to the whereabouts of his wife he replied that she had gone to stay with a sister in Port Credit.
"I wouldn't have taken you if I had known that your wife was going to leave you," stated the landlady.
"Oh, she's only gone for a few days. She'll be coming back," he replied.
"Why don't you go with her?" he was asked.
"I don't get along with her sister very well," was his excuse.
"I thought McCullough was in the United States all the time," asserted Mrs. Kinsella to the Star today. "I never once suspected."

At first, Mrs. Kinsella reported that McCullough "stayed in the house every day." He spent his time "reading continuously."

He seemed particularly interested in the news of his escape and would read to the landlady every night all the news concerning McCullough, and the reports concerning his whereabouts. He would always tell the landlady when there was another post card received concerning him. One night while he was reading, Mrs. Kinsella exclaimed: "Poor man, I guess he's safe across in the States by now." "Perhaps he is," commented McCullough. . . . "One day when we were talking about McCullough, I said, 'I hope he wouldn't get caught.' He asked me then if I liked McCullough, and I said, 'I didn't know anything about him, but I hoped he got away.'"

Mrs. Kinsella then allowed to reporters that McCullough did leave the house on occasion, especially after he had managed to "buy" a bicycle. "When he came in with it last Friday night, he honked the horn and exhibited it to everyone in the house. He told her it cost $55, and one of the young ladies in the house was informed that he paid $43 for it." Since that day, she went on, "he has alternatively walked and ridden for his exercise." In fact, "during the day time McCullough used to make repeated visits to a grocery store two buildings to the south of the rooming house. . . . Three or four, or even five times a day, after the departure of his companion, he would go to the grocery store for ice cream cones and similar wants. . . . They say he was nearly starving when they took him to the police station. Well, let me tell you he was eating here all day long, day and night he walked into my pantry. He was eating nearly all the time. I never saw such a man in my life for eating. He used to buy 10 to 15 ice cream cones a day."[5]

After Vera's capture, McCullough spent a total of sixteen days at 78 Bathurst, trying the patience of Mrs. Kinsella (although there was evidently affection for him in the household). Without hope

of seeing Vera again, he resolved to flee the city once his prepara-
tions were complete. His most pressing need was money to get
away. It was, in fact, his need for money that explains much of
McCullough's movements while in hiding.

On the night he supposedly left a rain-soaked Vera in the dark
outside the Toronto Jail, McCullough went on to hide in the dilap-
idated British Welcome League building at the northwest corner
of Spadina and Front. The building had long been deserted, after
having been used as a stopover for British immigrants arriving
in Canada. "The place is practically boarded up and a flashlight is
necessary to locate even the fireplaces in the various large rooms."[6]

While working as a breadman along Spadina, McCullough had
used the British Welcome League building to conceal stolen property. There, in the flooded basement, he had hidden money in a
fireplace for future use. There, too, he had stashed the "China silk,"
stolen from a freight train in Port Credit. The silk alone had an
estimated value of $16,000.

One can imagine McCullough's anguish when he discovered
that both the money and the silk were missing. Who had betrayed
him? As a burglar, McCullough was a loner – except, that is, for his
mysterious accomplice Albert Johnson. Had Johnson, the man who
had bolted out the front door of Cross's Livery, leaving McCullough
struggling with Williams, gone on to steal McCullough's only
resources? This was the same man McCullough had refused to
describe to police ("I am no snitcher") in order to give him time
to get away.

McCullough's only hope was Vera, who either accompanied
him that night or agreed to meet him later at the Welcome League
building.[7] Although also a fugitive from the law, she was not
under sentence of death. Thus, while McCullough hid in the cav-
ernous building for three days, Vera went in search of money
and food.

It was during this ordeal that she approached her old neighbour on Spadina for money and was heard to declare in the restaurant on Queen Street that rather than be taken she would use a

drug "which would put her to sleep for 150 years." Even the forlorn Harry Berman received a visit. "He said she looked bedraggled and that her face was dirty. She had told him that the police were after her and that she had been sleeping in empty houses. She wanted some money to buy a drug, which he gave her."[8]

Though money was a problem, the greatest difficulty was Bart Cronin. McCullough actually saw the detective searching along Spadina one day when he peered out the basement window. His nemesis was getting close.

On the fourth day of hiding, McCullough left the building himself, "and in going out fixed a board across the doorway, as a trap, so that anyone entering the place would move the board." While McCullough was absent, "Detective Cronin made an investigation and happened to knock the board down. On his return, McCullough noticed that the board had been moved and was consequently afraid to enter the building again."[9] Later that morning, "Mrs. Vera Knight" made inquiries at 78 Bathurst.

So began McCullough's sojourn under Mrs. Kinsella's roof. Despite the company of the two female boarders, and Mrs. Kinsella's unfortunate son, McCullough grew restless. Vera was gone, he needed a way to make his escape from Toronto, and he needed money. He knew that at the jail, Vera was quietly praying for him to go. But he was not as careful as he should have been.

It was not long before McCullough's presence became an open secret in the neighbourhood. Not one of these neighbours, however, contacted the police to take advantage of the $1,000 reward. "Not a man in the neighbourhood cheeped a cheep, and there were many who knew there was a man upstairs in a small room at the back of #78. The women in the neighbourhood also knew that a man was hiding in the house. Not a word was said, and when the capture was made . . . the neighbours told The Telegram that it was too bad and that they felt sorry for McCullough."[10]

He was a favourite with the children. He "used to go down to the woodshed at the back and get the kids playing about to go and buy his papers." He "was generous. . . . He'd throw them a nickel and ask for two papers, and let them keep the cent. Every day he was out in the back. He didn't seem to be afraid of nobody."

There were repeated trips during the day to the store "kept by foreigners" where he bought ice cream. At night he would venture forth in disguise to ride his bicycle "for exercise" and in search of money. A house at 627 Crawford Street was broken into and jewellery, money, and articles of clothing were taken. A local telephone lineman reported his tools and uniform were missing.[11]

But in spite of these local burglaries and the widespread knowledge of McCullough's whereabouts, the neighbours at King and Bathurst remained silent. Here among them was a convicted murderer, a man who had killed a policeman in their own neighbourhood, and yet they were unwilling to turn him in for the $1,000 reward.

McCullough was liked. Indeed, after his recapture the women in the neighbourhood told the endearing story of how Mrs. Kinsella "started to scrub the floor one morning, when McCullough came down and, seeing her, said, 'Oh, Granny, you are too old for that work. Let me do it.' And he took the scrubbing brush, got down on his knees, and did the job."

There was laughter among the men over the unloved William Cross, owner of the livery around the corner on King, who seemed to be the only person in the neighbourhood not in on the secret. The fool worked below McCullough's window!

The livery stable and yard runs south, and reaches right to the back of the house where McCullough was in hiding. For two weeks William Cross, whose evidence secured the conviction of the murderer, worked in the stable and out in the yard, almost directly under the window of the man who had been doomed to death at the trial at which Cross was the main Crown witness. Had McCullough fostered any spirit of revenge against Cross he would have had ample opportunity for securing vengeance. At times Cross

worked alone, up till two o'clock in the morning, out in the
yard under McCullough's window.[12]

It was learned further by reporters that "McCullough frequently visited the Memorial Park on Portland Street [near
Bathurst and Front]. He there met several of his former companions and . . . they supplied him with food. He wore goggles when
he was making trips in the day time and walked like an old man."[13]

Who were these "companions"? Since Vera's arrest, and that
of Currell, it was evident that the so-called "organized gang of
thieves" who supposedly helped McCullough to escape never
existed. Suspicion was aroused among reporters when it was
learned that, one night during his hiding, McCullough visited
Alfred Amory's house at 344 Bathurst. As well as being a member
of McCullough's death watch, Amory was a member of the Church
for the Stranger.

Amory's wife, alone at the time, "heard a knock on the back
window and when she raised the blind a man, cap pulled down
over the eyes, glared at her from outside and asked, 'Is Mr. Amory
in?'" He was not. "Mrs. Amory thought the man bore a resem-
blance to McCullough," and without waiting to speak to her
husband contacted the Claremont Street police station. The
intruder was not found.[14]

The Amorys flatly refused to speak to reporters after
McCullough's recapture and "referred the reporters to the police."
The police acknowledged the visit and admitted that McCullough
had approached another home in Parkdale, and that the owner
"was also a member of the Church for the Stranger."

The *Star* added that two other members of the church living
in the west end had been visited by McCullough. Without saying
so directly, the implication was clear: members of the Church for
the Stranger had been assisting the escaped prisoner.[15]

This was why Nelles repeatedly emphasized after the escape
that there had been no connection between him and McCullough.

The reverend knew intuitively what he didn't want to know, which was that members of his own flock were supplying food and money to a convicted murderer in violation of the law.

When the secret was out, Nelles, "when asked by The Star as to McCullough's soliciting for money, refused to discuss the matter." When asked by the *Telegram* "in regard to himself and several members . . . having been canvassed personally by McCullough," he declared, "That statement is absolutely false!"[16] The church was rescued by Chief Detective George Guthrie, who, when approached by reporters concerning the matter, "declined to give the names of the people, taking the ground that it was of no interest to the public." Neither did Guthrie wish to press charges, since those charges could implicate a sizeable portion of the congregation.

McCullough's plan was to ride his bicycle out of Toronto disguised as a telephone lineman. He had the uniform, lineman's spurs, goggles, and a complete set of lineman's tools that he had stolen for this purpose. The elaborate route he had planned and drawn on a map progressed through small towns in Ontario and Quebec, eventually crossing the border into New York, where the final destination was marked as Schenectady.[17] Schenectady was fifty miles from Westville. Did the lost boy Leroy want to go home?

All that was holding him back was a lack of money.[18] Then one day McCullough looked out his side window, and spied Bart Cronin, knocking on doors along Bathurst Street. Over the next few days, McCullough saw Cronin in the neighbourhood at least five more times. On Thursday, May 7, he saw the detective enter a house down the street.[19] McCullough resolved to leave Toronto on the Saturday. But the very next day, Cronin received the information he needed to bring about McCullough's recapture: "You got me a day too soon, that's all."

McCullough remarked later to one of his guards that "Cronin was the gamiest man he had ever met and he had met many and all varieties. He was glad it was Cronin who arrested him and knew that if he were ever caught in Toronto he was positive Cronin would be the man to trap him."[20]

## XV

# Mr. Unknown

While I appreciate that no decent citizen would harbor or try to shield a murderer intentionally from the law, few people would accept money for turning a criminal over to the police.

— William Cross, May 19, 1919

His return to the death cell triggered a depression in Frank McCullough.

Sgt. R. F. Eyre, the hardened soldier who replaced Currell on the death watch, reported that McCullough was "no longer the bright, clear eyed youth who took his recapture with a smile." He was "despondent," unable to eat, "looks downcast and even ill," and "only arouses out of his stupor . . . for short intervals." In the succinct words of the *Evening Telegram*, he "is now a nervous wreck." McCullough "did not say who, the guard explained, but expressed the opinion that someone had informed the police about his whereabouts."[1]

McCullough was right. Someone had betrayed him for the reward. The search for the informant's identity became the next preoccupation of reporters, with the cruellest speculation of all being that it was Vera herself who had turned him in. One reporter apparently surmised it was possibly Vera's betrayal, more than his recapture, that was causing McCullough's despair. What is significant about this conjecture – the source of which remains unknown – is the overwhelming public disavowal it provoked. There was an absolute and vehement rejection of the thought that Vera would do such a thing.

Even "the detective force paid a high tribute to the sterling qualities evinced by Vera de Lavelle, who . . . had proved beyond doubt that she could stand nobly by a friend through thick and thin and would also sacrifice anything to such an end." "That such a woman as this would willingly . . . return her lover to the hangman's hands, is almost beyond belief."[2] The story of Frank and Vera had become a popular romance, and it was essential to keep it so.

The effect that this suspicion had on Vera can only be imagined. But the poignancy of the lovers' predicament was not lost on those involved with the case, nor on the public at large. Here they were, imprisoned behind the same stone walls, only yards apart, yet unable to communicate with each other.[3] The guards were under strict orders that any breaches of the regulations, in particular the carrying of letters, would result in immediate dismissal and criminal charges. Frank and Vera might as well have been at opposite ends of the world.

There was only one thing to do, and Vera did it. Just before her second appearance in court, she wrote a letter and gave it to W. B. Horkins, her artful lawyer, who released it directly to the press.

Dearest Frank:

A few lines, dearest one. I know that you are not the same man as you used to be, but I love you just the same as I ever did. If you should ever get a life sentence, dear one, take it and I will always be true to you.

How I have suffered. I was told that you were told that it was me who gave you away dearest. I swear before God that I never said one word to anyone that would put you in such trouble.

I am going up for trial on Thursday, but I do not know how things will turn out. I will always come and see you if you do get life sentence, and darling, please, oh, please, do not distrust like that. It is just like you said, like coals of fire on one's head. I am so worried myself, dearest, that I do not know what to do with myself. But try and be cheerful. Oh, darling, what would I give if only I could hear you say with your own lips that you don't distrust me. And dearest, believe me when I say that I will come and live near you wherever they send you. Excuse this paper, dear, I could not get any more. And dearest, send some message if you still believe in me. Please trust me, Frank. I wish you every luck and God bless you, but I will always look to you, that is, if you will let me.

> I am yours with x x x x x x x
> Vera

McCullough's answer found its way to Vera by the same route she had taken: "If Vera came to me on her knees and said she betrayed me I would not believe her." According to the *Telegram*, it was "a romance which the shadow of the gallows intensifies."[4]

But if Vera hadn't betrayed him, who had? What "squealer" had informed the police of McCullough's hiding place? Whose bank account now contained the "blood money," the "thirty pieces of silver"? In their race to identify the informer, the newspapers openly used these terms of derision. According to the *Globe*, "Nine tenths of the people one speaks to express contempt for whoever it was that sent McCullough to the gallows for one thousand dollars."[5]

At first it was not clear whether the authorities would release the name. "Will you tell the name of the person that gave the

information about McCullough's hiding place?" inquired a
reporter for the *Star*, speaking to Chief Detective George Guthrie.

"Not at present."
"Will the person's name ever be divulged?" "Some time."
"When?" "I won't say."
"Do you know who it was?" "I refuse to answer that
question. I don't wish to be impolite, but don't ask me that."
"But you will tell?" "Yes – some time, I suppose."
"Has anybody claimed the McCullough award?" asked
the Star at the Provincial Secretary's Office. "No, not yet,"
was the reply.[6]

There were several candidates. One was the sorrowful Harry
Berman, who had been forsaken by Vera for McCullough: "I
didn't know the man, and had nothing to do with it." Another
was Irene Marks, a known police "stool-pigeon," desperate for
money, who had testified against Vera at her trial. Marks was
rescued by the police, who simply stated she had no involvement.
Perhaps it was a member of the Church for the Stranger (Nelles:
"I don't know anything about it"). Mrs. Kinsella, the landlady at
78 Bathurst, was "nettled" by unkind speculation that it was her
silent son, the "invalid suffering from paralysis of the brain." Then
"the Globe received a name on what appeared to be pretty reliable authority, and submitted it to Inspector Guthrie. 'It's wrong,'
he said, 'Guess again.'"

Everyone's favourite candidate was the odious William Cross,
owner of the livery, who received letters and telephone calls and
was frequently stopped on the street "to be sarcastically congratulated on winning the $1,000 'blood money.'"

Cross "declared emphatically" that he was not the man. He was
even willing to sign one of the petitions to commute McCullough's
sentence. He said, "While I appreciate that no decent citizen would
harbor or try to shield a murderer intentionally from the law, few
people would accept money for turning a criminal over to the

police." To avoid further harassment, Cross said he "was going to urge Inspector of Detectives Guthrie to publish the name of the man who laid the information."

But by this point it was dawning on the authorities that releasing the name could have serious consequences. In future police investigations, would a potential informant be willing to cooperate if claiming the reward meant notoriety? And wouldn't the authorities somehow be liable if McCullough's "squealer" was harmed or his property damaged?

Mr. Hartley Dewart, K.C., MPP, leader of the Opposition, was pressed to raise the matter of the informer's identity in the provincial legislature.[7] Dewart wisely declined to do so and "was not very hopeful that a question in the House would bring from the Attorney General the name of the person who received the $1,000." The attorney general himself, the Honourable I. B. Lucas, expressed the view that the "name may never be given out if the claimant objects and has a satisfactory reason for desiring that there be no publicity."

Thus the newspapers were left to their own devices. The *Evening Telegram* was the first to claim reliable details concerning "Mr. Unknown." He (not she) was "not a resident of the Bathurst street neighbourhood." "He is a married man with a family, and is described as a respectable citizen, not connected with the police department . . . nor is he, nor was he, employed by the Government in any capacity." It was reported that McCullough thought he knew the man's identity. "He does not, however, hold any animosity against him, strangely, as he says he should forgive him as he would ask to be forgiven."[8]

"Forgiven"? Here was the pious McCullough emerging once again. Now recaptured, he needed the help of Nelles's onward Christian soldiers more than ever. McCullough let it be known he had "not lost my faith by one bit." He was continuing to read The Good Book "as usual," and wished above all for Nelles to return.

But Nelles had been badly burned by McCullough. He had rallied his congregation around the man's conversion, and had sought publicity for his church by supporting McCullough's cause, only to be slapped in the face. McCullough's escape strongly suggested he had been dissembling all along. Moreover, it now seemed that while some church members had been found supplying him with food while he was in jail, an even larger number had known of McCullough's hiding place after the escape and had protected him against the law. Poor Reverend Nelles! He had done his best for his church and for McCullough, and was betrayed by both.

Nelles had to tread very cautiously. "If McCullough asks for your spiritual advice again, will you accept?" asked a *Star* reporter of the minister. "There are a number of considerations connected with the work and until I have fully taken the matter under my consideration I should not care to say."

This language suggests that Nelles was deliberating, most likely with his church elders. If the Church was "for such cases" and was "not confined to the home," as Nelles had pronounced earlier, could it now abandon McCullough for fear of criticism? Wasn't their "brother" all the more in need of the pastor's presence now that his neck was back in the noose? And yet Nelles couldn't proceed without the full consent of his elders; to do otherwise would risk disunion if the McCullough venture were to go badly again.

McCullough, as usual, knew the right buttons to push. He wrote a pleading letter to Nelles, again released to the newspapers:

I tried to make it [the escape] no worse than I could help and I did not forget your teaching, Mr. Nelles, although I certainly committed a burglary [lineman's tools?]. It was, however, only a last extremity for I certainly did my utmost to obtain money and clothes honestly and took some desperate chances in order to do so, but I made up my mind if I could not make my mistake without violence, that I would not go. . . . My escape was a gamble and I took the chance as I guess almost anyone would under the circumstances. That will not make one bit of difference as far as my soul is concerned, because I still believe and am happy in that belief regardless of everything.

Nelles was reportedly "overwhelmed" with letters beseeching him to take up McCullough's cause again, including one "from the mother of a soldier killed overseas, asking that his efforts on McCullough's behalf be continued." In the face of such public pressure, the elders relented, and on May 15 the pastor made a much publicized return to the jail. "Frank McCullough was almost overcome with emotion when Rev. Nelles visited him in the death cell.... McCullough was most profuse in his regrets for the trouble occasioned friends by his escape. The visit cheered the condemned man considerably." According to Nelles, McCullough was now "in fine spirits" and eating well. "He expressed a desire that Mr. Nelles inform those people who had confidence in his reformation that he was trying to do his best." Nelles had returned and so too, it seemed, had the prodigal son.

A renewed petitioning campaign got underway at once. "The young women of several churches are circulating petitions in the places where they are employed." Individuals not associated with church-organized efforts arrived at Robinette's offices with signed petitions. "The heads of several large firms had phoned him [Robinette].... A cartage agent brought a petition very heavily signed, stating that he had taken a day off and had worked from morning until after midnight to secure the names."

These reports were not without embellishment. "Rev. Nelles cites another case of interest. An aged woman, past seventy, a semi-invalid, on crutches, visited a large factory in the west end and secured practically every available signature in the building to a petition for clemency."[9]

Although the testimony against Vera had been persuasive at her trial, there remained a final compelling means by which to determine her guilt. Before delivering his judgement, Judge Emerson Coatsworth ordered that Mrs. Kinsella and her boarders be asked to formally identify Vera as the woman who had secured McCullough's Bathurst Street room.

Accordingly, on the morning of May 11, Bart Cronin and a fellow detective arrived by appointment at 78 Bathurst to deliver Mrs. Kinsella and her two boarders, young Jeanne Brodie and Murrell Kelly, to the jail. "Mrs. Kinsella, an Irishwoman who had never ridden in a motor car in her life, refused to enter the vehicle, but on the persuasion of Detective Young finally agreed."

At the jail, "the police picked out three other female prisoners and, placing them in the warden's office, had Vera placed in the centre of them." In 1919, there were no screens or one-way mirrors at line-ups. "Mrs. Kinsella was called into the room and positively identified Vera as the woman to whom she had rented the room." She went over and touched Vera on the arm without speaking. Brodie and Kelly were then called in, and both "were firm in their opinion that the Lavelle woman was the only one who had engaged the room." Vera apparently "wilted under the identification" and there were tears. Afterwards, "begging leave to speak to Mrs. Kinsella, Lavelle said to the old lady: 'I'm sorry for what I have done and if I have caused you any inconvenience.'" Vera was taken away.

While waiting for her ride outside the jail, Mrs. Kinsella received $9.50 from Cronin for the rent McCullough owed her. "Where is the car that was to take us home?" asked one of the young women with her. "Oh, it's coming, like that young man's moustache," Mrs. Kinsella replied, nodding at a youthful policeman. "Do you know," she continued, "this is the worst picnic I was ever in. But say, I feel more sorry for that young man than I do for myself." One of the young women said, "I'll bet all I have got that he won't hang. He really was a polite young fellow and seemed quite nice."

The next morning, several reporters arrived at 78 Bathurst to question Mrs. Kinsella further about her identification of Vera.

She refused to speak to them. The morning papers had arrived, and Mrs. Kinsella, unused to notoriety and disturbed by what she had read, remained secluded in the house. When reporters refused to leave until they spoke to her, she suddenly emerged with an air of defiance:

> You can just write down what Mrs. Kinsella thinks about McCullough – write it down as I tell you now – them reporters writing about me going down to the jail – I'd like to scald them. I never was in jail before in me life. It's a nice clean place what I seen of it. Well, they brings out the girl who came here with McCullough, and, I knew her as soon as I laid my eyes on her, and I goes over and touches her on the arm. You can't help but feel sorry for the girl – the trouble she's in. Vera was very pleasant to me when she'd come downstairs to cook a bit of meat for McCullough, but after she left I fed him.[10]

And as for McCullough:

> Now this is what I think about him – take it down – I think he has softening of the brain and hungry diabetes. Why, that man would sit at the table and eat enough for three men, and then he would come in to the pantry at night and eat everything in sight, and all I got out of him was three dollars for the first week. Then he went out and bought himself cakes and ice cream as well. I don't know who told on him no more than the man in the moon, but it weren't nobody in this house, I know that.

It was the *Toronto World* that broke the full story on "Mr. Unknown." The article opened with the observation that the informer had displayed "a knowledge of the ways of police and newspaper reporters quite unusual in an ordinary citizen."

The man sent a letter to the police identifying McCullough's location "written on a peculiar and little used class of paper, in a tint of ink seldom seen, and written with a pen not in fashion today." The letter was unsigned, and in it the informant declared that an exact copy in the same unusual materials would be presented to the police by a solicitor acting on his behalf.

The solicitor, Mr. R. F. Webb, had been approached by a "quiet man" whom he did not know, who was "methodically determined to avoid publicity for himself and his family." The two registered an agreement whereby Webb was given full authority to receive the reward money on the man's behalf.

According to the *Toronto World*,

> There is extreme cleverness in this scheme, as when the cheque is drawn for the reward it will be issued in Mr. Webb's name and he will draw the money from the bank in his own personality and hand it over to the informer in cash. That closes the channels of the government's treasury office, the audit office and the bank from obtaining any knowledge of the man's identity.

This is precisely how the transaction was completed. Chief Detective Guthrie and Webb proceeded to the attorney general's office and made formal application for the reward, "the detective stating he was satisfied as to the identity of the informer." The cheque was issued to Webb, and the Honourable I. B. Lucas, attorney general, issued a statement saying the name of the informer would not be released. In the words of the *Star*, the name would "remain forever shrouded in mystery."

"Yes, surely, the informer is a clever man, but it is a pity he is not known, for to study this mentality would be interesting.... As to whether he is an employer or employee Mr. Webb was dumb, but one is almost inclined to the belief that he comes under the former heading."[11]

A subdued Vera de Lavelle appeared in court for judgement on May 15.[12] "Curiosity as to the fate that awaited the girl . . . was responsible for another large crowd which included many women." Vera "betrayed little or no interest in the buzz and close attention which followed her."

Judge Coatsworth was brief: "There are so many condemnatory facts – her connection with McCullough, her interview with Currell, the guard, for some purpose on the night when the escape was made, her going into hiding immediately afterwards, and her efforts to keep away from the police . . . showing clearly her connection with this escape, and I therefore find her guilty as charged."

The judge postponed sentencing until the end of the session. The maximum penalty was seven years. Vera "received the decision with the same apparent indifference that has marked all her appearances in court." Her "face was firmly set, but as she looked up at the Clerk of the court, she smiled."[13]

If one is to believe the newspapers, the majority view by this point was that McCullough shouldn't hang. "The fact that he did not resist capture and that the original shooting was in the heat of passion are said to be large factors in the public's sympathy." But the decision over McCullough's fate was not the public's to make. The responsibility fell to the acting minister of justice in Ottawa, the Honourable Arthur Meighen. At this time, the forty-five-year-old Meighen was caught up in a whirlwind of postwar government activity that by the end of May was dominated by the Winnipeg General Strike.

On the same day that Vera appeared in court – May 15 – nego-
tiations with management in the building and metal trades in
Winnipeg broke down and a general strike was called. Thirty
thousand workers laid down their tools and, along with striking
public-sector employees, brought the city of Winnipeg to a halt.
The government was faced with a massive display of labour defiance that had the potential to spread to other cities also suffering
from unemployment and inflation. Speculation ran rampant:
were these the opening salvoes in Canada of the working-class
revolution that was consuming Russia and threatening Europe?

Much of the burden of dealing with this explosive situation
fell to Meighen, who was minister of the interior as well as acting
minister of justice.[14] Meighen's career was still in a swiftly rising
trajectory. Elected to represent Portage la Prairie in 1908, his striking ability as a debater soon brought him into prominence. He
was made solicitor general in 1913, member of the Privy Council
in 1915, and successively secretary of state and minister of the interior in 1917. Within the cabinet, he quickly earned a reputation for
"blood and iron." Within a year of his involvement in our story,
he replaced Sir Robert Borden as prime minister.[15]

As chance would have it, McCullough couldn't have been given
a more heartless politician to decide his fate. Meighen was arrogant, rigid, humourless, and legalistic. He was also a man driven
to achieve political dominance. He was "clever, destructive in
debate, crushing in criticism, but there it ends. No one possessed
of such qualities can command heart loyalty."[16]

Conservative by nature, as well as by political vocation, Meighen
had no sympathy for lawbreakers, or for disloyal Winnipeg strikers
organized by "alien scum." He held firmly to the conviction that
in an unhappily changing world, law and order – especially the
law and order of big business – must be obeyed or civilization
would be consumed by anarchy. The timing of the decision to be
made over McCullough coincided exactly with the chaos in
Winnipeg. What would this minister of justice, this defender of
law and order, decide in the matter of a condemned murderer

who had killed a policeman and subsequently escaped from jail? But Meighen had not yet made his decision. In fact, a short statement released by his office in early May (probably written by J. D. Clarke) was so noncommittal as to invite further organized activity on McCullough's behalf. It stated blankly "that unless clemency be exercised, McCullough will be executed on June 13, the date fixed by the court at Toronto." At the same time, by internal memorandum, Meighen directed that further consideration be given to the case on June 1, and that "no action as to appeal for clemency to be taken meantime."[17]

Perhaps it was astute to reserve a small example of mercy on one hand, if federal troops were ordered into Winnipeg on the other. Perhaps from the perspective of Ottawa, McCullough was only a pawn in a larger political game.

Responding to the innocuous statement from Meighen's office, T. C. Robinette confirmed that "a deputation of prominent citizens" was being appointed to visit the minister in Ottawa. "It is nothing short of amazing the amount of sympathy that is being shown. Even at my home, businessmen from all over the city are phoning me regarding McCullough. We have received hundreds of postcards from people even outside the city." "Last night in the downtown district," added the *Star*, "petitions were being handled on the streets, particularly on Queen Street, east of Yonge Street, three being signed as rapidly as the crowd could get to them."

Two trips were made to Ottawa, the first by Reverend Nelles alone. He was followed shortly afterwards by Arthur Hill, the foreman of the jury, accompanied by "a party of businessmen." There was considerable fanfare at Union Station when Nelles departed on May 18. It was announced that an unidentified "labourer" had requested that "he and some friends of his be allowed to defray the expenses of Rev. Bertram Nelles's trip to the Capital."

The trip proved to be a disappointment. As fate would have it, Nelles's train pulled into Ottawa just as Meighen's train was leaving for Winnipeg.[18] The two ministers could have waved to each other. Nelles was left standing on the platform as the train

of Canadian history passed him by. He was also left in the hands of
the imperturbable J. D. Clarke, who spoke to reporters after their
meeting:

> "Mr. Nelles told me just the things you would expect a
> spiritual adviser to say."
> "What will happen now?"
> "I will pass them [petitions and letters] on to the Acting
> Minister of Justice."
> "But he is out in Winnipeg."
> "Well, when he returns. There is plenty of time. If Mr.
> Meighen is kept out there any length of time, another
> Minister will be appointed to act in his place, and I shall
> lay Mr. Nelles' representations before him."

On his return to Toronto, Nelles was met at Union Station by
a party of McCullough supporters carrying a single petition
"bearing over 2,000 signatures organized by three young women."
Nelles declared his mission to Ottawa accomplished, in the sense
that "there is nothing more to be done at present. The plea will
probably come before the [privy] council when the Acting
Minister returns from Winnipeg."

As for the city of Ottawa itself, Nelles reported that the churches
were similarly organized on McCullough's behalf. "The public are
evincing the greatest interest here, but in Ottawa the church forces
are doing remarkable work. Last Sunday Rev. Dr. Aitkens, former
pastor of the Metropolitan Church, offered special prayers for
McCullough, and two prayer meetings are being held in Ottawa
this week. Last week a similar service was held."

Nelles praised the three Toronto women for their work on
McCullough's behalf, and announced that the previous evening a
single petition "bearing 4,000 names" had been delivered to
Robinette's law offices. "This included signatures of practically
all the patients in one of the hospitals." The *Evening Telegram*
reported that the same day, a Saturday,

. . . proved a good day for petitions. Young women from various churches were on the ferry boats and at the ball game [Toronto versus Jersey City] where over a thousand signatures were collected. Both ball teams signed to a man. Several members of the Toronto Police Force have also added their names.

Arthur Hill and a party of "businessmen from the Riverdale district" travelled to Ottawa on May 22 "at their own expense," and were reported by the *Telegram* to have had "an hour and a half conference with the Acting Minister of Justice and with Parole Officer Archibald." It appears, however, that, like Nelles, they saw only Clarke, who recorded the interview in a memorandum to Meighen: "The jury were, Hill points out, absent from the Court room for several hours discussing the verdict they should bring in. They would, he says, have brought in a verdict of manslaughter, but for the declaration of the trial judge."[19]

By the end of the month, there was little more to do than wait for Meighen's return. During this interval, feverish activity continued with "many women patrolling the streets presenting lists of names to passersby." Meighen's impending decision "turned into a gambling event in some quarters in the down-town section. Many business men are offering and betting three to one that McCullough will not pay the penalty on the gallows. Much money is being wagered. . . ."[20]

But there was one more sensational event still to come before the end of May. On May 29, reporters were suddenly called to the jail. "Jail officials . . . sheepish, and not in a communicative mood" nevertheless had an announcement to make. They left "it to reporters to 'tell it first' to Sheriff Mowat and Inspector Dunlop, who lost no time in visiting the jail."[21] The announcement was a simple one: Vera de Lavelle had escaped.

# XVI

# Vera the Elusive

The whole trouble with Vera de Lavelle has been that the authorities have failed to appreciate . . . the undercurrent of cunning which possesses the woman. . . . To see this frail, good-looking woman with an almost innocent face, without ostentation and quiet mannered, standing in the dock, a non-student of human nature would put her down as just an ordinary woman. But behind her mask was a burning, clever, constructive brain, more subtle in its organization and more deceptive in its planning than any of the police officers gave her credit for. But they know now.

– *Toronto World*, May 30, 1919

Vera's escape from the Toronto Jail was "so simple" it left the authorities "dazed when they think of how coolly it was accomplished."

Because she was awaiting final sentencing, Vera was not required to work like other inmates. Nevertheless, she offered to help out in the laundry, which was housed in a wooden extension to the main jail building. Here, nine female prisoners were put to work. The clothes were hung to dry outside in a laundry yard enclosed by the prison wall.

Vera "worked well, willingly and happily." She was a favourite of the laundry matron, who considered her "a harmless and much-wronged woman." The other women enjoyed her company, and it was here, in the laundry, that she befriended a skittish, seventeen-year-old Ruby Masten, who was doing time for vagrancy and a "charge of incest."

On the morning of May 29, Vera and Ruby Masten were sent outside to hang sheets on the lines to dry. With the permission of the matron, they took with them a four-foot stepladder that was used for various purposes inside the laundry. But somehow during the lunch break, a painter's ladder, which was supposed to have been locked up, was concealed under piles of laundry in the yard. This ladder was ten feet tall.

After lunch, the two women were assigned to continue hanging laundry. At 1:30 p.m., masked by the sheets hanging on the lines, Vera and Ruby simply secured the long painter's ladder to the top of the four-foot stepladder, "playfully" climbed the eighteen-foot prison wall, and "lowering themselves to the full extent of their arms, dropped to the ground."

Once over the wall, they faced a six-foot board fence, and while climbing it Ruby twisted her ankle. "It was a minute or two before they could proceed. While Masten rested on the ground, Vera Lavelle stayed with her, although every second was precious. . . . When her companion was able to proceed, Vera aided her to reach the shelter of the trees on the east side of the Park, where they parted."

By 2:00 p.m., as the pile of washed sheets grew visibly larger, the matron "thought it might be just as well to see if Vera and her helper were getting on with their work or chatting over social events." Her dismay at finding the ladders propped up against the wall and the yard empty "may be better imagined than described in print."

The alarm was sounded immediately. Guards from the jail searched the surrounding streets. The police, including a squad of plainclothesmen, were sent to scour the east end of the city. Later

in the afternoon, a carefree Ruby Masten was found sauntering
down Yonge Street and was arrested. There was no sign of Vera. In
fact, she spent her first hour of freedom close to the jail, praying
in a church.

By the end of the day the police were still confident that Vera
would be captured "in a few hours." But the newspapers were
equally confident that "one of the shrewdest, coolest and cleverest
schemers" Toronto had ever seen, one who had "matched wits with
the police and beat them at their own game in broad daylight,"
would never be caught.

> Lavelle is known to have many good and true friends in the
> city, and she will undoubtedly seek aid both in money and
> millinery. . . . If one can judge from overheard conversa-
> tions on street cars, in the streets, and even in the homes of
> the most law-abiding, there are few men and women in
> Toronto today who would not, if they met Vera de Lavelle
> by accident, slip her a five- or ten-dollar bill and wish her
> godspeed in her getaway.

Reporters interrupted a meeting at City Hall to inform Sheriff
Mowat. His job still in jeopardy over the McCullough escape,
the sheriff "raced straight to the jail in his motor." The provincial inspector of prisons, W. W. Dunlop, was contacted by a *Star*
reporter and exploded:

> If I have my way, the person who is responsible for this
> escape will not have a job. I'll have this "Picnicish" Jail
> cleared up. It's the smallest jail in the Province, the smallest
> part of my work, yet it causes me more work than the whole
> of the rest of it. I could handle the King's business better
> than the Toronto Jail.

Said Mayor Tommy Church: "It's not a jail at all – it's simply a
stop-over place." He was "strongly of the impression that an

immediate investigation into the management of the jail should be made. The city is a big contributor to the maintenance of the jail and should find out as quickly as possible what is wrong with its administration." Mowat and Addy were in hot water again.[1]

Ruby Masten, wearing "black silk hose and black patent leather oxfords," appeared in women's court the next morning, where Crown attorney Corley asked the presiding judge for a remand. "You won't leave the jail, will you?" asked Corley, turning to Masten and her lawyer. "No I won't," she replied with a broad smile. "All right, if you will promise to do that, because it's so easy to get away." To her lawyer, Corley said "with a smile, 'This remand is strictly on the understanding that your client won't leave the jail,' amid a ripple of laughter in the court, which caused Inspector Gregory to demand order." A giggling Ruby Masten was taken away.[2]

At City Hall, the board of control moved a second resolution that the government conduct a "public investigation" into the management of the jail. "I'm surprised that these departing prisoners aren't presented with an illuminated address," the mayor remarked. He observed that the jail was under the control of the government and was not the city's responsibility. "Yes, but we have to pay the guards and officials," Controller Joseph McBride added. "Joking aside, there should be an investigation open to the public."

> Controller Cameron: "The poor guards are so overworked that they are utterly fagged out."
> Controller Robbins: "We have no power to make any alterations at the jail."
> Controller McBride: "We can make a request for a public inquiry."
> Controller Maquire: "The Government will never agree to a probe that will reflect on themselves."
> Mayor Church: "It's well they haven't the Kaiser down there."
> Controller McBride: "They wouldn't keep him very long."
> Mayor Church: "The Sheriff's got to take the men the Government sends him. They're political appointments."

The resolution passed, but with little effect, in part because the government had already conducted its inquiry. W. W. Dunlop's report, never released, had pointed directly to the incompetence of Sheriff Mowat, but Mowat still held his job. Somebody had to pay, and so the finger went down the line to those closest to the trouble. The laundry matron as well as Tanny Soady, head matron and notorious cook, were fired.

The next day, a cartoon featuring Controller McBride and Mayor Church appeared in the *Toronto World*. Entitled "A Different Law for Women," it protested the fact that two women had been sacked while Sheriff Mowat and Chief Turnkey Addy still held their jobs.

> Josophist [Joe McBride]: "The two matrons, out of defer-
> ence to an incensed public opinion, have resigned."
> The People's Church [Mayor Church]: "What about the two
> men appointed higher up [Mowat and Addy]?"
> Josophist: "The rule of fifty-fifty covers all such indiscre-
> tions."[3]

The editor of the *Toronto World* contended that the two escapes, first Frank's and then Vera's, were "part of the plan to empty the jail and have it closed up entirely."

> We were told, it will be recalled, that when Rev. Chambers
> was retired long ago, the jail would be closed immediately.
> The management is doing its best to bring about the
> desired consummation. . . . It is understood there are still a
> few more prisoners who have not yet vacated their apart-
> ments. Alarmist reports should not be heeded. The jail will
> undoubtedly be closed some day.[4]

For T. C. Robinette, still awaiting word from Ottawa, Vera's departure was a mixed blessing. McCullough was scheduled to hang in two weeks, on Friday, June 13. While Vera's escape would technically "have no bearing on the case of McCullough, if the jail can hold him," still, it just didn't look good at all. "She was foolish to escape at this stage," observed a police official. "It suggests that both she and McCullough are a bad lot. . . . It will, if anything, be a factor against his sentence."

On the other hand, Vera's "spectacular escape" certainly maintained public interest, which was all-important in the matter of pressing Ottawa into leniency. And it suggested that Vera had some sort of plan. Perhaps she knew something others didn't that would save McCullough in the end.

After a Saturday visit to the jail, Robinette announced that "McCullough was glad when he was told that his sweetheart . . . had escaped." "Frank" wanted to hear details, "and when told that she was still at liberty expressed the opinion that she had fled in effort to help him."[5]

For the hapless Ernest Currell, Vera's escape meant she couldn't testify at his trial on June 5. Currell was charged before Judge Emerson Coatsworth on two counts: aiding and abetting and also "permitting the prisoner [McCullough] to escape." He appeared in court "quite composed, neatly attired, and wearing two military buttons." The ancient hand wound allowed Currell's lawyer to characterize his client as being "invalided home after receiving wounds in action."

Henry Addy was present to defend himself and blame Mowat: "I gave instructions that nothing was to be carried in, and guards were not to sleep." He claimed that because Currell was a new man, he "was given more careful instructions," especially since "the night watch would be the most trying."

> Greer: "How is it that Currell, the newest guard, was given the hardest work?"
> Addy: "The Sheriff fixes that. Those men are employed by the Sheriff and my own guards are not to go in."

For his part, Currell complained that Addy had not cautioned him sufficiently: "The only instructions he gave me was not to take any penknives." He was told nothing about parcels and letters. But Currell did admit to sleeping on the job: first on the table in the cell, once in a chair, and finally on at least two occasions "on the edge of the bed in which McCullough was sleeping."

Greer: "You were told by Mr. Addy that McCullough was a shrewd and dangerous man?"
Currell: "No sir, he didn't say dangerous, but shrewd."
Greer: "By this time your sympathy had been aroused?"
Currell: "Yes sir, so far as the love affair between McCullough and Miss Lavelle was concerned."
Greer: "Did you not have any instructions not to go to sleep?"
Currell: "No, I did not. Mr. Addy only told me to cheer him up and prevent him from committing suicide."

Admitting that he had slept on the job appeared to clinch the matter. Judge Coatsworth concluded in his charge to the jury: "This man did act contrary to his duty." He brought in parcels and letters, and "he went to sleep several times when he was at the post of duty, the very things that a soldier is shot for – and he was a soldier himself – yet he went to sleep several times." If Currell presented himself as a soldier, could he complain at being treated as one?

The jury was out for more than two hours, "and from the sounds issuing from the jury-room, it was evident that they had a hard time reaching a decision." Currell "remained composed during their absence . . . but on their return it could be plainly seen that the prisoner was anxious."

They found the former wounded soldier guilty of aiding and abetting, but innocent on the charge of permitting McCullough to escape. "The jury made a strong recommendation for mercy, which Judge Coatsworth, in reserving sentence until Wednesday, said would be duly considered." Currell's lawyer, retained by the GWVA, "intimated that an appeal would be taken to a higher court."[6]

By the end of the first week in June, Vera's first week at liberty, there was still no word from Ottawa, even though Arthur Meighen had returned from the unrest in Winnipeg. Did the delay mean that Ottawa was seriously considering commuting the sentence?

> This is the question being raised in police and domestic circles all over the country. The date of the execution has been set for June 13, exactly six days from today, and no authentic word has been received. The petitions circulated by [McCullough's] counsel are all in the hands of the Hon. Acting Minister, Arthur Meighen.

McCullough, "entombed in the death cell in the grim Don Bastille," was reported to be "calmly awaiting" final word. Nelles was "confident in the mercy" of the authorities and was visiting McCullough "every few days, but not with the same regularity as before the escape," while Robinette believed "the prospects are bright. Today he is making telegraphic appeal to Hon. Arthur Meighen."

It was important, at this crucial point, for any information from the jail concerning McCullough's state of mind to be carefully managed. In this, Addy was helpful, reporting that McCullough had "dropped all pretence of gayety" and was in an "introspective mood." Nelles rushed into print to dispel the impression that his less-frequent visits to the jail reflected waning interest. "Engagements outside Toronto have made daily calls during the past week an impossibility."

> McCullough deserves just punishment by imprisonment. Personally I have done my best, and if the Church of God

has no message to give to the 'least of these, His brethren' –
and McCullough is included – it seems to me the Church
has lost its vision after the Christ fashion. . . . McCullough
wishes to express through me his gratitude to those who
have had an interest in his spiritual welfare. . . . Personally I
would rather be in Frank McCullough's shoes today than
in those of some others who cry with the mob of old, "an
eye for an eye." . . . "He that is without sin let him cast the
first stone."[7]

All of this sounded rational and was pitched perfectly towards
Ottawa. But Robinette's impatience got the better of him. Fearing the worst, he announced after a weekend visit to the jail that
"he was firmly of the opinion that McCullough was mentally
deranged," and that on the following Monday a team of three
doctors would report on the sanity of the prisoner. "The terrible strain of the past few months and the nervous exhaustion
brought on by the escape and its attendant consequences has
preyed on McCullough's mind and he is bordering on imbecility,"
said Robinette. "He talks incessantly and there is no continuity
of thought."

Not only did Robinette fail to consult with Reverend Nelles in
this hasty strategy – here was the minister declaring "spiritual
conversion" and the lawyer "imbecility" – but the venerable
doctors themselves didn't seem to know much about their
reported assignment.

On Monday afternoon, reporters following up on Robinette's
announcement sought news of the psychiatric examination.
"From inquiries made last night it seems very doubtful if any of
the selected medicals saw the condemned man yesterday. Dr. C. K.
Clarke,[8] 34 Roxborough East, who is to head the investigation,
refused to do so unless instructed by the attorney-general; Dr. A. J.
Johnson[9] of Bloor Street knew nothing about the matter, and the
third doctor mentioned, Dr. Claire, could not be found." Robinette
was unavailable for comment.[10]

What were Vera's thoughts? And where was she? Various sightings had been made. A merchant reported that she had bought a hat on Yonge Street "and passed two plainclothes officers without being detected." She was seen on a King West streetcar, in another church, "at a ball game at the Island Stadium in company with another woman," and "entering Scarboro Beach." It was believed she was still in the city, although she had "submerged herself as completely as a submarine boat. It remains to be seen if the authorities possess a deep sea bomb of sufficient strength to bring her to the surface."[11]

Eventually, however, she surfaced on her own, by means of a letter to Frank released to the press by her lawyer, W. B. Horkins. Except for her belaboured claim to be outside Toronto, it sounded pitifully genuine.

Dear Frank,

This is just a line, dear, which I hope is not the last, to let you ever know that my thoughts are all on you. . . . I pray to God almost all my time, and since my escape my life is hardly worth living. I cannot even reconcile my mind to anything else but to you. If my life were accepted in preference to yours I could say, "Take it," and say it with a smile; but yours, it almost drives me insane. I cannot sleep, and even if I do, I wake up with the horrors of the jail or that I am caught. Even if you do not get a reprieve, it will surely look as if God had forsaken even us, but if you do, and get life sentence, bear it with a smile.

It is nice and warm weather where I am. I forgot to tell you, dear, I am not in the city, but I have one friend whom I can trust and am sending this letter to them, so that they can repost it for me and so not give anyone information as to my whereabouts. When I was told that I would be kept in the jail till after the 13th., my life was unbearable, and I had to do something, so I could see what was going on about you. I never cease reading the papers, and I get all of them. Even the thought frightens me so much that I would to God it were never to happen, but you will always be to me my own. You know, dear, I could never breathe a word or tell our secret. As I sit writing this letter to you, my heart aches for you, darling, and if some only saw the good side of you, what a difference. But some cannot see it as I can.

I do not know if you will ever get this letter, but I trust that you might, because I thought this much, that even the last note from me to you would only give you a little comfort, and God only knows you need it, "Mon Cher Mari." I will close, and last of all, should you get a reprieve, I will in all cases do my sentence, and after I get through I will write to you, as I could never forsake you. Now, dear, be brave, even for my sake. God bless you.

I am, with love,
Your Vera

So that was it. She couldn't stand being in the jail if he were to be hanged, and in the absence of any information concerning his plight, she had been forced to do "something." According to the *Globe*, "the great question being asked is whether she is working her nimble wits to assist McCullough in another break for freedom, and whether she will immediately put into effect an already prepared plan to aid him to escape."[12]

But what was their secret? "You know, dear, I could never breathe a word or tell our secret."

On Monday, June 9 – four days before the scheduled hanging – there was still no word from Ottawa. Robinette was livid. "There are over 20,000 names on petitions up there, and they can't make up their minds." The activity of the "McCullough sympathy movement" continued unabated. "The Labor Temple was keenly interested in the fate of Frank McCullough today and on his behalf many of the strongest labor organizations in the city sent telegrams to Ottawa requesting the exercise of executive clemency." That night, an ominous gathering took place outside the jail that should have forewarned the authorities.

> A curious crowd congregated on the south side of Riverdale Park . . . in the hope of catching a glimpse of McCullough, in the death cell. They were rewarded by his appearance at the window. Greetings and signals were exchanged by the prisoner and the watchers. . . . He appeared to be quite cheerful. "He signalled and blew kisses to the people," said a witness at the scene, "and then he took a newspaper and by signals spelled out the question 'any news?' "[13]

The news came the next day. Telegrams from the undersecretary of state were sent simultaneously to Justice Rose, Sheriff Mowat, Henry Addy, T. C. Robinette, and Reverend Nelles. Addy's telegram "reached the jail by special messenger," and he immediately went to McCullough's cell.

When the chief turnkey entered, McCullough was occupied writing letters. He greeted his visitor with a cheery good morning. " 'Well, what is the news – good or bad – let's have it?' said the condemned man. 'It's bad, Frank.' – 'That's what I expected,' said McCullough." "He did not show the slightest sign of breakdown when told of his fate and calmly chatted to the guards. He later talked to Mr. Addy briefly, stating that he might as well be hanged as to spend his life in jail."

> Probably the only man to whom McCullough shows any real inner nature is the Rev. R. B. Nelles. McCullough spends much of this time reading his Bible and does not seem to weaken at the thought of his fate. No nervous collapse is expected. The Rev. Nelles spends much of his time with the condemned man. . . . Hangman Ellis is expected to be in Toronto on Thursday morning when he will visit the jail and inspect the scaffold and test out the rope which will be used for the execution. This will be done with bags of sand.[14]

Meighen had made his decision the week before. Although it was claimed by Justice Department officials that the "case was reviewed in all its details," in reality the matter was handled with all the peremptory efficiency Ottawa's distance from the scene permitted.

On June 4, J. D. Clarke sent a succinct memorandum to a harried Meighen "again submitting the capital case of McCullough for final decision on the application for clemency." Clarke noted, "There has also come to hand additional petitions on the prisoner's behalf; and the foreman of the jury, as well as the spiritual adviser, have seen me and have made pleas for clemency." It concluded, "I have altered the date of your recommendation, made earlier in April, presuming that you intend it to stand."

Attached was Meighen's earlier recommendation, prepared as a memorandum to the governor general, which had been drafted before McCullough's escape. Referring to Rose's reports, the trial transcript, petitions, and other documents, the memorandum concluded, "Upon careful consideration of all which, the undersigned respectfully recommends that the law be allowed to take its course."

Meighen signed.

The fact is that Rose had previously given Meighen the perfect excuse to commute McCullough's sentence. In his second report, the judge had stated loud and clear that the crime was, "in its moral aspect, manslaughter only [and] . . . the moral aspect is considered by the Acting Minister in dealing with an application for the exercise of executive clemency."[15] But Meighen, dealing with disorder in Winnipeg, opted for the law rather than moral considerations. Or possibly he never even saw Rose's reports and was influenced in the decision entirely by Clarke.

Two days later, on June 6, the clerk of the Privy Council appended his signature to a covering form, attached to Meighen's memorandum, stating that "The Governor General is unable to order any interference with the sentence of the court." The telegrams were issued and the deed was done – or so it seemed.[16]

In Toronto there was outrage. "Public sympathy is exceedingly strong in favour of McCullough and there are numerous people in Toronto today who would like to see him reprieved and think that the department of justice has been unusually severe in this case."

Hundreds of people stood in Riverdale Park last night outside the jail yard, and waved handkerchiefs and papers to McCullough, who stood at the window of his death cell and waved his hands through the bars. The crowd became so large that a policeman was assigned to keep the spectators from going too near the jail wall. One man used field glasses to see McCullough. Shortly after nine the light was turned on in McCullough's cell and he could be seen quite plainly. A grey-haired old woman who could hardly walk, forced her way through the crowd and waved her hand, while two little girls stayed till nearly midnight. McCullough stayed at the window for many hours.

Was Vera hidden in the crowd? "There is little doubt," said the *Toronto World*, "that she is still in the city."[17]

# XVII

# Victory Over Death

The responsibility of deciding on the fate of McCullough is
one of the most anxious that I have ever been compelled to
undertake.

— Arthur Meighen, June 10, 1919

It was an accident. He never carried arms. He's as good a
man as ever went overseas.

— Returned soldier, June 12, 1919

EXTRA RUSH

TORONTO ONT, JUNE 12TH 1919
MINISTER OF JUSTICE, OTTAWA
FOURTEEN HUNDRED MACHINISTS OF TORONTO LODGE
NO 235 INTERNATIONAL ASSOCIATION OF MACHINISTS
REQUEST THE REPRIEVE OF FRANK MCCULLOUGH ON
ACCOUNT OF HIS YOUTH AND CIRCUMSTANCES SUR-
ROUNDING THE WHOLE AFFAIR JUSTICE CAN BE SERVED
WITHOUT KILLING THIS YOUNG MAN

— THOS. A. WHITE, SECY

Thursday, June 12, 1919, was to be Frank McCullough's last full day on earth; "unless," observed the *Star*, "another attempt to spirit him out of the death cell should prove successful."

The day began with bright sunshine. Following his custom, "McCullough reserved one slice of bread from his meal to place on the ledge of his barred cell window, where birds, who have been attracted by the practice, fluttered about, twittering their thanks."

McCullough asked Henry Addy that the following morning he "be shaved and fixed up to look his best," and that his breakfast consist of ham, eggs, toast, and tea. He planned to spend his last day writing letters and "reading the Bible with Rev. Mr. Nelles. McCullough asked for a large amount of writing paper and it was supplied to him."

The closer McCullough came to death, the more serene he seemed to be. Perhaps the time spent with Nelles had had an effect after all. Or perhaps McCullough's serenity was part of his strategy to achieve a last-minute reprieve. Perhaps it was both. McCullough had shown that he could at once be many things to many people. He was a "gallant blackguard" in the pages of one newspaper, and "just the best boy in the whole world" in another.[1]

The previous day, the newspapers had published what McCullough called his "Confession and Profession," in which he described the influence of Nelles's teaching. Gradually, "as day by day I looked for this peace," he could "feel the Spirit taking hold of me" and "my load of care grow lighter and lighter." This had not happened all at once. "I have read in various tracts where the Light came suddenly. But it did not come that way to me."

> All who read this, believe that I go with happiness in my heart that I can come fully prepared to meet my Maker. And right now, while I am writing this, I am happier than ever I was before. I haven't a care, for did not Jesus die to save me? I want all who read this to believe there is nothing on this earth that can equal the joy that fills your heart if you will only believe in God and trust Him, and put your

care on Him and pray to Him to forgive your sins. The sting
is taken from misfortune and death if you have faith.

The newspapers also published the brief account McCullough
gave of his past, in which he claimed he had fought in Mexico with
the U.S. army and had been wounded. Thus, while McCullough
claimed to place his life in the hands of God, he continued to lie.

Meighen's final decision had put Robinette in fighting mood.
He would not be ignored or manipulated. He would not be cowed.
The firm of Robinette, Godfrey, Phelan & Lawson would not take
Ottawa's eleventh-hour decision as the final word. Why had they
delayed? Did Ottawa think that releasing the announcement at
the last minute would minimize criticism? "The dirty work is
always deputized," added the editor of the *Toronto World*. "The
degradation is always laid on the shoulders of another. There
would be no hangings if those responsible had to do the hanging."[2]

Robinette fired off a telegram to Meighen:

I WOULD URGE YOU TO WIRE JUDGE ROSE FOR HIS
OPINION TO BE SENT BY WIRE I KNOW THE JUDGE IS
ANXIOUS ABOUT THE MATTER AND I AM CERTAIN HE
WILL BE PLEASED TO SEE THIS MAN COMMUTED PUBLIC
OPINION IN TORONTO WITH ALL CLASSES IN HIS FAVOR
THE MEN AT THE NATIONAL CLUB WHERE I GO EVERY
DAY BIG BUSINESS MEN ARE TWO TO ONE FOR HIS
COMMUTATION THE ORDINARY PUBLIC IS NINETY PER
CENT THOUSANDS OF NAMES ARE BEFORE YOU AT
OTTAWA THESE PETITIONS WERE ENTIRELY UNSO-
LICITED AS MCCULLOUGH HAD NO MONEY TO SPEND
UPON HIS CASE IN MY CASE AS TO COUNSEL FEES
ENTIRELY A MATTER OF DUTY AND STICKING TO THE
FELLOW HIS ESCAPE A FOOLISH MOVE DOING NOBODY
ANY HARM SAW HIM A FEW DAYS AGO AND HE IS A
CHANGED MAN I BELIEVE IN THE WORK OF REV MR
NELLES WITH HIM MY VIEW IS HE SHOULD BE KEPT AN

ASSET AND WORK FOR THE COUNTRY A NUMBER OF
YEARS AND NOT BE KILLED ON FRIDAY TORONTO AND
OTHER CITIES WILL BE PLEASED TO HEAR OF HIS COM-
MUTATION LET ME URGE YOU WITH ALL OF MY POWER
WITH MY KNOWLEDGE OF THE CASE AND OF CASES OF
THIS KIND TO ALLOW THIS POOR FELLOW TO LIVE
YOURS SINCERELY T. C. ROBINETTE

Meighen (or Clarke on his behalf) wired back:

REFERRING YOUR WIRE CASE HAS BEEN DECIDED AND
DECISION APPROVED BY GOVERNOR GENERAL TRIAL
JUDGE HAS FULL PRIVILEGE OF REPORTING AND
RECOMMENDING AND OF MAKING SUPPLEMENTARY
REPORT IF HE DESIRES NOT PRACTICE UNLESS THERE
ARE SPECIAL REASONS TO ASK FOR FURTHER REPORT
AFTER REPORT MADE IN WRITING SINCERELY A.
MEIGHEN

Robinette had used this ploy before, after the trial, when he
had manipulated Ottawa into asking for a second report from
Rose. Did Robinette really think that Meighen would now ask the
judge for a third? And Meighen's telegram in reply was correct: as
the judge in the case, Rose did indeed have the power to submit
any report or supplementary recommendation any time he
wished. If Rose was as "anxious" as Robinette claimed he was, why
wasn't he doing just that?

A personal letter from Meighen also arrived, by courier:

Dear Mr. Robinette,

I have just read your wire . . . and have answered [by
wire]. I need scarcely add that this case has been the subject
of a great deal of deliberation and care. The responsibility
of deciding on the fate of McCullough is one of the most
anxious that I have ever been compelled to undertake. I was

ready to make a recommendation at the time of his escape and had then come to a conclusion which sometime later, on a new recommendation was approved by Council and by His Excellency. The escape of McCullough did not weigh with me in the least, nor do I think it weighed with any member of Council.

The case was reviewed and considered and decided on the same principles that have governed in the determination of all capital cases that have come before the Government since I have been a member thereof, and I think on the same principles that have been applied in years prior thereto.

I realize and indeed appreciate the generous services you have rendered the unfortunate man and the contribution you have made thereby to the cause of justice. I regret indeed to say that there does not appear any reason why the subject should now be reopened or any hope that if it were, a different conclusion could be reached.

Yours truly,
Arthur Meighen

Robinette threw up his hands in despair. All of this pretty bureaucratic language – replete with "thereof's" and "thereto's" and "thereby's" – said nothing, or at least nothing Robinette wanted to hear.[3]

W. B. Horkins, Robinette's partner in the case, walked down to the jail that morning to see McCullough. When he entered the cell, McCullough was "playing checkers with Rev. Nelles." McCullough jumped up and held Horkins firmly by both shoulders: "I have waited for this opportunity and it was good of you to come and say good-bye. I did not have a cent to spend in my defence, and Mr. Robinette and yourself have spared neither time nor money in looking after my interests. I cannot thank you too much."

The visit lasted only five minutes, leaving Horkins deeply

moved by McCullough's expressions of gratitude. The man could do that to you. He could commit murder, then win you over, and finally leave you in tears. When Horkins said his last goodbye, "McCullough put up his hand and pointing his finger gave a playful demonstration of Mr. Robinette addressing the jury at the trial." As Horkins left, "McCullough was soundly beating Rev. Mr. Nelles at checkers."[4]

On his way back along Adelaide Street, Horkins suddenly stopped, then quickened his pace towards the office. When he arrived he burst into Robinette's chambers and called for another colleague, A. R. Hassard, to join them. In a matter of minutes, the three worked out a final scheme to force Justice Rose into granting another reprieve.

A "cool and efficient" Arthur Ellis arrived in Toronto by train on Thursday morning and proceeded directly to the jail.

With a determined pace and without comment, the executioner inspected the death chamber, giving particular attention to the "workings of the trap and the hempen rope which will be used." McCullough was then taken to the basement of the jail to be weighed. Other than ordering him to stand on the scale, Ellis said nothing. As Ellis "abruptly" adjusted the weights, "McCullough smiled at him."

After the prisoner was taken away, Ellis filled a bag of sand to the same weight and had a guard carry it up to the death chamber. The bag was tied to the rope and "sent with a crash" through the trap. When Ellis was satisfied that all was functioning smoothly, the chamber was locked under his supervision and he vanished as suddenly as he had appeared, returning to his hotel.[5]

What about Vera? Could she remain in the city and not attempt a final meeting with her lover? "This was the first question to enter the minds of many citizens when the news that McCullough's doom was sealed reached the city." There was a report that she had been seen in the crowd outside the jail the night before, and was a "silent fellow passenger" on a streetcar afterwards. Reporters were stationed at the jail "in the chances of Vera coming forward. . . . It is argued that her faithfulness to him . . . might inspire this quixotic and dramatic act, which would end her own freedom."[6]

Early in the afternoon, a letter sent through Robinette's office was delivered to the jail and released to reporters:

Mon Cher Mari,

Dear, I can hardly realize what it means for you. Even after getting the paper today, and reading of your case, which says but little hope, I dare not think what it means. . . . May God give you strength to stand what is before you. . . . It seems to me if they do take your life, dear, there is hardly anything in my life worth living for. If I could only see you for a moment. I would come and see you. But they would never give anyone such a privilege as that, and especially to me.

I have your picture in front of me, and it will always be near me. Sometimes I can see you plainly before me, as if you were there in reality. My dear Frank, my heart is broken. I could never tolerate the thought of your death, and really now I only realize it to be too true.

God has almost always answered my prayers, and if they are not answered this time, I will never believe in religion again. The outside world, dear, has worked splendidly on your behalf, and I cannot realize that Ottawa's answer has really been given out. Anyway, dear, even if you do pay the penalty, I know you will go knowing that I love you just the same. Never in all my life on this earth will I forget you. Well, "cher de la mien," this will be my last letter to you, darling, and oh, God bless you, dear.

Yours always, with love,
Vera de Lavelle

At City Hall, there were reports of "an unusual number of requests for passes to see the execution." Sheriff Mowat "refused to give any, except to the officials who must be present and one reporter from each newspaper." Mowat himself begged off. He was "unable to be present" and would be represented by a deputy.[7]

A determined Hassard in the company of Horkins interrupted Justice Rose's assize court hearings that afternoon. Hassard did the talking, in the belief that Rose had grown impatient with Robinette and Horkins. He asked permission to argue later in the day for another reprieve, in order to give time for a point of law to be considered by the Court of Appeal.

A silent Rose listened intently to Hassard's justification. The lawyer argued that the reprieve Rose had granted after McCullough's escape, which was scheduled to end the next day, was "illegal." According to section 1063 of the Criminal Code, argued Hassard, a reprieve could be granted by the judge in a case under two cited conditions only: if there was a point of law the judge believed should go to a higher court, or the judge believed that further time was required for executive clemency to be considered.

But, argued Hassard, Rose had granted McCullough's reprieve as a matter of "convenience," merely because McCullough had escaped. The reprieve was purely a mechanism to avoid another trial if McCullough were recaptured after the scheduled date of execution. In other words, the reprieve was not granted in conformity with the two specific conditions laid down by the code. Consequently, as Hassard argued, "in the eyes of the law the man is already dead. I contend that the giving of a reprieve when McCullough escaped . . . is not covered by section 1063, and was not even thought of by Parliament when the Act was passed."

After hearing him out, Rose's single comment was, "It is pretty late now, Mr. Hassard, but all right." He would hear the motion following *Seleck v. New York Life* later in the day, and he ordered Horkins to notify the attorney general's office to be represented.

Outside the courtroom, a voluble Hassard outlined his complicated argument again before a pack of jostling reporters. He pointed out that Rose "would have to grant another reprieve in order for his argument to be considered by the Court of Appeal." And "even if" this appeal were finally turned down, Horkins interjected, "McCullough might never hang, as there is an unwritten rule in the Department of Justice that a man condemned to death should not twice be harassed by the anxiety of looking forward to his execution."[8]

What were Rose's thoughts during a tedious *Seleck v. New York Life* that afternoon? Where should a reporter be for the most sensational story in the case: in Rose's court, or at the jail? "And who can help a sneaking desire for this final reprieve?" asked the *Toronto World* as a warm summer evening began to fall upon the city of Toronto.

Henry Addy very soon realized there was going to be trouble. From his office window at the front of the jail, he saw pedestrians filing up to the building all afternoon. By 5:00 p.m. his chief guard, Harry Denning, came to tell him he was worried. Addy went outside and walked around to the rear of the jail, where he was astonished to find a thousand people already gathered and calling for McCullough. Addy immediately telephoned the police department to suggest they better send constables over to maintain order.

This was the first of many calls made that night by an increasingly frantic chief turnkey. It is difficult to determine precisely how many people ultimately gathered at the jail in the remaining hours. One estimate put the crowd at twelve thousand. But people were coming and going all night long, so it was difficult to tell. From early in the evening, "automobiles lined Broadview Avenue from Gerrard up to Woolfrey," and "the streets in the vicinity became almost impassable with motor traffic hastening to the environs of Don Castle." It would be fair to conclude, as did Magistrate Cohen the following day, that some ten thousand people came to the jail during the course of the disturbance.

By 7:30 p.m., the crowd had reached twenty-five hundred, and was boisterous but not violent. At first they were mainly women, "with a goodly number of boys and girls and a minority of men." Women "brought their children in baby carriages, soldiers hobbled on crutches, anything to get within view of the window." By standing in the park, at some distance from the rear wall of the jail, the crowd could see McCullough's cell. There they lingered, "standing in suspense," hoping McCullough would again appear.

The children played and romped in front of the crowd, near the wooden jail fence, climbing in the trees only to be chased down by a constable. They got together in groups and sang, on one occasion, "Till We Meet Again." Groups of boys assembled with a lead: "Three cheers for McCullough." They responded, "Is McCullough down hearted?" and then a substantial: "No!"

McCullough made his first appearance before 8:00 p.m. He came to his window, "held up his hands for silence and could be heard singing."

A woman who had been standing back in the crowd edged her way up and inquired of a constable, "What is he singing?" "Nearer My God to Thee," replied the officer. McCullough could be seen waving his arms to beat time with the music and holding a book in one hand. The distance from the park to the cell is about one hundred yards so that his voice was not discernible.

Inside, McCullough had been writing letters and praying with Reverend Nelles. Nelles spent most of the day with him, leaving at eight with a promise to return first thing in the morning. "I read to him a number of his favorite passages in the Bible. Frank picked them out himself. One was John 14." When the commotion outside began to interrupt their vigil, McCullough asked Nelles, "What does it mean?" "It means they love you, Frank, and that whatever happens tomorrow, they know you are truly a changed man."

As dusk fell, the crowd became larger and louder. More men were arriving now, "including many returned soldiers." At 8:40, "in response to loud and long cheering, clapping, shouting, singing and general noise," the lights in McCullough's cell were turned on and he suddenly appeared.

> The sight of him drew a tremendous prolonged cheer from the throng, in fact, such a cheer as has not been heard even at welcoming Toronto's troops home. Hands were waved up in the air; handkerchiefs waved, hats thrown to the wind. McCullough seemed to stand back and gaze out at the throng, then wave his arms, reach out through the bars and wave his hands again. Then he stopped a second, and threw three kisses. After this he clapped both hands together as illustrative of a handshake, turned, jumped, and was gone. As he disappeared the cheers stopped abruptly and the crowd stood in silence. After a few minutes' wait the cry was again taken up: "McCullough! We want McCullough!" "Reprieve! Reprieve!"

As the crowd at the jail was calling for reprieve, A. R. Hassard brought his formal appeal before Justice Rose to an end. *Seleck v. New York Life* hadn't finished until eight, whereupon Hassard addressed the court for forty-five minutes in the role of "amicus curiae, or one who wishes to help the cause of justice." As expected, he argued that Rose had reprieved McCullough for reasons not specified in the Criminal Code. The reprieve had simply been a strategy to avoid a second trial if McCullough were recaptured after the date of execution had passed.

Once Hassard had concluded his eloquent presentation, Rose dropped a bombshell. The court listened in silence as he read from a document. It was the governor general's order, altering the expiry date of a reprieve issued in Ottawa so that it coincided with the date of June 13 set by Rose. Those present in the courtroom, including Robinette, Horkins, and Hassard, until now had never known about the governor general's reprieve.

It all went back to that unanswered telegram sent to Toronto by J. D. Clarke in Ottawa to inquire whether Rose, as the judge in the case, had been approached for a reprieve.[9] This failure in communication had resulted in two differently dated reprieves: one issued by the governor general and the other by Rose himself. To rectify the problem (and Toronto's negligence), Clarke had arranged for the governor general's reprieve to be revised so that both documents bore the same date. There had been a sigh of relief when this was accomplished without Robinette discovering the fact that two dates for the execution existed. For if he had known, Robinette would surely have tried to manipulate the matter to McCullough's advantage.

Now, in Rose's courtroom, the very evening before the scheduled hanging, Robinette and his colleagues were finally hearing about the two reprieves. They were not at all pleased. Rose's bombshell completely destroyed Hassard's carefully contrived argument. While Rose's power to grant a reprieve was arguably constrained by the two conditions cited in the Criminal Code, the governor general had absolute authority, unfettered by any condition. It wiped away any argument Hassard might make about an "illegal" reprieve issued outside the two conditions cited in the code.

How ironic! Normally, a bureaucratic mistake allows the prisoner to get off. In this case, however, because of a single unanswered telegram, the sentence was now to be carried out. If the bureaucracy hadn't bungled the matter earlier, there would have been one reprieve only: Justice Rose's. And this might have allowed Rose to accept Hassard's argument that his own reprieve went beyond the cited conditions in the code. Rose might actually have allowed Hassard's challenge to go forward to the Court of Appeal by granting another last-minute reprieve.

But it was all academic now. "It was not a pleasant duty in refusing the plea for a reprieve, said the learned justice, but much as he would have liked to have divided the responsibility with a court of appeal, he had his duty to perform."

Hassard looked at Horkins, Horkins looked at Robinette, and a defeated Robinette "declared there was no use in urging the matter further, and it was dropped." Outside the courtroom, Robinette told reporters that "it was a chance and I did the best I could." Frank McCullough was going to hang.

➤➤  ◄◄

The mob at the jail was becoming more rowdy. Addy "walked out among the crowd, and was astonished at the scene, which has never been enacted during his service at the Jail." Fearing that the throng might storm the jail, he called Chief Grasett for more constables. He also called Ellis at his hotel, urging the hangman to come to the jail at once. There was one obvious way for the crowd to prevent the hanging, and that was to prevent Ellis from entering the jail to do his "public duty."

> Wildly talking women, with their children, formed no small part of the growing crowd that by ten o'clock had reached near five thousand. Police sought to persuade them to go to their homes. They declared their intention to stay all night. Irresponsible youths and returned soldiers were among the most boisterous.

"Like tinder to the rising flame," McCullough continued to appear at his window at half-hour intervals. "The row could be heard ten blocks away."

> At 10:15 he merely extended his hand from the floor of the cell, which could be seen in the window, and merely the sight of his hand waving was sufficient to warrant cheers

and handclapping. The hand was shown until after eleven o'clock, when he appeared and lit a cigarette, standing back from the window and smoking.

"Reprieve! Reprieve!" roared the mob. "Cheers for McCullough," shouted some. "For he's a jolly good fellow," commenced another group. Voices sang, "We won't go home until morning." "Then a sacred touch entered the throng when 'Nearer My God to Thee' was sung by a number of people, and 'Jesus Loves Me' which were promptly howled down by others."

By midnight, the crowd was enormous, extending far back into the park and around to the front of the jail. "At least thirty or forty automobiles were being parked continuously on Broadview Avenue." Now the horde "included many returned soldiers." Some had emptied out of the Gerrard Street Military Hospital; some "wore khaki," while many others had "their service buttons displayed." Three mounted policemen arrived and a "strong cordon of police and detectives paraded outside the prison fence" under the command of Insp. John Beattie. No effort as yet was made to clear the crowd.

McCullough made several attempts to communicate directly with the crowd in spite of the distance between them. He held up his arms requesting silence, and "many in the mob seemed to understand that he wanted to say something." But it was difficult to obtain the silence required to hear him. "Just as he appeared to be about to say something, an odd interrupter would break in with a remark: 'All right, Frank, let us have it! Tell us something, Frank!'"

On the following occasion, he repeated his request for silence, which was granted, and the mob stood quiet and still. Just on the psychological moment, a woman's voice piped out: "It's Doris, Frank!" The voice issued from the front of the throng, and several people made an attempt to find out who it was, but failed.

It was "little Doris" Mytton.

Using his arms, McCullough then attempted messages by semaphore "and on this occasion he distinctly wrote 'Vera.'" "Hushed" voices could be heard in the crowd: "Is she here?" "Vera, are you here?" "Come forward, Vera, we'll protect you!" But no one stepped forward, and "the word went through the crowd that she was there in disguise. 'Yes, Frank. Vera is here!' 'She's here, Frank!' 'We love you, Vera!' to tremendous cheers and applause." "Children waved their handkerchiefs. Women urged a rescue. A returned soldier in the crowd hotly defended the criminal. 'It was an accident. He never carried arms. He's as good a man as ever went overseas.'"

Why Inspector Beattie waited until this moment to make a move is hard to determine. Perhaps he realized that the crowd could only become more unruly, and that it was better to act sooner rather than later. Afterwards, the police maintained that because the "attitude of the crowd became so boisterous . . . and the noise made by them so distressing to patients in the isolation hospital and to local residents" they had simply decided to clear the park.

But as a cordon of constables pushed through the throng, ordering them to disperse, the crowd parted, then regrouped around them. At this point Lillian Furguson, who was arrested and later charged, had words with the police. "The police found her in Riverdale Park screeching wildly." When ordered to go home, she replied, "Oh move off yourselves, you pot-bellied bastards."

Beattie called for reserves and an additional squadron of constables. Mounted police "were posted outside the jail, on the streets and through Riverdale Park. Other reserves were kept in different police stations on duty all night." Soon, a second effort was made to clear the park, "but even the reserves could do nothing and the crowd was constantly augmented by hundreds of newcomers."

An alarmed Henry Addy reported to Chief Grasett that bottles were being thrown against the front of the jail, where the offices and main entrance were located, and that "a serious attempt would be made to raid the jail and release McCullough." Meanwhile, at the rear, "as the crowd became decidedly hostile in character, bricks began to fly above the heads of the police and the order to charge was given to the mounted men." The mounted police "obeyed the order at the gallop only to be driven back to the jail walls with volleys of missiles."

At this moment, "a reserve of sixty policemen and a number of plainclothesmen and detectives" sent by Grasett came racing up Gerrard Street in a number of vehicles. The policemen pushed their way through the crowd at the front and entered the main doors. This contingent of reinforcements remained stationed inside the jail under command of Assistant Deputy Chief Geddes, while the plainclothesmen and detectives fanned out to assist the mounted police at various points around the jail.

With their numbers strengthened, "at last, by sheer persistency, rallying," the mounted police pushed a good portion of the crowd out onto Broadview Avenue at the back of the jail and onto Gerrard at the front. "Here a pitched battle took place, ending in many arrests including returned soldiers." In the meantime, many "gathered again in front of the jail. Word was sent to the military authorities, and MPs in motor trucks were speedily hastened to the scene."

The worst of the violence occurred at the intersection of Gerrard and Broadview. As the mounted police "charged down Broadview and the crowd ran," a group at the intersection turned on the police and "bricks, stones and milk bottles were flying in all directions." "Come on. We'll fix the bastards!" cried Robert Allen, a returned soldier with a brick in his hand. "Call out the boys!" yelled one George Glover. "Bricks and sticks were used," and a signboard torn from the Salvation Army building at the intersection was hurled at the mounted police as they charged. "What the hell are we waiting for? Let's get the ___!" yelled another returned soldier, Robert Rooney, to the crowd. "We fought the Hun there, and we'll fight the police here!" "We'll stay as God-damned long as we like!" "Brickbats and milk bottles were flying through the air." "Wildly talking women used filthy language." "The soldiers aggravated the crowd. . . . The crowd threw rocks and used terrible language. The mounted police were repeatedly charging the throng and dispersing them only to have them gather again."

Several police were injured; two mounted police, constables Raney and Milton, were struck on the head and thrown from their horses to the pavement. "A returned soldier who stood watching the scene suddenly swooned and fainted."

The violence was ended at approximately 3:00 a.m., when the last of those arrested were carted off in patrol wagons. Thirty-five people were taken into custody that night, half of them returned soldiers. Some policemen were then withdrawn from the streets to join the contingent inside the jail. Here they encountered a terrified Arthur Ellis roaming the corridors and shaking nervously, who confessed he had "never before seen such a demonstration at a hanging." For the first time, the "cool and efficient" Ellis was frightened; for the crowd, now milling about waiting for daybreak, was also waiting for him. Ellis couldn't stay in the jail forever.

Apparently the only person not in a state of agitation was Frank McCullough. Although the noise kept the neighbouring community up all night, he somehow managed to sleep between 2:00 and 5:00 a.m. Then he rose, washed, and made his bed. "The bursting light of a bright June morning shone through the barred window of his cell, and he greeted it with song." He sang hymns, and while dressing broke into his favourite song, "He Wore a Tulip and She Wore a Big, Red Rose." His breakfast of ham, eggs, toast, and tea he ate heartily, "and left no morsel of his meal unfinished."

Reverend Nelles arrived at 6:00 a.m. "to the cheers of the throng outside the jail." McCullough "greeted him affectionately," and they spent the remainder of their time together in meditation. Although the crowds were calling repeatedly for McCullough to appear at his window, he had decided to wait. He asked Nelles to read the 23rd Psalm and dropped to his knees. "In simple fashion he called on the Almighty to bless the several guards whose names he repeated. The girl, Vera, he commended to the care of God. The man's absolute calmness . . . was remarkable."

When Nelles commented on his peace of mind, McCullough explained, "This is not bravado. It is not the same thing as nerve like I showed in other times. I'm quite calm and peaceful, that's all I can say. It is like victory over death." He took a signet ring from his finger and gave it to Nelles. "I earned the money for that by hard work, he said."

As the time approached, the cries for McCullough to appear became incessant. "A night without sleep did not dampen the spirit of the crowd which again became boisterous." Inside, "while waiting for the time of execution, Hangman Ellis wandered around the corridors and mixed with the police and admitted several times that he was 'feeling rotten and his nerves were in worse shape than any other time.' "

At 7:40 a.m., a "quiet" Henry Addy emerged from his office and joined the deputy sheriff (replacing the squeamish Mowat), two guards, and Ellis, who were waiting. When the party "walked toward the heavy iron gate that separates the Jail offices from the main part of the Jail, to go upstairs to McCullough's room, their way was barred by a score of constables who stood leaning against the bars, gazing up to the second floor." When the gate was finally opened, at least two unauthorized persons "managed to slip by, one citizen saying he was a newspaper man." As the officials began to make their way up the stairs, Nelles said to McCullough, "They're coming, Frank."

With this cue, McCullough at last rushed to the window, "and his appearance was greeted with tremendous cheers and cries lasting for minutes." "The condemned murderer might well have been a patriot leader, so loud were they in their demands for his release." McCullough stretched his arms straight out through the bars as though he were about to embrace the throng before him. Amidst the deafening noise of the crowd, there were cries of derision against the authorities. "Damn you ___ hypocrites!" was heard. "Bloody murderers!" "Bring him out! Bring him out here in the open!" shouted others. "See what you can do to him against us." Then McCullough vanished as quickly as he had appeared.

When the officials arrived at the door of the cell, McCullough "met Ellis with a smile." As the crowd roared outside, he quietly declined the offer of morphine while his hands were bound behind him. "He was 'the coolest man I ever saw,' said Dr. T. Owen Parry. 'He refused to take any stimulants and only smoked cigarettes.'" When asked by the deputy sheriff whether he had anything to say, he replied, "No, except that I would like it known that Frank McCullough's death is a warning to other boys who start on the wrong path in life."

That said, and "dressed only in a silk striped shirt and trousers belted at the waist, he walked the forty paces from his cell to the scaffold with a firm step, and appeared to be the least affected of those present." Nelles led the way, followed by Addy and Ellis. Then came McCullough, a guard on either side, with the deputy sheriff in the rear. "Entering the death chamber, the strong electric light that flooded the chamber made him blink, but he stepped on the trap, and turned and faced the officials and spectators." Twenty observers were present, including reporters, jail officials, detectives, policemen, and doctors. As McCullough faced them "a smile played about his face." He then turned to Reverend Nelles and said, "This is going to be harder on you than on me," and as the hood passed over his mouth, he said, "Goodbye, Mr. Nelles, God bless you – Goodbye, boys."

After adjusting the cap Ellis, who appeared very nervous, worked fast and Mr. Nelles in a firm voice started to recite the Lord's Prayer. When it came to "Deliver us from evil" Ellis sprung the trap and McCullough dropped out of sight.

Fifteen minutes later, Dr. Parry declared life extinct and the body was cut down. Dr. W. J. Maybee conducted a post-mortem, which showed the neck had been broken. A coroner's jury under

Dr. Latimore Pickering conducted an inquest at the scene and rendered the verdict: "That Frank McCullough was hanged by the neck until he was dead in due execution of the law."

Outside, the crowd fell silent and some began drifting away. "He's gone now. McCullough's gone." "Rest at last," remarked one, while a few sang hymns and wept.

Minutes later, the quiet was shattered by a crash and the roar of an engine as a police wagon raced from the jail enclosure with hangman Ellis crammed in the back, accompanied by a police guard. As the vehicle careened onto Gerrard Street, the crowd yelled, pounded the hood and roof, "and expressed hostile sentiments against him," until the wagon disappeared in the distance down the street.

There was to be no funeral. By law, the body of a hanged man was to be buried immediately in the jail yard – in an area known as "murderers' row" – without any ceremony. But that afternoon, an unusual event occurred.

At 2:00 p.m., "the remains of McCullough, which had been placed in a casket, upon which rested a single bunch of flowers, the offering of Mrs. Nelles, were carried to the jail yard, preceded by the pastor." At the pit that had been dug in murderers' row, a private service was conducted, as if McCullough had died of natural causes.

Afterwards, Nelles was interviewed by reporters outside the jail, where he said, "I only did my duty as a minister, but I have, as his spiritual adviser during the past four months, become greatly attached to him."

About a score of people tried to obtain admittance to the jail to visit the remains. They were told to go away, but as they persisted in hanging around the doorway they were warned that unless they dispersed the police would be called. On Gerrard Street and in the park small knots of people also hung around until after 3 o'clock.

The mourners who had attended the private funeral service conducted earlier by Reverend Nelles were four prisoners acting as pallbearers, along with Henry Addy – and the entire staff of the Toronto Jail.[10]

# XVIII

# Epilogue

Frank McCullough will live forever in the calendar of crime as one of the most romantic figures in its history. From his murder of Williams, to his escape from the Don Castle, to the similar flight of his sweetheart, to the moment when for the last time he waved his hands in a brave farewell to the thousands who cheered from below, he has been a gallant blackguard.

— *Evening Telegram*, June 13, 1919

The Duke of Devonshire,[1] Canada's governor general, spent the day of McCullough's hanging visiting the town of Oshawa, not far from Toronto. "Simcoe Street, from the centre of the town out to Alexandra Park was gaily decorated with flags and bunting." Schoolchildren sang "The Maple Leaf Forever" as the vice-regal party climbed a platform facing the crowded grandstand. Returned soldiers, members of the GWVA, and hundreds of cadets stood at attention on the surrounding racetrack.

The Governor General praised the good people of Oshawa for their patriotic work and support of the Red Cross, then planted a maple tree as a reminder of the occasion. The afternoon concluded with "a general reception held in a large tent on the grounds."[2]

Arthur Ellis, the man who carried out the governor general's "Order" a few miles away, said later in life that McCullough's was the only execution in his entire career at which he feared being lynched himself.[3] The hangman went on to decapitate a woman in 1935: "The noose came flying back up through the trap."[4] He retired to Montreal and hoped to live out his years in anonymity as "Mr. Arthur English." He joined a lawn-bowling club in Westmount. One Sunday afternoon, an officer in the Royal Canadian Mounted Police came to the club as a guest of its president. Suddenly, he gazed at one of the bowlers in surprise. " 'What is the hangman doing here?' he asked the president. The president, flabbergasted, looked from the inspector to the bowler. 'You can't be serious. That's our secretary-treasurer, Mr. English.' "

His anonymity broken, Ellis turned to drink. The owner of a department store "once, during the Christmas rush, employed him as a salesman in the basement of the store." A shopper recognized Ellis and complained, "so they had to let him go." He died of malnutrition in 1938 – alone, in a rented room.[5]

Canada's last hanging occurred at the Toronto Jail in 1962. Capital punishment was abolished fourteen years later.

Frederick Mowat was never fired. The "family compact" was alive and well.[6] Appointed sheriff in 1888 (when his father was premier of the province), Mowat remained in his position for thirty-six years. In an official history of Toronto in 1923, it was said that "Mr. Mowat has won the sincere confidence and esteem of the people, and holds an assured position, also, in the social life of the city."[7]

He died the following year in his home on Russell Hill Road at the age of seventy-three.

The less privileged and more competent chief turnkey, Henry Addy, suffered a massive stroke while on duty at the jail in 1925. He died two days later at the Western Hospital, having served as chief turnkey for thirty-seven years.[8]

Time and a good lawyer proved to be in Ernest Currell's favour. Before his sentence was to be delivered by Judge Emerson Coatsworth, Currell's lawyer went to Chief Justice Sir William Meredith to request a referral of Currell's case to the appellate division. The lawyer (C. E. MacDonald) argued that there was insufficient evidence to convict Currell, and that Judge Coatsworth had directed the jury improperly. "There was a question as to the propriety of the remark by the judge to the effect that if Currell had fallen asleep while on duty as a soldier he might have been shot."

"There is nothing in that," commented Sir William Meredith. "Who tried the case?"

"His Honor Judge Coatsworth, with a jury," returned Mr. MacDonald.

"He refused to state a case?" asked Sir William.

"Yes," returned the lawyer.

"He was probably right," commented Sir William. "If Currell fell asleep on duty, was he not properly convicted?"

"He wasn't charged with falling asleep," said Mr. MacDonald.

"Wasn't he charged with not doing his duty?"

"No, he was charged with assisting the prisoner to escape. The whole result of the trial was a paradox."

"If he went to sleep while on duty didn't he assist the prisoner in escaping?"

"That is what the good judge charged."

"Isn't that good law?"

"I submit not."

"Well," remarked the Chief Justice, "I think you will have to leave the motion over till we have finished the present case."

"When will that be?" asked Mr. MacDonald.

"Friday," smiled Justice Hodgins.

"I don't think the court will be sitting on Friday," said the Chief Justice. "You will have to wait and see."[9]

There is no record that the case was ever heard again. Nor is there a record of final sentencing. The jury in Currell's case had previously appealed to Judge Coatsworth to show leniency. Perhaps they were successful. For all we know, Currell might have been fined and released.

Ernest Currell died in Toronto in 1957. The sickly, "wounded soldier" outlived all the main characters in the case of Frank McCullough. All, that is, with the possible exception of one, as we shall see.

Frank McCullough's case brought an end to political appointments at the jail. Two weeks after the hanging, the provincial government decided a governor was required, and "that the appointment should go to a person who has handled desperate men, and is able to conduct the jail in an efficient manner."

This decision had beneficial results. The job went to a decorated Maj. George Hedley Basher, who had the right stuff. During the war, at the age of twenty-four, Basher had run a French military prison at Rouen, which held a thousand men. He whipped the Toronto Jail into shape and then took on a reorganization of the Langstaff Jail Farm. Basher re-entered military service in 1939 to become known "as the toughest commanding officer in the Canadian army." He led the Royal Regiment in Italy during the Second World War and was awarded the Order of the British Empire. "The Basher" owed his first civilian job to Frank McCullough, whom he never met.[10]

↦　↤

Bart Cronin was promoted to inspector of detectives in 1924. He served on the force for a total of thirty-seven years, retiring without fanfare in 1937. On his death in 1944, the closing notation in his personnel file said it all: "good conduct, meritorious service."[11]

T. C. Robinette died of a stroke only nine months after the hanging. McCullough was his last famous case, "the only subsequent criminal case of public interest being that of Vera Lavelle." The funeral for the "friend of publicans and sinners" was large, "wreaths and sheaths of flowers coming not only from the Bar and Bench, but from individuals who had been helped by the lawyer when in trouble." Peter White, Robinette's opponent at McCullough's trial, spoke after the funeral to reporters.

> I had known him ever since his student days, when he was considered one of the most brilliant men in college. I have several times had the honor, as representative of the Crown, of opposing him in important murder trials, and always found him a most difficult as well as a splendid antagonist, courteous, generous, and, above all, scrupulously honourable.

Among Robinette's five children at the funeral was young John Josiah, who went on to become the patriarch of Canada's trial lawyers.[12]

Justice Hugh Edward Rose's lucid orthodoxy contributed to "conspicuous success" as "among the best trial judges Ontario has known in this generation." His most celebrated case was the libel action of Sir Arthur Currie against W. T. R. Preston in 1928.[13] In 1939, Rose was appointed chief justice of the High Court of Ontario.[14] He died in 1946 at the age of seventy-six.

J. D. Clarke retired in 1919 to his garden at 10 Somerset Street in Ottawa. His arrogant superior, the Honourable Arthur Meighen, became prime minister in 1920. Meighen was crushed in a general election the following year, then outwitted and humiliated again in 1926. He remains one of Canada's greatest political failures.

"If I Were a Boy Again" – a "remarkable message addressed to the boys of North America by Frank McCullough." This was the advertisement for Nelles's evening sermon at the Church for the Stranger on the Sunday following the hanging. "The service is not intended to be sensational, but an invitation is extended to friends of every creed or no creed to attend. Doors open at 6:30, illustrated song service at 7:00 o'clock. Come early."[15]

Pulpit antics such as these could not avert decline at the Church for the Stranger. The church *was* sold, for $70,000 in 1923, "as the pressure from the Jews was getting intolerable."[16] Its new custodians transformed the building into a synagogue, and it became, once more, the centre of a vibrant community.[17]

At the time the church building was sold, Nelles, a Presbyterian, proposed that the members of the Congregational Church for the Stranger take the proceeds from the sale and amalgamate with a struggling Presbyterian church nearby. In this way, they could remain in the Spadina area. When his Congregational predecessor, the garrulous Rev. J. W. Pedley, heard about the plan, he phoned up an official of the Presbyterian Church. "Well, you think you have a nice juicy morsel, don't you, but let me tell you you will find there is a bone in it, because I am going to fight it!"

Pedley came roaring out of retirement. He booked a theatre on Spadina, where he held religious services to draw back the more loyal Congregationalists in Nelles's flock. He eventually obtained a court injunction to prevent the transfer of the church's $70,000 to the Presbyterians. The conflict tore the Church for the Stranger apart and became a denominational disgrace at a time when Protestants the world over were proclaiming their capacity to unite. It was a bitter end to Nelles's creedless ministry on Spadina Avenue.[18]

Reverend Nelles left Toronto. He spent the remainder of his ministerial career moving from place to place: Drummond Hill, Montreal, Port Hope, Madoc, Hamilton, Bala, Pembroke, and finally Lancaster, where he died in 1948. His preaching changed over the years. "It was marked by deep spiritual insight, as well as the literary culture in which he delighted."[19]

Nelles's grandson, Mr. R. B. Nelles of Agincourt, Ontario, remembered his grandfather saying near the time of his death that his "most horrible experience in life was to have attended a hanging." The family still has the ring McCullough gave to Nelles in the death cell.

What about Albert Johnson, McCullough's thankless companion who broke through the door of Cross's Livery? The only Albert Johnson of subsequent notoriety in Canadian history was the "Mad Trapper" of Rat River.

In 1932, the Royal Canadian Mounted Police travelled for days in the Yukon Territory to arrest a reclusive Albert Johnson, who had been illegally raiding traps. Johnson's origins were unknown. He was suspicious of the police, had an unusually large amount of money with him,[20] and had secluded himself in a fortresslike cabin in the isolated forests near the Rat River.

There was a shoot-out at Johnson's cabin, after which he led the police on a famous forty-eight-day chase across 150 miles of the Arctic at temperatures reaching forty degrees below zero. Johnson was so adept at survival that the police had to bring in a bush pilot, and former war airman, to track him down.[21] After killing a policeman and wounding two others, Johnson was finally killed himself on the Eagle River in the Yukon Territory.

The identity of the "Mad Trapper" has never been established, but he was estimated to have been between thirty-five and forty when killed. Our Albert Johnson, McCullough's companion, would have been the same age. The subject of the "Mad Trapper" has spawned several books, a movie, and "has given millions of armchair detectives an opportunity to give vent to their opinions."

> [He] was either obsessively bent on self-destruction, or hiding something in his past which he knew doomed him if he did surrender. Whether the Mounties killed a lone "gone mad" trapper, or a ruthless killer, or whether Albert Johnson was the hapless victim of a series of unfortunate circumstances, are unanswered questions which are now a part of the lore of that raw, mysterious land of the great Arctic forests.[22]

Vera de Lavelle was outside the jail on McCullough's last night, dressed in disguise. She stayed late, but could not bear to be present during the hanging. In the morning, when she knew McCullough was dead, she paid $10 to a florist for a funeral wreath on her way to Union Station, and left for Buffalo to stay with friends.

Two weeks later, Vera returned to the city and rented a room at College Street and Beverley, across from the University of Toronto. She wanted to bring her fugitive existence to an end. She told her neighbours and other people who she was, and waited for the police to arrive. She fully expected to be arrested for the charges against her: aiding and abetting McCullough in his escape, and her own escape from jail.

No one cooperated. "Many persons living in the vicinity of College and Beverley have been aware that she was a neighbour, but forebore reporting her whereabouts to the police." She tried to force the matter. "I was up and down Yonge Street all the time. I was also at the Grand, Hippodrome, Regent, Rialto, and other theatres." The fact is, the police did not want to arrest her. She "passed scores of detectives in her travels," and even asked one "what sort of detective he was."

The authorities had had enough of the McCullough case, and enough of public criticism. They feared Vera's martyrdom and simply wanted her to go away: "It is no secret that the police were well aware that she was in the city, and that they had but little desire to arrest her."

So Vera decided she would do the cowards' job for them.

On July 22, she telephoned her lawyer, W. B. Horkins,[23] and instructed him to tell the police and the newspapers that she would give herself up. Horkins went to City Hall, where he informed Assistant Inspector of Detectives Wallace that the following day he would guide the police to Vera's location. He also told reporters what was about to happen. "WHY DOESN'T VERA BREAK BACK INTO JAIL?" was the headline in one newspaper that evening. With the newspapers involved, how could the police refuse to do their duty? "She has forced herself upon them, and therefore they are forced to accept her whether they like it or not."

Accordingly, the following day, a police car was sent to Robinette's Adelaide Street offices to pick up Horkins. The lawyer climbed in beside Detective McConnell, and together they started out.

They were not unobserved by the vigilant eyes of the press, and close behind came another motor filled with eager young reporters. It was all quite in the true spirit of the "feature fillum" and a merry chased ensued. Along Adelaide to Jarvis, then north to Shuter and across to Sherbourne and north again to Wellesley and east to a garage on Bleeker Street. Here the lawyer sprang from the car and entered a high-power machine driven by "Babe" Burkhardt, a well known rugby player and friend of Mr. Horkins, and again the chase was on. With a roar and crash, the big car with the lawyer and detective therein, shot off westward on Wellesley Street and soon out-distanced the laboring motor with its load of pressmen.

They raced round the King's College Circle at the University of Toronto, almost hitting some university employees smoking outside the president's office, then down to College and Beverley, where Vera was found pacing up and down, awaiting the arrival of the police. "Hello, Vera!" said Detective McConnell as he stepped from the car. "I suppose you think it is a pleasure in arresting me," she told him saucily. "It is no pleasure for me to arrest the likes of you," replied the detective. "We get no medals for this."

She was "whirled" over to City Hall, where other reporters had gathered. They were prevented from speaking to her, and Vera was quickly escorted up through the main doors to the detectives office. It was noted that she was wearing a black velvet dress and "looked tired and careworn." "Her sombre garb, which included a large black bow at her throat, was taken to indicate that she was mourning for McCullough."

Vera was formally questioned. Afterwards, she reported to the police that the florist had never delivered the funeral wreath she paid for. She told them that she "fully expected the $10 will be refunded to her."

"Has Miss Lavelle a statement to make?" asked The Star, speaking to Mr. Horkins, her counsel. "All she said is that she has nothing to fear," stated Mr. Horkins. "The only emotion she showed was when she asked if she would be taken to the jail. Upon being told that she would be placed in the Court street cells over night, she was greatly relieved."

She appeared again before Judge Emerson Coatsworth the following morning. "I have considered the circumstances connected with this case and I don't impose a heavy sentence," he said. "Poor McCullough is gone, the thing is all over, and I suppose you have suffered a good deal in connection with it one way or the other, so I am going to impose a sentence of two months on the Jail Farm in this case [her own escape], and two months' imprisonment at the Jail Farm in the other case of assisting McCullough to escape, the sentences to run concurrently."

"Of course, you will serve your time?" the judge enquired. "You won't attempt to escape again?" "No, sir," replied Vera with a smile, and an evident feeling of relief that she knew her fate at last. "Will you say what you intend doing when you have served your sentence?" The Star inquired of Miss Lavelle, while she was waiting to be taken to the Jail Farm. "After I come out I am going to start life all over again," she replied, with emphasis on the last three words.

While passing through the corridors on her way to the waiting vehicle, "several people walked up to her and shook her hand." Robinette encountered her in the corridor and wished her good-bye, saying, "Now you be a good girl!"

She was. She worked in the kitchen at the jail farm, "and according to the matron, proved herself to be a good cook." She completed her sentence and was released on September 13 after signing her name in the jail register. That is the last trace of her. She vanished completely.

"You know, dear," she had written three months earlier to McCullough, "I could never breathe a word or tell our secret." What was their secret? It could be only one thing: she was carrying their child.[24]

The night before McCullough was hanged, he wrote the following letter to the youngest son of Reverend Nelles:[25]

To my Friend Bob Nelles:
    Well Friend Bob I just want to tell you how I would do were I a boy again. First of all Bob, I would obey Mother

and Dad always for they know best always and would tell them my worries and troubles, and would learn all I could at school for schooldays are over in a few short years and never come again. I would be careful of what I read outside of school hours. I would ask my Sunday School teacher what books to read. I would go to Church and Sunday School always rain or shine and study my lesson for next Sunday, not take it home and forget it till next Sunday. For when you get older you realize what it all means to you. There are always a lot of bad boys who steal apples, laugh at unfortunate people and make fun of them and who gamble on the corner or back lot. I would keep away from them Bob Boy. For when you get older you would get into more serious trouble and have a hard name and make Mother and Dad sorry and ashamed that you were their boy. And would always do my work cheerfully for work is play then.

When I went to bed at night I would always pray like this. My Father in Heaven I thank you for your blessings to-day and be with me during my rest tonight, help me to be a good boy, so that Mother and Dad are proud of me, help me to do right always. Bless papa, Bless mama, and granny and grandpop, Bless me, Bless everybody. Amen.

This is all this time Bob, be a good boy and we will meet in heaven.

God Bless You Little Friend,
From Your Friend Frank

# Notes

CHAPTER I: THE CRIME

1. That is, he was the first to be slain while on duty since the establishment of the Toronto Police Force in 1839. In the eighty years since 1918 there were thirteen other officers similarly killed: Roy McQuillan, 1930; Edmund Tong, 1952; Fred Nash, 1962; David Goldsworthy, 1969; Michael Irwin, 1972; Douglas Sinclair, 1972; James Lothian, 1973; Henry Sneddon, 1978; Michael Sweet, 1980; Percy Cummings, 1981; David Dunmore, 1984; Todd Baylis, 1994; William Hancox, 1998.
2. *Evening Telegram*, June 13, 1919.
3. Flags were flown at half-mast in Toronto, but there was surprisingly little ceremony attending Williams's death. The war effort still dominated all aspects of the city's affairs.
4. He was promoted to "acting" because approximately 150 policemen were in service with the Forces overseas. Those who survived were guaranteed their positions upon return.
5. "Madame May's High-Class Dress Exchange," located at 372 College Street, claimed to be "Canada's largest and most up-to-date second-hand dress exchange," accepting Victory Bonds as cash with "change given in cash." It is now the She Said Boom! record and bookstore opposite the restored fire hall.
6. The livery's location is now the site of the Planet Car-Van Wash at 689 King Street West.

7. Clinton *New Era, News Record*, November 21, 1918; *Globe, Evening Telegram, Daily Star*, November 20, 21, 1918; *Frank Williams Inquest*, Copy of Evidence, Public Archives of Ontario (PAO), RG 22, York County Criminal Assize Case Files, Box 278, McCullough, 1919; *The King v. Frank McCullough*, Trial. Public Archives of Canada (PAC), RG 13, Vol. 1497, File: McCullough, F., Vol. 1, Part 2.

## CHAPTER II: INQUEST AND INVESTIGATION

1. At this time, police headquarters and the detective department were housed in the old City Hall at Queen and Bay (then Teraulay) streets. Most constables and detectives worked directly out of eleven police stations at various locations in the city.
2. *Frank Williams Inquest*, Public Archives of Ontario (PAO), RG 22, McCullough, 1919, p. 37.
3. *Evening Telegram*, November 27, 1918.
4. After the coroner's inquest, Cronin's notes were miraculously preserved amongst some papers relating to Williams's death.
5. Now the location of the Liquor Control Board of Ontario (LCBO) store adjoining the tracks at Yonge and Cottingham Streets.
6. McCullough was arrested for housebreaking by Constable Ewing at the corner of Ontario and Queen streets in 1917. McCullough claimed that the whisky bottle belonged to the constable.
7. For Burwash, see Martin L. Friedland, *The Case of Valentine Shortis* (Toronto, 1986), pp. 239–45. McCullough would have known Shortis at Burwash.
8. *Frank Williams Inquest*, p. 40.
9. The classic description of the psychopathic personality remains H. Cleckley's *The Mask of Sanity*, 4th ed. (St. Louis, 1964). Cleckley cites the following characteristics (pp. 362–63): "(1) Superficial charm and good 'intelligence.' (2) Absence of delusions and other signs of irrational 'thinking.' (3) Absence of 'nervousness' or psychoneurotic manifestations. (4) Unreliability. (5) Untruthfulness and insincerity. (6) Lack of remorse or shame. (7) Inadequately motivated antisocial behaviour. (8) Poor judgment and failure to learn by experience. (9) Pathologic egocentricity and incapacity for love. (10) General poverty in major affective reactions. (11) Specific loss of insight. (12) Unresponsiveness in general interpersonal relations. (13) Fantastic

and uninviting behavior with drink and sometimes without. (14) Suicide rarely carried out. (15) Sex life impersonal, trivial and poorly integrated. (16) Failure to follow any life plan." The term used today is "sociopath," or "antisocial personality disorder"; in the past it was "psychopathic personality." See *Diagnostic and Statistical Manual of Mental Disorders* (DSM-III-R) (Washington, 1987), pp. 342–46.

10. *Globe, Evening Telegram, Daily Star*, November 20, 1919. An honest Herbert Jenkins admitted later at McCullough's trial that he did not trip McCullough deliberately. As he rushed to the corner, more out of curiosity than anything else, McCullough suddenly veered south towards the lake and the two collided.

11. *Post-Mortem Examination*, PAO, RG 22, McCullough 1919.

12. See Henry James Morgan, ed., *The Canadian Men and Women of the Time*, 2nd ed. (Toronto, 1912), p. 583; *Globe*, January 25, 1921; *Star*, June 10, 1921; Biographical File, Academy of Medicine, Toronto. The ever-pragmatic Johnson was the author of *Inquests and Investigations: A Practical Guide for the Use of Coroners Holding Inquests in Ontario* (Toronto, 1911): "Before going to an inquest the Coroner should see that he has with him convenient writing materials – a good pen and ink, a box of adhesive seals, some double sheets of foolscap, together with certain forms." (p. 15).

13. *Globe*, May 23, 1949. Greer was a "doughty fighter" in the courts, whose earlier career as a semi-professional baseball player put him through the University of Toronto. His batman overseas was the trainer for the "Toronto Hockey Leafs." It was normal procedure for a Crown attorney to conduct questioning at inquests. See W. F. A. Boyes, *A Practical Treatise on the Office and Duties of Coroners*, 4th ed. (Toronto, 1905), pp. 17, 327–28.

14. Billy club, or the baton.

15. *Evening Telegram*, November 21, 1918.

16. *Frank Williams Inquest*, pp. 41–47.

CHAPTER III: MR. T. C. ROBINETTE, K.C.

1. The shop was part of the William Davies retail meat chain that Joseph Flavelle made so successful. "The William Davies Company was the largest pork-packing company in the British Empire. People were starting to call Toronto 'Hogtown.'" See Michael Bliss, *A Canadian*

*Millionaire: The Life & Business Times of Sir Joseph Flavelle, Bart.,*
*1858–1939* (Toronto, 1978), pp. 52, 111–14.

2. *Evening Telegram*, November 26, 1918.

3. *Globe*, November 22, 1918. Emphasis mine.

4. A lawyer appointed counsel to the Crown during the reign of a king
is a King's Counsel, and thus entitled to wear a silk gown. The designation today is Q.C. (Queen's Counsel), although the appointment
has been discontinued in Ontario.

5. Charles G. D. Roberts, and Arthur L. Tunnel, eds., *A Standard*
*Dictionary of Canadian Biography* (Toronto, 1934), pp. 332–33.

6. J. E. Middleton, *The Municipality of Toronto*, Vol. III (Toronto, 1923),
p. 131.

7. *Globe*, July 29, 1919, March 15, 1920; see also Jack Batten, *Robinette*
(Toronto, 1984), pp. 18–23.

8. *Daily Star*, January 23, 1919; *Evening Telegram*, April 21, 1919.

9. Denison served as Toronto's senior police magistrate for forty-four
years. "Since I was appointed in 1877 until the end of 1919, there have
been 650,000 cases dealt with in Police Court. The majority of these
have been dealt with by me, as for the first twenty years I had no
assistant. . . . I paid little or no attention to any rules that are often
followed blindly, if in the particular circumstances they would have
interfered with fair and impartial administration of justice between
litigants." George T. Denison, *Recollections of a Police Magistrate*
(Toronto, 1920), pp. vi, 9. See also Carl Berger, *The Sense of Power*
(Toronto, 1970), pp. 12–22.

10. *Evening Telegram*, November 27, 1918.

CHAPTER IV: THE FIRECRACKER

1. *Otsego Farmer*, September 23, 1898.

2. *1900 Census*, New York, Otsego County, Town of Middlefield; *Otsego*
*Farmer*, October 12, 1894.

3. *Conveyances*, Otsego County, Liber 238, p. 47; *Otsego Farmer*,
January 29, March 26, April 16, 1897.

4. *Otsego Farmer*, November 25, 1898.

5. My evidence for this is that McCullough stayed in school until he
was fourteen, read voraciously (partial to James Fenimore Cooper),
could write well himself, and had a fairly sophisticated vocabulary

and a talent for drawing that was remarked upon by others. School records have not survived.

6. *Oneonta Herald*, May 15, 1902.

7. *Deed Records*, Otsego County, Liber 453, p. 81. Chauncey Ward's architectural ability and the craftsmanship of his brother, Gaius, can be seen at Oak Hill, the magnificent farmhouse built by the Green family of Westville. I am indebted to Mr. Ward Green for information concerning the village and the location of the Swart property.

8. The address was 1617 Summerfield Street (now Schaefer), on the border between Queens and Brooklyn.

9. The same place and time gave rise to Al Capone. See Robert J. Schoenberg, *Mr. Capone* (New York, 1992), pp. 17–36.

10. *Daily Star*, June 11, 1919. This account, or "Life Story," reportedly written by McCullough himself, is typical of his obfuscation. Some of the facts are correct, but most are half-truths and lies. It was written with an eye to obtaining executive clemency.

11. McCullough said he bought his ticket with ten dollars "from the proceeds of a boyish stamp collection."

12. *Daily Star*, June 11, 1919.

13. From the *Kansas City Star*, January 16, 1911: "Leroy Swart of Brooklyn, 19 years old, pleaded guilty to burglary in the criminal court this morning. Swart confessed to robbing five houses. Judge Latshaw sentenced him to ten years in the penitentiary." See also Missouri State Archives, Jefferson City Penitentiary, *Register of Inmates*, Vol. 23, August 1909–June 1911, prisoner #12222.

14. It appears that his sentence was reduced from ten to five years immediately after his court appearance. McCullough claimed later that after two years of incarceration he wrote to his parents to explain his predicament, and that through their intercession his sentence was reduced to five years. This is unlikely. McCullough's initial jail registration records a five-year term. He also claimed later he was fifteen when sentenced when in fact he was nineteen.

15. Completed in 1858, Fort Adams "was the most elaborate work of its kind in the United States when it was built." It was a massive naval and artillery fortification overlooking the entrance to Narragansett Bay, which operated as a command centre for the coastal batteries of the northeast. Eisenhower used the commanding officer's residence as a summer White House. Kennedy berthed his presidential yacht inside

the fort. It is now the site of the Newport Jazz Festival. See Irving Opperman, "Fort Adams, Rhode Island" in *The Book of Newport* (Newport, 1930), p. 15; *Newport Daily News*, November 5, 1964.

16. The United States entered the war within two weeks of his desertion, on April 6, 1917.
17. National Archives and Records Administration (U.S.); Records of the Adjutant General's Office; RG 94; General Correspondence: 2565389. I am indebted to Mitchell Yockelson, reference archivist at the Military Reference Branch, for this information.
18. *Toronto World*, May 14, 1919.
19. It was the receipt for this shipment, giving his address on Palmerston, that Sergeant Umbach found in McCullough's effects.

CHAPTER V: THE TRIAL – DAY ONE

1. The soldiers arrived in Toronto at the North Toronto Station on Yonge Street. There were 398 Canadian soldiers with an additional six travelling on to the United States. The truly large contingents were yet to come. In April and May alone, 104,848 soldiers returned to Canada from overseas.
2. They lived at 86 Roxborough East. *Canadian Who's Who*, Vol. 2, 1936–37, p. 940; *Globe*, October 15, 1945.
3. McCullough actively assisted Robinette in the selection of jurors. This was remarked upon by reporters, who recalled McCullough's "remarkable ability" in questioning witnesses himself at the coroner's inquest.
4. White was also "distinguished as a breeder of shorthorn cattle and for his taste in poultry." *Canadian Who's Who*, Vol. 2, 1936–37, p. 1,130; *Globe*, November 28, 1949.
5. *The King v. Frank McCullough*. Trial. Public Archives of Canada (PAC), RG 13, Vol. 1497, File: McCullough, F., Vol. 1, Part 2. Unless otherwise indicated, the quotations in this and the following chapter are taken from the trial transcript.
6. For a full text of the code, see *Revised Statutes of Canada*, 1906, p. 2419 ff.
7. *Daily Star*, January 22, 1919.
8. Rose to secretary of state, February 7, 1919.

CHAPTER VI: THE TRIAL – DAY TWO

1. *Daily Star, Evening Telegram, Globe,* January 23, 1919.
2. Emphasis in this quotation is mine.
3. As the arresting officer in charge of the case, Cronin spent a considerable amount of time with McCullough. He was always present when Robinette interviewed his client at the jail. During the trial, Cronin transported McCullough back and forth from the jail "shackled to myself." They had much time to talk.
4. *Globe,* January 23, 1919.
5. *Toronto World,* January 23, 1919.
6. *Daily Star,* January 22, 1919.
7. Rose to J. D. Clarke, April 2, 1919.
8. *Globe,* January 23, 1919. The addresses to the jury are not recorded in the trial transcript. For these I have relied on newspaper accounts and Justice Rose's bench-book notes preserved at Osgoode Hall.
9. *Daily Star,* January 23, 1919.

CHAPTER VII: ALBANIAN MOHAMMEDAN

1. Frank W. Anderson, *Hanging in Canada* (Calgary, 1973), pp. 57–80.
2. William II (1859–1941), German Emperor (Kaiser) and King of Prussia, managed to secure asylum in the Netherlands in November 1918 to avoid execution.
3. *Toronto World, Daily Star, Globe, Evening Telegram,* January 3, 4, 1919. Of the five hanged in Toronto in the decade before 1919, one was Macedonian, one Italian, one a Russian Pole, and the fourth an American described as "coloured," in addition to the "Albanian Mohammedan." When it came to hanging, Toronto certainly displayed an early adherence to multiculturalism.

CHAPTER VIII: THE DEATH WATCH

1. A new section was opened in 1958, by which time an estimated one million prisoners had passed through the old jail. In 1977, following reports of brutality, the provincial minister of correctional services announced that the old section would be demolished and replaced by a "massive flower garden" to be maintained by inmates for the

benefit of patients at the nearby Riverdale Hospital. It didn't happen. The building still stands and McCullough's cell is still there. See *Report of the Royal Commission on the Toronto Jail and Custodial Services*, Vol. II (Queen's Printer, 1978), pp. 185–207.

2. *Globe*, June 8, 1907.

3. Chambers was the last of the "political appointments" to the position of governor. It was a standing public complaint that jobs at the jail were filled by the provincial party in office. McCullough's case contributed to the termination of this practice.

4. "The Late Rev. Andrew B. Chambers, An Appreciation by Rev. S. D. Chown, D.D.," *New Outlook*, March 23, 1927, p. 20.

5. *Globe*, May 30, 1919.

6. The death cell was reserved for prisoners awaiting execution. Executions were conducted by hanging behind a metal door in a "death chamber." In 1919, the death cell was located around a corner on the same floor as the death chamber.

7. In 1919, the jail held an average of 115 prisoners on any given day, of whom 15 were usually women. There were 10 male guards and 2 female matrons who worked 72 hours per week. See "In the Matter of the Prisons and Public Charities Act and Inquiry pursuant to Section 9," Public Archives of Ontario (PAO), RG 63, A-8, Box 747, File 473, referred to hereafter as *Jail Inquiry*.

8. *Jail Inquiry*, p. 44.

9. *Attestation Paper*, No. 202077, Ernest Currell, "Medical History Sheet."

10. "Etaples was a masterpiece of organization. . . . Each battalion at the Front had its own Field Dressing Station; patients were then transported to a Casualty Clearing Station, usually equipped with an emergency operating room and always located on a railway line, and then on to Etaples. Here, there were more than forty thousand beds and a score or more of hospitals – including several operated by the Canadian Army Medical Corps. . . ." Sandra Gwyn, *Tapestry of War* (Toronto, 1992), p. 449.

11. Located on the site of the Canadian National Exhibition.

12. *Daily Star*, *Evening Telegram*, April 16, 17, 19, 1919.

13. *Daily Star*, January 24, 1919.

14. *Ibid.*, January 28, 30, 1919.

15. This description of the letter was that of W. B. Horkins, of Robinette's firm. *Evening Telegram*, April 19, 1919.

16. Clarke to Meighen, May 22, 1919.
17. Hill to Robinette, March 12, 1919; J. D. Clarke to Meighen, May 22, 1919.
18. Rose to secretary of state, February 7, 1919, p. 6.
19. *Evening Telegram*, April 21, 1919.
20. *Jail Inquiry*, p. 25.
21. Doris's mother, Gladys Mytton, was also fond of McCullough ("he always appeared to be so manly"). While it was said that her conviction for receiving stolen property was the reason Edward Mytton removed the family from Toronto, it is likely that the attraction both mother and daughter felt for McCullough was also a factor.
22. *Jail Inquiry*, p. 28.

CHAPTER IX: THE CHURCH FOR THE STRANGER

1. *Jail Inquiry*, p. 4.
2. They formed the United Church of Canada in 1925. A few Congregational churches and roughly one-third of Presbyterians voted to stay out of the union.
3. "Record of Interview with Reverend J. W. Pedley," Dec. 16, 1930. File: *Western Congregational Church*, United Church Archives.
4. The church is now the site of B. Silverstein & Sons, Dry Goods. See also Steven Spiseman's outstanding *The Jews of Toronto* (Toronto, 1979), pp. 69–96.
5. Nelles, "pre-eminently a man of the people," was a great user of lantern-slides. He "covered the pipes of the organ with a lantern screen. . . . All the hymns were thrown on to the screen by the lantern, a device that is more conducive to good congregational singing than any quantity of hymn books." *Star*, February 1, 1919.
6. Within two years, attendance at Sunday-evening services grew from twenty-five to seven hundred. "How has this change been wrought? By a big pastor with a big program and lots of push; . . . by a program that meets the needs of the neighbourhood, and his [Nelles's] energy is so contagious that there is something doing – and generally several things doing – every night at his church." *Ibid.*
7. This was the estimate of the *Mail and Empire*, June 10, 1919. The six large boxes of petitions preserved in the National Archives contain at least that many names, if not more.

8. *Evening Telegram*, March 26, 1919; *Daily Star*, February 27, 1919.

9. Robinette to Guthrie, March 26, 1919. Guthrie was acting for Charles Doherty, minister of justice, then at the Versailles Peace Conference with Prime Minister Robert Borden. Guthrie was succeeded at the end of March by Arthur Meighen, who dealt with McCullough's case.

10. Clarke to Robinette, March 18, 1919.

11. Robinette to Guthrie, March 29, 1919. Emphasis mine.

12. Clarke to Rose, March 30, 1919.

13. There was more than one law on this point: Criminal Code, section 1064; Sheriff's Act, R.S.O., 1914; Prisons and Public Charities Inspection Act, R.S.O., 1914; Order in Council, June 22, 1903.

14. *Jail Inquiry*, pp. 9, 20, 37.

15. *Ibid.*, pp. 20–36.

16. *Globe*, April 10, 1919; *Evening Telegram*, April 16, 1919; Rose to Clarke, April 2, 1919.

17. *Jail Inquiry*, p. 27.

18. *Daily Star*, April 15, 1919.

CHAPTER X: MISS VERA DE LAVELLE

1. That is, the first recorded escape in Canada of a prisoner awaiting sentence of death. To my knowledge this is true. *Daily Star, Mail and Empire, Globe*, April 16, 17, 21, 1919.

2. *Toronto World, Mail and Empire, Globe*, April 17, 1919. Emphasis mine.

3. *Toronto World*, April 23, 1919.

4. *Daily Star, Evening Telegram*, April 16, 1919. "Daisy" was slang for an astounding person. The contemporary word, for those of a certain age, is "doozy." Both terms may go back to the "Daisy Duesenberg," a luxury car of the period. The world land-speed record of 156.03 mph was set in a Duesenberg in 1920.

5. *Globe*, April 16, 1919. Robinette also said, "Robert Bickersdike, ex-M.P. of Montreal, who has fought to abolish hanging is also interested in the case."

6. I have corrected McCullough's spelling. He wrote "perpetuated" instead of "perpetrated." McCullough used fairly sophisticated language ("introduced into the night guard's coffee"), which is both a reflection of his schooling and his ability to pick up language by osmosis. His spelling was usually impeccable.

7. *Daily Star, Globe*, April 16, 17, 1919; *Evening Telegram*, April 17, 1919.

8. Returned soldiers discharged from military service could no longer wear uniform. They displayed a discharge button on their civilian clothes to show they had done their duty. See Desmond Morton, *When Your Number's Up* (Toronto, 1993), p. 55. "In 1916, men rejected from service on account of health or age could finally obtain a special badge so that the myrmidons of patriotism would not shame them as 'slackers.' For the same reason, returned soldiers received a discharge button from the Patriotic Fund."

9. *Globe*, April 18, 1919.

10. *Jail Inquiry*, pp. 28–29; *Daily Star*, April 19, 1919.

11. *Evening Telegram*, April 19, 1919.

12. *Mail and Empire, Evening Telegram*, April 17, 19, 1919; *Daily Star*, April 21, 1919.

CHAPTER XI: IN THE MATTER OF THE PRISONS

1. *Daily Star, Toronto World, Evening Telegram, Mail and Empire*, April 19, 21, 1919; *Globe*, April 22, 1919. The "woman in the case" who called Buffalo was not identified.

2. *Toronto World, Mail and Empire*, April 22, 1919.

3. *Globe*, April 23, 1919.

4. As it turned out, the Conservative government was thrashed at the polls in October 1919. The provincial secretary, W. D. MacPherson, was demolished in the riding of West Toronto. The Conservatives were replaced by the United Farmers of Ontario under the leadership of E. C. Drury, who formed a coalition with labour.

5. Thomas Langdon Church, mayor from 1915 to 1921. "During this period all privately owned light, power, and transportation systems were united into publicly owned bodies, becoming the Toronto Hydro-Electric Power Commission, and the Toronto Transportation Commission." *Canadian Who's Who*, 1948, pp. 199–200. Church was elected MP for Toronto-Broadview in 1921.

6. Sir William Ralph Meredith, editor, *Canadian Municipal Manual* (Toronto, 1917). See sections 374, 379, and 384 of the Municipal Act.

7. *Daily Star*, April 16, 21, 23, 1919; *Globe*, April 23, 1919.

8. *Evening Telegram, Daily Star*, April 21, 22, 1919.

9. *Evening Telegram*, April 17, 22, 1919; *Jail Inquiry*, p. 13.

10. *Globe*, April 28, 1919; *Evening Telegram*, April 17, 21, 1919.

11. *Globe*, April 23, 1919.

12. *Mail and Empire, Toronto World, Daily Star*, April 23, 1919.

13. *Daily Star, Evening Telegram*, April 23, 1919.

14. *Jail Inquiry*, pp. 45–53.

15. *Jail Inquiry*, pp. 45–53; "Supplementary," pp. 1–14.

16. *Evening Telegram*, April 26, 1919.

17. *Rules and Regulations Pertaining to County Gaols*, Section 14: "No person shall be allowed access to any prisoner for the purpose of interviewing him or her with a view to publishing such interview."

18. *Daily Star*, April 28, 1919; *Evening Telegram*, April 29, 1919.

19. *Daily Star*, April 29, 1919. McBride's motion won by a majority of fifteen to nine. Because the vote did not meet a required two-thirds majority, the motion was lost. The mayor voted against the motion.

## CHAPTER XII: ADMINISTRATIVE INCOMPETENCE

1. Mowat lived at 416 Russell Hill Road.

2. Dunlop to Mowat, April 29, 1919.

3. Mowat to Dunlop, April 30, 1919.

4. Dunlop to MacPherson, April 30, 1919.

5. Mowat to MacPherson, May 2, 1919.

6. Dunlop to MacPherson, April 29, 1919.

7. *Daily Star*, May 2, 1919.

8. *Globe*, May 2, 1919.

9. Clarke to Cartwright, April 23, 1919; Cartwright to Clarke, April 24, 1919; Clarke to Cartwright, April 26, 1919; Meighen to governor general, April 28, 1919; Privy Council of Canada, 899; Mulvey to Mowat, Mowat to Mulvey, April 30, 1919; *Globe*, May 2, 1919.

10. Bayly to Mulvey, Newcombe, May 9, 1919; Mowat to Mulvey, May 9, 1919; Cartwright to Clarke, May 3, 1919; Meighen to governor general, May 12, 1919.

11. Greer had examined McCullough at the coroner's inquest.

12. *Globe*, May 7, 9, 1919; *Evening Telegram*, May 8, 1919.

## CHAPTER XIII: THE TORONTO RIOTS

1. "He is now a child of God since being converted . . . he is your brother and mine. If you are a Christian, which I hope you [the governor

general] are, you will show the spirit of our Master, which was love, joy, long suffering, gentleness and peace. If Jesus saw any one in trouble he helped them out, he didn't hang them. . . . So be careful what you do with God's property as Frank McCullough is now." A. Sympathizer, Ottawa, June 9, 1919.

2. "It does seem the world has not lived up to its highest ideals. What a blight and stain it puts on countries that uphold capital punishment. Sometimes people go by hundreds to witness the awful tragedy. Do you not think thousands of murderers are made in such an act? Certainly so." Mrs. Annie Rex MacDonald, Rochester, Minnesota, June 3, 1919.

3. "For four years the world was in a state of war, which if it did nothing else should have taught everyone in it that there is something more besides hard and fast rules. Right now the same world is in a war of Bolshevism, which is going to last until the men in high places discover that the days for the same old hard and fast rules are over. This is a new day, and we as inhabitants of the earth must live by the new methods." Ida L. Webster, *Toronto World*, June 12, 1919.

4. A statement claiming that manslaughter was the more appropriate charge for McCullough prefaced most of the petitions sent to Ottawa. The wording was drafted initially by Robinette's office and went through various adaptations. It is unlikely that the majority who signed petitions were aware of the legal technicalities of the case. Most simply felt McCullough didn't deserve to hang, and the argument about manslaughter sounded convincing.

5. See the letter from "Tom Fairplay" at the beginning of Chapter x.

6. To my knowledge there is still no thorough study of the riots.

7. The majority of Canada's Armed Forces were in service overseas and would not return until 1919. In the twelve months following the armistice, 267,813 returned across the Atlantic. During the peak months of April and May 1919, when McCullough was at large, 104,848 soldiers arrived in Canada, many of them disembarking in Toronto before moving on to other locations. *Daily Star*, May 29, 1919; Desmond Morton and Glenn Wright, *Winning the Second Battle* (Toronto, 1987), p. 112.

8. Most of these men were outpatients. In addition, there were in excess of 1,300 hospital beds reserved for soldiers: Christie Street (600), Davisville (425), College Street (125), Spadina Street (69), Euclid

Hall (36), Toronto General (14), Toronto Asylum (11). There were also beds at St. Andrew's Military Hospital, the Base Military Hospital, and Hart House at the University of Toronto. See *Department of Soldier's Civil Re-Establishment, Annual Report*, December, 1919, Sessional Papers (Canada), No. 14, 1920, pp. 21–22, 28; No. 140 (unpublished), 1921.

9. This distinction was shared with Montreal. See Morton and Wright, pp. 23–24, 124.

10. The city claimed to have given 65,000 men for service overseas, from a population of approximately 547,000. This figure is 12 per cent of the population, and does not include women who served in various capacities. Approximately 5,000 men from Toronto were killed and over 25,000 suffered casualties. Toronto gave for all war purposes a total of about $30 million, and manufactured munitions for the Allies in the amount of $200 million. See *Toronto City Directory*, 1919, pp. 35–36.

11. One had to be a citizen before enlistment was possible. Resident non-citizens, or "landed immigrants" today, were exempt from war service and taxes. Those resident in Canada from Allied countries had to return home before they could serve. There was a push to forge agreements among the Allied powers so that Allied residents could enlist for service (and go straight to the Front) without having to return home first. The war was over before the bureaucracy could achieve this objective. Canadian residents of axis powers – "enemy aliens" – were stuck in a difficult position. They couldn't enlist for Allied service even if they wanted to (and many did); and, of course, were not permitted to return home for fear they would fight for the enemy. The returned soldiers wanted these people interned, or released under licence to work at war wages, and taxed.

12. *Globe*, September 28, 1918. The Department of Public Health estimated that 60 per cent of Toronto's restaurants were operated by "aliens" and that 35 per cent of these were of Greek origin. See *Daily Star*, August 8, 1918.

13. It was rumoured that Cluderay was an amputee, but this does not appear to have been true. An earlier incident, however, did involve a disabled soldier. The same White City proprietor commented on the character of a Private Nicholson's companion. *Daily Star*: "Did Nicholson express any indignation at this remark?" Major Bailey:

"Yes, he did, but as he was a double amputation, he could not do much. Personally, I would have knocked the man down." *Daily Star*, October 3, 1918.

14. Shrapnel Corners was the unofficial headquarters of the returned men. It was a small park with benches near the College Street Hospital and the Great War Veterans' Club on Carlton.

15. There were only 73 policemen on duty that night in all of Toronto. This explains the inability to marshal sufficient strength in time to deal with the outbreak. There were a total of 435 constables on the Toronto force at this time. An additional 85 consisted of officers and support staff. The force was not at full strength because approximately 150 men were in active service overseas. See *Daily Star*, September 20, October 19, 1918.

16. The formal explanation for this refusal to intervene was that the military police were responsible for men in uniform only; that is, men still in service, who were apparently few in number at the White City. Returned men who had been discharged from service were not permitted to wear uniform (it was illegal for them to do so) and were identified by their discharge buttons. These men were formally the responsibility of the civil police, because they were no longer soldiers, but civilians. It was generally believed, however, that the military authorities used these technicalities as an excuse to cover their sympathy for the rioters.

17. *Daily Star*, August 3, 1918. The restaurants demolished on the first night were: Superior (257 Yonge), Palace (271 Yonge), Vendome (283 Yonge), New London (311 Queen), Colonial (349 Yonge), White City (433 Yonge), Star (441 Yonge), Klees' Butcher Shop (504 Yonge), Marathon (822 Yonge), Alexander (750 Queen), and the Sunnyside (Roncesvalles and Queen). The estimated damage on the first night was $40,000, a considerable sum in 1918.

18. Church claimed, "There were a large number of foreigners, Socialists and idlers in the crowds, and, I am told, numbers of Germans and Austrians." In other words, enemy aliens had provoked the violence against enemy aliens!

19. District No. 2 included the Toronto region. Military headquarters were located at Exhibition Camp, which, since 1878, was the site of an agricultural fair that in 1912 was officially renamed the Canadian National Exhibition.

20. Bickford's staff estimated that only 25 per cent of the rioters were uniformed soldiers.

21. This occurred at the destruction of the Sunnyside Café at Queen and Roncesvalles. Not only did constables smoke cigars, their commanding officers, inspectors Mulhall and Crowe, stood in silence across the street, watching the looting, and gave no orders even to try to intervene. Mulhall later took full responsibility and early retirement.

22. A veteran of the first contingent of the Canadian Expeditionary Force (CEF) to go overseas in 1914.

23. During the second battle of Ypres (or "Wipers," as the soldiers called it), when the Germans used poison gas for the first time.

24. Before his discharge, Hunter managed to return to France attached to the Princess Patricia's Canadian Light Infantry and participated at Vimy Ridge. See *Globe*, May 2, 1957.

25. The rioters presented a list of grievances to Mayor Church that included the following demands: "That all the unmarried men of the Toronto police force who participated in the outbreak of Saturday night be drafted into the C.E.F [Canadian Expeditionary Force]"; "That immediate steps be taken to repress disloyalty and sedition in Toronto among the foreign elements of the population of this city"; "That the police force be instructed to disarm all aliens, it being a well known fact that the majority are in possession of firearms. Furthermore, we, as returned men, offer our services freely in this direction, if the police cannot cope with it." Church was eventually forced to read a proclamation from the front steps of City Hall, warning a crowd of thousands "against congregating on the streets and holding meetings, and gave notice that should rioting continue the Riot Act will be read, giving power to the police and soldiers to fire upon the crowd." *Evening Telegram*, August 7, 1918.

26. The author of the inquiry's report was none other than Col. George T. Denison, who was police commissioner as well as magistrate of the police court. The report concluded that "it was much better to have the riot put down in that way [police using batons] than to have called on the military to come out with rifles and ball ammunition to fire upon citizens, and although some few citizens were hurt, that the general result was infinitely better than if the Board had taken the offer of the military authorities and given them the power of acting." See *Star*, October 19, 1918.

27. *Daily Star*, August 3–7, September 18–19, 25–30, October 1–7, 19, 1918.

28. Letter from a Mr. Robert Redford, Lafayette Hotel, Buffalo, New York, May 12, 1919.

29. *Evening Telegram*, May 19, 1919.

CHAPTER XIV: 78 BATHURST STREET

1. *Daily Star*, May 8, 10, 1919.

2. This was not J. J. (John Josiah) Robinette, who went on to become perhaps the greatest of Canada's trial lawyers, but an older son who was working at City Hall.

3. *Daily Star*, *Evening Telegram*, May 8, 1919.

4. *Evening Telegram*, May 8, 1919.

5. *Daily Star*, May 8, 9, 1919.

6. *Evening Telegram*, May 12, 1919.

7. She claimed she hid in a vacant house at Spadina and Adelaide, but it is almost certain the two were concealed together in the British Welcome League building.

8. *Globe*, May 8, 1919.

9. *Daily Star*, May 10, 1919.

10. *Evening Telegram*, May 8, 1919.

11. *Ibid.*, May 12, 1919; *Mail and Empire*, May 9, 1919.

12. *Evening Telegram*, May 13, 1919; *Daily Star*, May 9, 1919.

13. *Evening Telegram*, May 13, 1919.

14. *Daily Star*, April 30, 1919.

15. *Ibid.*, May 10, 1919.

16. *Ibid.*, *Evening Telegram*, May 12, 1919.

17. He planned to travel through Myrtle, Bathney Junction, Havelock, Hungerford, Smith Falls, Winchester, Glen Norman, Vaudreuil, Montreal, St. John's (Quebec), Plattsburg, Loon Lake, Tupper Lake, Prospect, and Herkimer.

18. This, at any rate, was the reason McCullough gave for staying so long in the city after Vera's capture.

19. The fact that Cronin made so many inquiries in the area is further evidence that neighbours were lying to conceal McCullough's presence.

20. *Daily Star*, May 12, 1919.

CHAPTER XV: MR. UNKNOWN

1. *Daily Star*, May 9, 1919; *Evening Telegram*, May 16, 1919.
2. *Toronto World*, May 9, 1919.
3. Upon his recapture, McCullough was placed in a cell at the very back of the jail, not far from the death cell from which he had escaped. Vera's cell was in another section of the jail.
4. *Evening Telegram*, May 19, 1919.
5. *Globe*, May 19, 1919.
6. *Daily Star*, May 12, 1919.
7. Precisely who was behind this effort is not known.
8. *Evening Telegram*, May 14, 15, 19, 1919.
9. *Daily Star*, May 9, 16, 1919; *Evening Telegram*, May 16, 1919; *Globe*, May 19, 1919; *Toronto World*, May 17, 1919.
10. *Daily Star*, May 9, 13, 14, 1919; *Evening Telegram*, May 12, 14, 1919; *Mail and Empire*, May 15, 1919; *Toronto World*, May 12, 1919.
11. *Toronto World*, *Evening Telegram*, May 14, 1919; *Daily Star*, May 20, 1919.
12. On the same page of the *Star*'s account of Vera's trial it is noted that a Morley Callaghan, aged 16, of 35 Woolfrey Avenue, had won first prize in the annual oratorical competition held at Riverdale Collegiate. His subject was "Canada's Claim to National Greatness." Callaghan received $20 in gold and $10 in books. *Daily Star*, May 15, 1919.
13. *Evening Telegram*, May 19, 1919; *Toronto World*, May 12, 14, 1919; *Mail and Empire*, May 14, 1919; *Daily Star*, May 15, 1919; *Globe*, May 16, 1919.
14. The other principal was Sen. Gideon Robertson, minister of labour.
15. See R. Graham, *Arthur Meighen: A Biography*, 3 vols. (Toronto, 1960–65).
16. Sir Joseph Flavelle, quoted in Michael Bliss's outstanding *Right Honourable Men* (Toronto, 1994), p. 98.
17. Handwritten note of Meighen's instructions by Clarke, May 10, 1919. Vol. 1497, File CC101.
18. Once there, Meighen described the strikers as "revolutionaries of various degrees and types, from crazy idealists down to ordinary thieves." See D. J. Bercuson, *Confrontation at Winnipeg* (Montreal, 1974) p. 136.
19. Clarke to Meighen, May 22, 1919.

20. *Daily Star*, May 15, 20, 22, 1919; *Evening Telegram*, May 9, 13, 14, 15, 19, 23, 1919; *Globe*, May 10, 16, 1919.
21. *Evening Telegram*, May 30, 1919.

CHAPTER XVI: VERA THE ELUSIVE

1. *Toronto Star*, May 29, 30, 1919; *Evening Telegram*, May 30, 1919; *Globe*, May 30, 31, 1919; *Toronto World*, May 30, 1919.
2. *Toronto Star*, May 30, 1919.
3. *Evening Telegram*, May 30, 1919; *Toronto Star*, May 30, June 5, 1919; *Toronto World*, June 3, 1919.
4. *Toronto World*, June 7, 1919.
5. *Toronto Star*, May 30, 1919; *Toronto World*, May 31, 1919; *Globe*, June 10, 1919.
6. *Ibid.*, June 6, 1919.
7. *Toronto Star*, June 7, 9, 1919; *Evening Telegram*, June 3, 1919.
8. After whom the Clarke Institute of Psychiatry is named.
9. The patriarchal Arthur Jukes Johnson, who presided as coroner at the Frank Williams inquest.
10. *Evening Telegram*, June 3, 1919; *Toronto World*, June 5, 1919.
11. *Toronto World*, May 30, 1919; *Globe*, June 10, 1919; *Mail and Empire*, May 31, 1919; *Evening Telegram*, June 5, 1919.
12. *Evening Telegram*, June 11, 1919; *Globe*, June 10, 1919.
13. *Toronto Star*, *Mail and Empire*, June 10, 11, 1919.
14. *Evening Telegram*, *Toronto Star*, June 10, 1919. The telegrams stated succinctly: "His Excellency the Governor General is unable to order any interference with the death sentence passed upon Frank McCullough."
15. *Globe*, April 10, 1919; *Evening Telegram*, April 16, 1919; Rose to Clarke, April 2, 1919.
16. Clarke to Meighen, Meighen to governor general, June 4, 1919.
17. *Toronto Star*, June 12, 1919; *Toronto World*, June 13, 1919.

CHAPTER XVII: VICTORY OVER DEATH

1. *Globe*, June 10, 1919; *Evening Telegram*, June 12, 13, 1919; *Toronto World*, June 13, 1919.
2. Editorial entitled "Criminal Psychology," *Toronto World*, June 13, 1919.

3. Robinette to Meighen, June 9, 1919; Meighen to Robinette, June 9, 10, 1919.
4. *Toronto Star*, June 12, 1919.
5. *Globe*, June 12, 1919; *Toronto World*, June 13, 1919.
6. *Globe*, June 10, 1919.
7. *Evening Telegram*, *Toronto World*, June 13, 1919.
8. *Toronto Star*, *Evening Telegram*, June 12, 1919.
9. See pp. 117–18.
10. *Toronto Star*, *Evening Telegram*, *Globe*, *Toronto World*, *Mail and Empire*, June 12, 13, 1919. McCullough's remains are still there today, under the paved parking lot behind the jail.

## CHAPTER XVIII: EPILOGUE

1. Victor Christian William Cavendish, ninth Duke of Devonshire, was reputed to be England's richest peer and largest landowner. He died in 1938 in his massive baroque mansion at Chatsworth, the county seat of the dukes of Devonshire.
2. *Mail and Empire*, June 13, 1919.
3. Frank W. Anderson, *Hanging in Canada* (Calgary, 1973), p. 68.
4. This occurred at the execution of Mrs. Tomasino Sarao at the Bordeaux Jail in Montreal. Ellis was not allowed to weigh Sarao before the hanging. The weight given to him on a slip of paper was her weight upon entry to the prison. She had gained forty pounds in the interval.
5. Anderson, pp. 57–80; Andy O'Brien, *My Friend the Hangman* (Toronto, 1970), p. 20. Ellis married Edith Grimsdale in 1915. After years of abuse, she left him in 1922 when she finally discovered his true profession. For seven years Ellis had told her he was a travelling salesman.
6. The "family compact" was a term of derision used to describe a small, powerful group of wealthy men and their families who dominated the affairs of government in Ontario during the first half of the nine-teenth century.
7. J. E. Middleton, *The Municipality of Toronto* (Toronto, 1923), Vol. II, p. 23; *Evening Telegram*, April 12, 1924. Mowat apparently attended Upper Canada College, "thereafter taking a course at Galt Grammar School." He tried farming, first in Manitoba and later near Downsview, Ontario, and then became the proprietor of Mowat's

Wharf at the foot of Yonge Street, after which he was appointed sheriff in 1888. His father, Oliver, was premier and attorney general of the province for twenty-four years, from 1872–96. Knighted in 1892, Sir Oliver Mowat was appointed to Canada's senate and became federal minister of justice in 1896. He left Ottawa in 1897 to become lieutenant-governor of Ontario.

8. Addy was born in County Cavan, Ireland, in 1857. He arrived in Toronto in 1876 and first "worked in the bush with a lumber company." He then worked as a guard at the Queen Street Hospital for the Insane, and was afterwards appointed a guard at the Toronto Jail. He became chief turnkey in 1888 (the same year Mowat was appointed sheriff) and lived for many years near the jail at 550 Gerrard Street East. *Evening Telegram*, April 4, 1925.

9. *Evening Telegram*, June 15, 1919.

10. "Majors were known to tremble more than privates when called before him to answer for breaking a rule." A Canadian Army song included the refrain: "We had to join up; we had to join old Basher's army." As a "penologist," Basher supported the death penalty and was a strong proponent of corporal punishment: "They thanked me for bringing them to their senses." He became deputy minister of the Ontario Department of Reform Institutions in 1952. That same year, he again took charge of the Don Jail after the spectacular escape of the Boyd gang. "With rumours spreading of a mass outbreak, he organized the tightest security ever experienced at the jail. A squad of OPP officers replaced six dismissed jail guards and city police stood round-the-clock guard outside the jail. The mass outbreak never came." Basher died at his home in Whitby in 1960. *Globe*, June 26, July 8, 1919; August 27, 1959; October 10, 1960.

11. "Bartholomew Cronin," Employee Personnel Records, City of Toronto; *Chief Constables' Report*, 1937; *Star*, October 2, 1944.

12. I am indebted to Mr. J. J. Robinette for information concerning his father and the McCullough case. J. J. Robinette was thirteen when his father defended McCullough. He could "distinctly" remember his father being "frustrated over the testimony of one witness" (this would have been Cross) and "very upset about McCullough's escape." J. J. Robinette died in 1996 at the age of ninety. *Globe*, March 15, 17, 1919. See Jack Batten, *Robinette: The Dean of Canadian Lawyers* (Toronto, 1984).

13. See Robert J. Sharpe, *The Last Day, the Last Hour: The Currie Libel Trial* (Toronto, 1988).

14. "When the reporter telephoned to the residence on Roxborough Drive, a feminine voice answered. Mr. Justice Rose was busy at the moment. Was there any message? A request was made for a photograph of the newly appointed chief justice. 'Just one moment, please. Judge Rose will speak with you now,' was the answer after a brief silence. The request for a photograph was repeated when a quiet voice came over the wire. 'May I ask the occasion for which you need my picture?' asked Chief Justice Rose, in somewhat bewildered tones. The reporter explained that Mr. Justice Rose was now Chief Justice Rose. Another request was made for a photograph. 'This is my first intimation of my appointment,' said the new chief justice." *Mail and Empire*, October 3, 1930; *Canadian Who's Who*, 1936, p. 940; *Globe*, October 15, 1945.

15. *Daily Star*, June 18, 1919.

16. See p. 72. These were the words of J. W. Pedley, Nelles's predecessor. Pedley's blatant anti-Semitism was not unusual for the time.

17. It was the Hebrew Men of England Synagogue from 1923 until 1961.

18. See C. E. Silcox's "Interview with J. W. Pedley" in the file *Western Congregational Church*, United Church Archives. A further issue was that Nelles was proposing amalgamation with a "non-concurring" Presbyterian Church, or a church declining to join the new United Church of Canada. Pedley believed that Nelles's plan was merely a way of siphoning Congregational assets away from church union, to support those who were opposed to union.

19. *74th General Assembly of the Presbyterian Church in Canada* (Glengarry Presbytery), June 2, 1948.

20. The remainder of the "China silk" money that McCullough hid in the British Welcome League Building? When killed, Johnson had $2,410 on his person.

21. The pilot was "Wop" May (Wilfred Reid May), who, as a novice pilot on the Western Front, was being pursued by Manfred, Freiherr von Richthofen, when the "Red Baron" was killed. May could have been the Red Baron's 81st victim, but instead went on to become one of Canada's leading bush flyers.

22. The books include Dick North, *The Mad Trapper of Rat River* (Toronto, 1972); Frank Anderson, *The Death of Albert Johnson*

(Edmonton, 1968). The film *Death Hunt* (1981) starred Charles Bronson and Lee Marvin (with Angie Dickinson as "Vanessa"). North, pp. 46, 127.

23. Because of illness, W. B. Horkins retired early, at the age of fifty. He died in 1952. His most notable case was as prosecutor of "the Blackhand Italian Underworld gang." *Globe*, May 6, 1952; *Canadian Who's Who*, 1936, p. 524.

24. To date, all efforts to discover what happened to her have failed. If still alive (in 2000) her child would be eighty. *Daily Star*, July 22–24, September 12, 1919; *Globe*, July 23, 1919.

25. I am grateful to Mr. R. B. Nelles for a copy of this letter.

# Index

Criminal Code, 36–7, 54, 67–8,
116–7, 119, 185, 188–9
Cronin, Detective Bartholomew,
16, 43, 49, 51, 56, 65, 84, 88,
142, 156; origins, 6–7;
cautions McCullough, 7, 17;
records Kennedy's questioning of McCullough, 8–9;
suspects McCullough
belongs to crime ring, 10;
reads charge against
McCullough in police court,
12; testifies at coroner's
inquest, 17–9; questioned by
Robinette in police court,
24–5; testifies at McCullough's
trial, 46–7; reports to Addy
appearances of woman in
Riverdale Park, 81; arrests and
questions Currell, 84–5;
arrests and questions de
Lavelle, 102; arrests
McCullough and transports
him again to City Hall, 137–8;
searches for McCullough in
the Spadina and Bathurst
areas, 145, 148; subsequent
career and death, 203
Cross, William, 2–5, 11, 14–6,
39–45, 48–9, 55, 89–90,
146–7, 152–3
Cross, Mrs. William, 4–5, 14
Cross's Livery, 2, 35, 39, 138, 144
Currell, Ernest, 64–5, 77–8,
84–5, 87–8, 92–5, 99, 105,
120–1, 125, 169–71, 201–2
Currell, Katharine, 91–3, 95, 105,
121, 141

Davidson, Alexander, 77
Denison, Colonel George T.,
24–5, 85, 103
Denning, Harry, 58, 69, 78–80, 186
Dewart, Hartley, 134, 153
Dickson, Samuel, 130
Drew, Harry, 106–10
Dunlop, W. W., 84, 92, 98–9,
104–7, 110, 113–6, 163, 166–7

Ellett, Nettie, 29
Ellis, Arthur, 59–60, 116, 175, 183,
190, 194–7, 200
English, Arthur. *See* Arthur Ellis
Exhibition Camp, Toronto, 64
Eyre, R. F., 149

Ferguson, Lillian, 192
Follis, Samuel, 63, 77–8, 101

Glover, George, 193
governor general, 75, 117–9, 176,
189, 199–200
Grant, Rev. G. D., 29
Grasett, Henry, 98, 100, 190,
192–3
Great War Veteran's Association
(GWVA), 94–5, 130, 134, 171,
199
Greer, Richard H., 13–8, 120–21,
169–70
Guthrie, Detective George, 12–3,
138, 140, 148, 152–3, 158
Guthrie, Honourable Hugh, 74–5

Harrington, Dr. Andrew B., 12, 36
Hassard, A. R., 20, 183, 185–6,
188–90